Frank

An International Journal of

Contemporary Writing & Art

NUMBER 18

Publisher/Editor: David Applefield
Managing Editor: Ethan Gilsdorf
Associate Editors: Lisa Pasold, Marie Doezema
Swiss Dossier Editor: Kristin T. Schnider
Design/Layout: Ethan Gilsdorf, Lisa Pasold
Web Site Editor: Sondra Russell
•

Frank, founded in 1983 in Boston, is published in Paris in English twice a year by **Frank Association** and distributed internationally. **Frank** attempts to promote diversely creative and original work that demonstrates excellence, innovation, vision, and engagement. The Editors look favorably on work that responds artistically to social, political, and global issues, as well as texts and images that reveal original and passionate perspectives on the world, its cultures, traditions, and languages. Work that falls between existing genres and helps redefine boundaries or all sorts is highly encouraged. Work that conveys a sense of necessity and implores readers to pay attention is what belongs on **Frank**'s pages. Unsolicited manuscripts of previously unpublished and original work of all kinds are welcome accompanied by International Reply Coupons or the equivalent amount of postage in check or money order in US $ or Euros. Electronic submissions as Word file attachments are welcome and should be saved in RTF, labeled with the author's last name, and sent to submissions@ReadFrank.com. See **www.ReadFrank.com** for additional guidelines.
•

Frank is distributed to the trade in the US by Midpoint Trade Books (New York, NY), in Canada by Mosaic Press (Oakville, ON, Canada), in the U.K. by Calder Publications (London, UK), in Switzerland by Bergli Books (Basil).
•

Individual copies are available at $10 US or 10 Euros plus $3 US or Euros for postage. Subscriptions (four issues): $38 US / 38 Euros. Institutions: $60 US /60 Euros. Orders can be taken on-line at **www.ReadFrank.com** or at www.amazon.com and www.bn.com.
•

All other orders, special requests, and queries should be addressed to:
Frank Association
32, rue Edouard Vaillant   Tel: (33) (1) 48 59 66 58
93100 Montreuil/ France   Fax: (33) (1) 48 59 66 68
email: editor@ReadFrank.com   Web sites: www.ReadFrank.com and www.Frank.ly
•

Dépôt légal: 3e trimestre 2001
ISSN: 0738-8299 / ISBN for Frank 18: 2-913053-01-7 / EAN: 9782913053014

Directeur de la publication: David Applefield
Frank is a registered activity of the French **Frank Association** *(Loi de 1 juillet 1901, but non-lucratif)*, (SIRET: 403 944 028 00014) and the U.S. not-for-profit organization **Frank Association USA** (pending). The journal, its trademark, and URLs ReadFrank.com and Frank.ly are under license from David Applefield.
•

Frank wishes to publicly thank **Pro Helvetia**, the Arts Council of Switzerland, for its generous support of this issue. **Frank** also wishes to thank the **Migros Kulturprozent** for its translation grant, **the Direktion für Bildung und Kultur des Kontons Zug** for its support of the translation of Elisabeth Wanderler-Deck's text, as well as the **Aargauer Kuratorium** for the translation support of Monica Cantieni's and Martin Dean's texts. **Frank** also wishes to thank its sponsor Absolut Vodka, the public relations firm News Pepper, Svetlana Sarycheva, Mme Di Fusco, Kevin Kennedy and Isabelle Sulek.
•

Cover Design: Cover photos of François Lamore's smock and shoes by David Applefield, Montreuil, 2001. Layout by Sophie Alvacet and Lisa Davidson.
•

Copyright: ©David Applefield, 2001. Reproduction in any form of any of the contents other than for review is prohibited without the prior written consent of the Publisher.

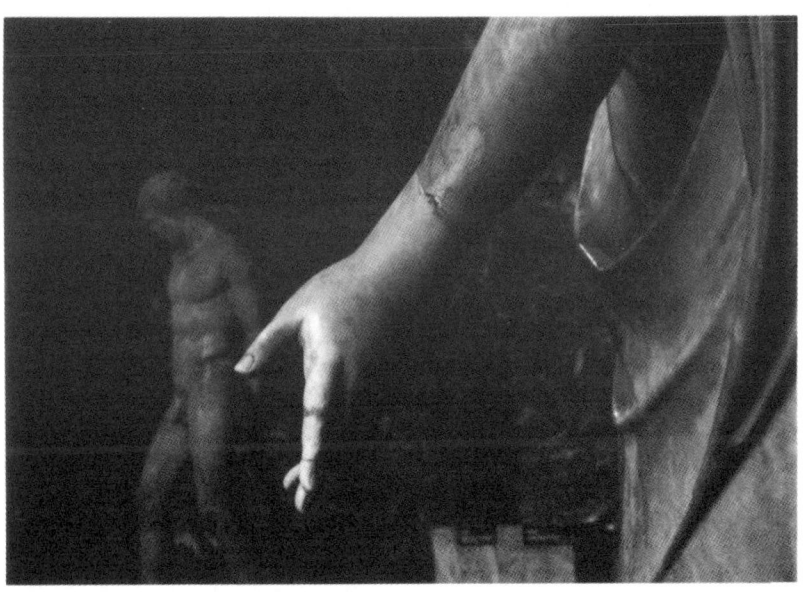

Dorothea Resch - *Louvre* - photograph, 2001

Frank 18 contents

Dorothea Resch		
photograph		3

FICTION & AMERICA 7

Duff Brenna & Thomas E. Kennedy
    A Literary Conference Call   8

Duff Brenna
    "I George"   39

Thomas E. Kennedy
    "The Sacrament of Vodka"   47

POETRY 61

Alain Campos
    drawing   61

Chris Agee
    Dark Hay   62

Virgil Suarez
    Poem for My Uncle Emilio ...   63

Louis Armand
    Jacques Cousteau est mort   64

Fred Johnson
    To the Horizon   65

Wyn Cooper
    Postcard of Saxton's River ...   66
    Postcard Looking at a Postcard ...   67

Jennifer Dick
    Rain   68
    Ruins   68

Robert Gibbons
    Match Point   69

Jill Alexander Essbaum
    A History Lesson   70
    Disengaged   71

Michael J. Dennison
    From Sky   72

Rick Mulkey
    Theoretically Speaking   73

Bono
    drawing   75

Raphael Dagold
    Dirt Heart   76

Carol V. Hamilton
    A Revelation   79

Michael Morse
    Mercury, Slickered   81

Billy Collins
    Tree   82

Sergey Gandlevsky
    Obedient to a gypsy itch...   83

Sandor Kanyadi
    Sigh (*Sohaly*)   84
    Sigh (*Sohaj*)   84
    Should be Abolished (*El kellene*)   85

François Trémolières
    The Oracle   86
    The Son of Abraham or Mad Love   87

Deborah Reich
    Coffee & Tits   89

IN OTHER WORDS 91

Bogdan Korczowski
    "The Only Way Out Against
    Nothingness"   92

José María Mendiluce
    Leila   96

Veronica Frühbodt
    painting   97
    painting   99

Robert Fagan
    Musée de l'Homme   100

Jean Lamore
    Wovoko   103

Damir Uzunovic
    The Quick and the Dead   111

François Lamore
    poem   114
    print   115

Alpha Oumar Konaré Presidential Interview Series: Mali	116
Bedri Baykam Down to the *Kemic*	122
Deepak Chopra Knowing God in Paris	126
Phyllis Cohen *drawing*	129
Wallis Wilde-Menozzi "my dear Ledig"	130
James Baldwin *Telegram*	133

FOREIGN DOSSIER: SWITZERLAND 133

Herzog & De Meuron *photograph*	134
Malcolm Pender Swiss Literature	135
Yves Netzhammer *graphic*	138

Fabio Pusterla
    Things with no Past
    from Buried in the Garden
    Landscape
    from Pietra Sangue Opposing Forces
	139
	140
	142
	143

Paul Nizon *from* The Year of Love	145
Ilma Rakusa *four poems*	149
Monica Cantieni Herr Pillwein and Frau Kulanek	153
Martin R. Dean The Blue Elephant	156
Aglaja Veteranyi Why the Child Is Cooking in the Polenta	164
Wolfgang Amadeus Breulhart Culture: An Instrument of Peace?	174
Claire Genoux *two poems*	181
Elisabeth Wandeler-Deck Rumor About Flying and Hearing	183
Yves Netzhammer *graphic*	188
Leo Tuor Giacumbert Nau—an Annotated Account of His Life as a Shepherd	189
Roger Monnerat The Trout	196
Hugo Loetscher A Nice Accent: On Impurities in Language...	200
Mariella Mehr The Eye of Thetis	206

Pierre Imhasly
    Switzerland is Different for the Swiss ...
    Thou Art a Worm ...
    You Have to See Them in Context
	210
	214
	215

Laurent Schweizer *from* Naso Lituratus	220

Christian Uetz
    two poems
    Nichte und andere Gedichte
	222
	224

Ruth Dreifuss Interview with the Swiss Minister of Culture	226
Anne-Lou Steininger The Sickness of Being a Fly	231
Kristin T. Schnider Her Father. Very Early.	234
Swiss Notables	238

CONTRIBUTORS 239

Phyllis Cohen *drawing*	242

fiction & america

Novelists, story writers, and their views on contemporary culture.

A LITERARY CONFE
DUFF BRENNA AND

In the spirit of encouraging direct access and a continued dialog between readers and writers, **Frank** is initiating here its first Literary Conference Call, published in connection with the **Frank** web site, www.ReadFrank.com and guest sponsor Absolut Vodka. Committed to expanding the creative process and bridging the static printed page and the interactive electronic page we attempt to join the two in a host of complementary ways. We extend the editorial richness of the page by offering online paths of shared experience. We invite **Frank** readers to respond to our featured writers, meet other writers and fellow readers; consult bibliographies; tap into calendars of literary events; and ultimately order each other's books. Just follow the online addresses indicated at strategic points in the interview.

The first Literary Conference Call took place exclusively via email and cell phone and was conducted between David Applefield in Paris, Duff Brenna in San Diego and Thomas E. Kennedy in Copenhagen. In-context, relevant guests have been contacted at selected occasions within the interview to comment on precise issues or questions.

We are reminded of the classic scene in Woody Allen's Annie Hall when Alvi Singer while waiting in line to see Sorrow and the Pity, nauseated by a pretentious New Yorker who pontificates about the work of media-visionary Marshall McLuhan, pulls from off-camera Mr. McLuhan himself, who confronts the man directly: "Obviously you understand nothing about my work." Allen breaks once more the imaginary plane of reality, approaches the camera, and speaks directly to the viewers: "Don't you wish life were really like this?" We all nodded "yes" back in 1977. Well, today the ideal world and the real world have taken a serious step towards each other as we possess the chance to go to the source. McLuhan left no trace of a post-humous email address, but there are plenty of McLuhan pages on the Web. We invite you to step out of line and add to the larger discussion that animates our pages, your pages. A magazine interview is nothing more than a first step for an even richer encounter. Please feel free to participate in this on-going process at www.ReadFrank.com/conference18.

PHOTO: A. GULDBRANDSEN

THOMAS E. KENNEDY

RENCE CALL

DUFF BRENNA

THOMAS E. KENNEDY

TALK WITH *FRANK* EDITOR DAVID APPLEFIELD

Literary friendships and literary rivalries have always been a significant aspect of American letters.

Duff Brenna and Thomas E. Kennedy labored alone on their fiction for decades—Brenna in the American mid- and southwest, Kennedy in New York and Europe. A few years ago, when both reached fifty, they learned about one another's existence through a mutual friend; they proceeded to read, admire, and talk about each other's work. Through a series of on-going and online discussions on the process of writing fiction, both novelists admit that they have grown in their understanding of what they aspire for in their books and their lives—and equally important, to what degree as writers they resist the pressures of a mainstream literary market that is driven now more than ever by raw commerce. **Frank** editor, David Applefield, invited Duff and Tom to interview each other on these pages with the condition that **Frank** be able to interrupt the discussion and provoke the writers throughout the exchange to go further and say more. The following is what transpired in **Frank**'s first Literary Conference Call.

TUNING-IN TO DUFF BRENNA

When Brenna was 15, he read Jack London's biography, *Sailor on Horseback*, and found it a self-defining moment. "I decided I would always take chances, dare myself and do it, and get as much as I can out of whatever time allowed. Now that I'm in my fifties, I'm beginning to slow down, half surprised that I've lived so long and yet finally realizing that I really, really will die and my reflexes aren't so fast anymore. I better cool it if I'm going to finish the series of books clanging around in my head." The author of three published novels *The Book of Mamie*, (University of Iowa Press, 1990); *The Holy Book of the Beard*, (Doubleday, 1996); and *Too Cool*, (Doubleday, 1998) as well as a collection of poetry *Waking in Wisconsin*, (Doubleday, 1998), Duff Brenna is a man who has paid his dues. At fifty-three Brenna has witnessed life from inside of a number of jails and foster homes, through the eyes of a truck driver, a crane operator, a steel worker, a dairy farmer who went bankrupt, an airborne soldier mobilized to "pacify" a Latin American "communist insurrection," a writer struggling to be published for twenty-five years, and as a husband and parent. As a summa cum laude college graduate, he eventually became a tenured associate professor at California State University, San Marcos, where he was named "Outstanding Professor" in the Department of Literature in 1994.

In 1988, his novel *The Book of Mamie*, which had been turned away by 23 agents and 23 publishers, won the AP Novel Award and, two years later, was published by the University of Iowa Press. 1990 was a good year for Brenna; it brought major reviews that hailed him as "an American treasure," and a new Twain, Steinbeck, and Flannery O'Connor. His success with *The Book of Mamie* also brought a movie option and a grant from the National Endowment for the Arts. His next novel, *The Holy Book of the Beard*, debuted to splendid reviews, and the third, *Too Cool,* even greater ones. Brenna's work and narrative style is unique in American fiction. His vision transcends the conventional consensus reality of the United States today. And, there is also exuberance, a rare commodity in a literary America of minimalist K-mart realism. Literary and entertaining, his characters are unlike those we have

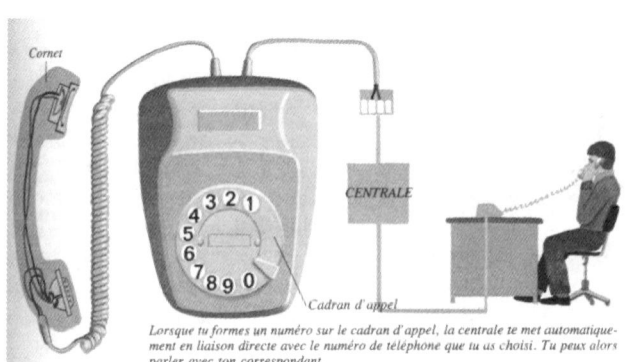

Lorsque tu formes un numéro sur le cadran d'appel, la centrale te met automatiquement en liaison directe avec le numéro de téléphone que tu as choisi. Tu peux alors parler avec ton correspondant.

come to expect from novels published by either literary or commercial presses. The main character of *The Book of Mamie* is a six-foot tall Wisconsin woman of enormous physical strength but with the intellect and savant wisdom of a precocious child. *The Holy Book of the Beard* is peopled with a low-life San Diego diner crowd who reflect, inter alia, the figures of the Judeo-Christian tradition. Triple E, the main character of *Too Cool* is a juvenile delinquent called upon to deal with a situation of grave seriousness in the snowy mountains of Colorado. Brenna's forthcoming novel, *The Altar of the Body* (Picador USA), excerpted here, deals with a passive Minnesota man whose life is taken over by an over-the-hill bodybuilder and his leggy, Las Vegas girlfriend and her aging mother, who, in her hallucinating mind, literally melts into the pages of a paperback western. Hilariously funny, Brenna's novels remain rivetingly serious, and his multitude of past lives inform his prose. Brenna is currently working on *Foggy Meadow Breakdown*, a collection of linked stories about a family that helped settle Foggy Meadow, Minnesota, and he has notes for a novel about the Alaskan experiences of Triple E, the delinquent protagonist of *Too Cool*. Brenna's work has been translated into Japanese, Finnish, and German.

TUNING-IN TO THOMAS E. KENNEDY

It took Thomas E. Kennedy 20 years to publish his first story, "The Sins of Generals" in Long Island University's journal *Confrontation* in 1981. In the 20 years following that first publication, he has published 13 books, 100 short stories, numerous essays, poems and translations, as well as photographs, a new passion. Among other awards, he has won an O. Henry Prize in 1994, the Pushcart Prize in 1990, the Charles Angoff Award in 1988, and first prize in the Gulf Coast Short Story Contest in 2000. Some of his work has been translated into Danish, French, and Serbo-Croatian. In 1997, the University of Missouri at Kansas City (BkMk Press) published a second collection of stories, *Drive, Dive, Dance & Fight*, and Wordcraft of Oregon published his third novel, *The Book of Angels*.

About *Drive, Dive, Dance & Fight*, Andre Dubus affirmed that Kennedy "writes with wisdom, and it is perhaps that wisdom which turns some of his stories of great sorrow into something triumphant."

Kennedy like Brenna has lived a variety of lives—as a shoemaker's helper, bank clerk, military stenographer, medical editor, translator, speech writer, lobbyist, writing teacher, and drifter.

Since 1974, he has lived in Europe, first in France, then in Denmark where he works as a writer and editor in the medical field while he serves as international editor of the American literary journals *Cimarron Review* and *Potpourri*, Contributing Editor of the *Pushcart Prize*, and as Advisory Editor of *The Literary Review*, for which he has guest-edited a number of special anthology issues. He has taught and read as a visitor at many American and European universities and has been a member of the fiction faculty at the

Emerson College International Writing Seminar in the Netherlands since 1990. In 1987, he guest-edited a Danish selection of work for **Frank** *6/7*. New novels—*Roaring Boys*, set in Queens, New York, on the brink of the Vietnam War; *Beneath the Neon Egg*, set in contemporary Copenhagen; and *A Passion in the Desert*, the story of a sixties survivor, as well as a story collection, *Mistress of the Sunrise*, are under editorial consideration. He has just completed another work, *Waiting for the Barbarians, A Love Story*, which is a novel disguised as a guide to the bars of Copenhagen—each chapter takes place in a different watering hole. A collection of essays on the craft of fiction, *Realism & Other Illusions*, will be published by Wordcraft in late 2001.

Kennedy has a B.A. (*summa cum laude*) from Fordham University, a Master of Fine Arts in Writing from Vermont College, and a Ph.D. in American literature from Copenhagen University. He has lived in Denmark since 1975.

La corde tendu boîtes doit faire Et bien sûr, il ne crier!

Connect...www.ReadFrank.com

THE ROLE OF INTUITION

Kennedy: I would like to start, if I may, with a question that has always intrigued me—the extent to which a story can be accessed, or the degree of consciousness a writer brings to the writing. How fully can fiction be *understood*? Do other people ever surprise you by pointing out things you yourself did not fully see?

KENNEDY: ONE OF THE MOST MADE WAS THE DISCOVERY

Brenna: I don't think fiction can ever be *fully* accessed or understood. After I've written a book and gone through the multiple drafts and revisions, I think that I understand everything in it, every word even, but I probably don't. Things slip into your writing that you're not aware of. An essay I read about *The Book of Mamie* pointed out parallels between Mamie Beaver and Steinbeck's Lennie in *Of Mice and Men*. Those observations enlightened me. I can see they are very true. There is no getting away from it, Mamie with her great size and strength and inarticulateness is akin to Lennie to some degree, as is their intimate, earthy association with nature. I've had other surprises, too, things critics have said in their reviews, some that are way off base, others that I'm delighted with and that actually teach me something. Such *revelations* point out that a hidden consciousness often dictates the creative process. The mind has a subtext that its critical self seems to know nothing about. What we understand of our work on the rational, day-tripping level is undone by the dreamy, uncanny layers lurking beneath the surface.

Frank: Okay Duff, but isn't it dangerous for a writer to be alerted to this "subtext?" Isn't this the literary equivalent of genetic engineering?

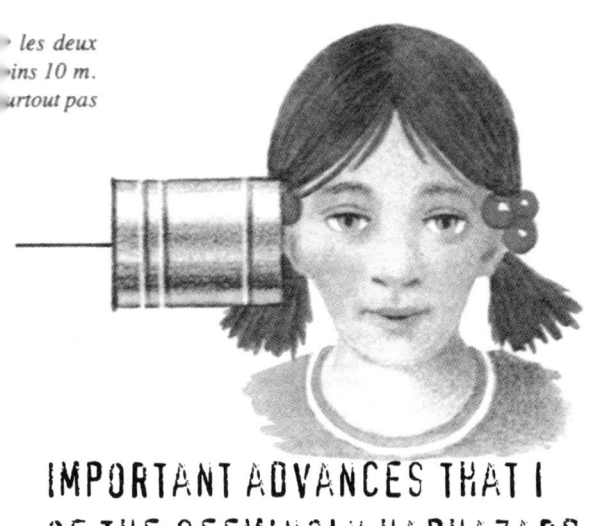

Brenna: Depends on the writer. I like learning about the subtext. It tells me something about the characters and the story and how in tune my subconscious is with what I think I'm doing. Knowing your subtext can enrich the story and give it a direction that it might not have taken otherwise. All books are engineered to some degree every time you revise. Even Kerouac's work was "engineered." Though he might not admit it.

Frank: Tom, how have readers surprised you?

Kennedy: For me intuition is essential. I don't want to have an intellectual understanding of a story I am writing, if ever, until long after it is done. I need not to have. And surprisingly, after groping through the dark of the character's actions to find the story, a fairly clear kind of 'meaning' often proves to be there anyway, constructed by my unconscious or whatever. If I understood the thing from the start, I would never write the story because if my writing doesn't yield a discovery to me, it is pretty worthless from my point of view as a writer. I write to understand, to discover what is there—not to explain what I already know. Sometimes after a public reading, the audience will ask questions, and it amazes me how smoothly the essence of a story is grasped by at least one of them—an essence which to me was inseparable from all the story's elements (voice, character, plot, language, movement, process) and which somebody suddenly sums up in a sentence. If I had grasped these instant summaries in advance, the "cliché gong" might have sounded in my head and killed the story for me before it was born, but once the story is written such a summary is okay. Other times, however, a reader's comment might seem beside the point—like the guy who once asked me why three sentences on page twenty-something of one of my novels began with an 'S' or another young fellow who asked me why there is sex in my fiction.

Frank: So, Tom, why *is* there sex in your fiction?

Kennedy: You got to get it somewhere! That's one of the writer's perks... imagination. No, really, sex matters, and I worry about some of the young Americans I run into on college campuses these days who seem positively terrified of sex. Not too long ago I was sitting in a café in Copenhagen watching all the incredibly beautiful Danish women in their summer dress and who should come literally marching down the street but a contingent of American youths with banners flying in the breeze on which were emblazoned the words NO SEX NO CRY! These kids were trying to picket Danes to institute premarital chastity! To give up free love! What a fucking misunderstanding! Akin to sending an army of uptight missionaries to 19th century Tahiti!

> BRENNA: WRITERS GET OBSESSED WITH WRITING, SO THEY CAN GET OUT OF THIS MESS OF A *REAL* WORLD

Frank: Duff, how great a role does intuition play in your writing?

Brenna: How come Tom gets the good questions? Intuition plays a big role. I almost never know where the story is going at first. I don't plan it, don't outline it or anything. But when I'm really into the flow of writing, ideas and images will come so fast that I have trouble keeping up. All my books so far have come from an image that gets locked in my mind: Mamie kissing the movie projector; Henry Hank storming into the diner and attacking Mary; Triple E and Jeanne trapped in a blizzard in the mountains. I put the images on paper and follow them wherever they may go, which always includes unexpected turns, new characters coming along, new twists in an unknown plot, actions not anticipated. And more often than not I run into dead ends, I'm going nowhere, nothing is coming to life, nothing compels me to go on, the energy evaporates, instinct fails, and the work flutters and dies. My files are loaded with these abortions. But now and then there is a story with *legs*, a story that gets up and takes off and fills my mind with what seems like infinite possibilities. The story leaps ahead and I follow; it really does seem that way, that I am not entirely in control. It is like some part of my brain has actually tapped into what Yeats called the *anima mundi*, the soul of the world, the hidden river of knowledge flowing everywhere, like the magnetic currents that envelop the earth. Every writer I've ever talked to has expressed a similar feeling, the alternate reality, or the point of the Eternal Now that Blake mentioned, the center where vertical and horizontal time lines meet. You wake from this state and three or four hours have passed, but it seems only an hour at most. It's very weird, and wonderful too, like you've stepped into a separate dimension. Maybe that's why writers get obsessed with writing, so they can get out of this mess of a *real* world and get back to that alternate dimension.

Frank: I think it's healthy for readers to hear that. People tend to think good writers know what they're doing, when it's precisely the opposite. The more available you are to what you don't know the greater chance for brilliant surprises to emerge.

Kennedy: Italo Calvino talks about this in his essay on *Lightness*—about "literature as an existential function, the search for lightness as a reaction to the weight of living...the sudden agile leap of the poet who raises himself above the weight of the world." Do your characters lead the way when you write, as Forster said his did in *A Passage to India*, or are they, as Nabokov claimed in reaction to Forster, galley slaves who do as they are told?

Brenna: Like an indulgent parent, I let the characters have their way. Then, when I have found out who they really are and what story I want them to tell, I pretty much make them behave.

Frank: Not to slide too far off topic, but is that how you bring up your kids too? Does art teach you how to live?

Brenna: Trial and error and learning from your own mistakes. Consistency. Discipline of mind that allows you to work continuously seven days a week to bring out the best that is in you and your "work-in-progress." Yes, some of the ideals of art seem to dovetail with the ideals of child rearing. As to art teaching you how to live. My son and daughter grew up surrounded by books and conversation about books and paintings and plays and movies. I took them to the Shakespeare Festival every year from the time they were in first grade. Did it make them better adults? I believe so. In other words, I believe that if you study Shakespeare, you are far less likely to become a serial killer or a rapist or some other grotesque horror than if you don't have Shakespeare or someone connecting you to the timeless and universal triumphs and tragedies of humankind. Art is the great web that bonds us in human sympathy with the past, present and future. Without art, life becomes a series of meaningless, mechanical motions.

Frank: Tom, at the end of the first chapter of *Neon Egg* your protagonist, Bluett, thinks about what he's done wrong in his family life. Does the act of writing, especially at this stage of your life, force you to contemplate how you have conducted your personal affairs?

Kennedy: There is no doubt that my aesthetic development is informed by my existential experience. One learns and grows from one's personal failures as well as from the occasional enlightenment or even triumph of emotion with which one is blessed. Having children greatly enhanced my capacity to experience existence, I think, and to experience love, and having been married for nearly a quarter century was a tremendous experience for me. So yes, I do contemplate my personal affairs constantly—as one reviewer said of one of my characters 'constantly assessing.' I want to know what has happened to me in my life, and to do that I have to think about it from as many angles as I can, and that experience is certainly closely related to one dimension of the progress of my writing. Other dimensions would include those of language growth and experience, philosophical expansion, historical perspective, immersion in the hated elements, etc.

Frank: Tom, earlier you brought up a good point about the pain of the writer and his or her galley slaves. As readers we connect to the lives and pain of the characters we spend time with, but we are obscured from what the writer endures. Tell us about your "weight of living." What have you been living, psychically, while writing *Beneath the Neon Egg*.

Kennedy: *Beneath the Neon Egg* started with my divorce and two images of Copenhagen—the frozen street lake beneath the window of my apartment and an animated neon sign on a brick wall on the other side of the lake; the sign depicts a neon chicken that goes through a series of movements resulting in its laying a big neon egg that I saw that winter again and again reflected in the black frozen ice of Black Dam Lake. The egg would glow there on the wall for a moment, then go out, and the chicken would reappear to go through the motion of laying the egg again. This neon sign has been there for many years—a dairy ad—and is a kind of emblem of Copenhagen. It became an emblem for me of the winter of my discontent—those frozen months following my divorce. In that state of mind, I somehow conceived a character named Bluett ("Blue" for short). Bluett is an Irish name pronounced "Blew It," but that association, believe it or not, managed to evade me while I wrote the book. Bluett, it turned out was a free-lance translator who, in order to survive financially, had to translate five pages a day every day. Bluett too is divorced and alone and wandering the frozen streets of winter, seeing that neon egg, and I followed him in my mind's eye to the end of the journey of a winter. In the background I've placed the music of John Coltrane's magnificent jazz symphony, *A Love Supreme*—the four parts of the novel are written in parallel to that symphony, one feature of which is the disintegration of musical notes into pure vibration preliminary to the creation of a new reality—the pure love of God, the supreme love.

So Bluett takes a journey through his isolation and physical longing to the beginning of an understanding of the divine connectedness of the human race. What the character experiences is pure fiction, but the emotional course beneath the fiction paralleled my own emotional life at that time. I suspect that most or many novels do that for their writers and hopefully also offer themselves to be translated into the reader's emotional reality as well.

> KENNEDY: I WANT TO KNOW WHAT HAS HAPPENED TO ME IN MY LIFE

The new novel I have just finished, *Waiting for the Barbarians*, begins in a spiritual sense from the other side of that discontent. It is subtitled *A Love Story*, and that is what it is—a story of a man's love of life and all that life can offer, even if his consciousness is defined by great pain. The starting image for me to write this was a true story of a mother who killed her children, husband and siblings in cold blood with a pistol. I met the only child to survive the bloodbath; he had hid away beneath a bed, listening to the mother searching to get him, too. Paradoxically, the novel was a pure joy to write because there is room in it for everything I care about—history, literature, music, physical joy, the intense pleasures of surrendering to the unimpeachable desire to live and be happy in spite of all.

FORM AND REWRITING

Frank: I've heard Tom ask the question whether writers needed to learn to "restructure the spontaneous." There is usually a pretty big difference in what one writes in a first draft and the finished work. Both of you do a lot of rewriting. Let's talk about this process. Duff?

Brenna: I'm obsessive about it. Really, it's the part of writing that I enjoy the most, the revisions, the search for the perfect phrase, the perfect word, the lean, well-balanced sentence. I cultivate a cold mind when I revise. I'm usually pretty calm, and at the same time ruthless. Nothing is sacred. I slash and burn, so to speak, and now and then I'm proud of the results, the purity of a line, the way it communicates, the way it seems to shine. I forget who it was that said, "I'm not a writer, I'm a rewriter." Whoever said that is a person after my own heart.

Frank: Do any examples come to mind, Duff, of how a changed word or phrase moved the writing from the banal to the sublime?

Brenna: I wouldn't say sublime. I've never read a sublime sentence. One searches for "sublimity" with the same understanding that one searches for "perfection," always knowing that you'll never get there, it will always be beyond your grasp. The Grand Canyon is sublime. The Horsehead Nebula is sublime. It seems to me that you have to go to nature to really view anything truly sublime. But what you can capture is a fine word or phrase, or as I said, "the lean, well-balanced sentence." In an early draft of *The Altar of the Body*, I wrote, "Slow as vodka logic it came, first the bumper and grill, then the interminable hood, the windshield, the long dull side in gloomy black." Then I go on to talk about a smiling, waving woman being inside the car. After several drafts, I changed the image to: "The first time I see her she is steering a Lincoln Continental through the neighborhood. Slow as vodka logic she comes, looking left and right, searching for something. Tree leaves reflect fractal patterns off her windshield, smearing her image, bringing her in and out of focus." To my mind those are three clean sentences, with each word pulling its own weight and adding to the other words around it. We get the woman, we get the car, and we get foreshadowing: fractal patterns connecting with the woman's smeared image coming in and out of focus. In the book, she is a liar and a manipulator and yet also a very good woman at heart. Life has overwhelmed her, fractured her, so to speak. I tear all my sentences down that way, go over and over and over them. And sometimes I feel like I've done well. Other times I'm not so sure and I wish I were smarter and more talented and had a clearer eye.

> **BRENNA: SLOW AS VODKA LOGIC SHE COMES, LOOKING LEFT AND RIGHT.**

Kennedy: I want to go deeper into this. I really envy the way you just muscle right in like that, Duff. I don't mean about seeking *le mot just*—of course, I do that, too. I'm talking about the very foundations of the work. Of course we learn our craft, we learn it long and hard so that when we come to our writing finally we are like carpenters or bricklayers or wire-lathers—we know how things go together and if we lay a crooked curbing, we curse and tear it out and start over. Not that. I'm talking about something else and I worry about it; I don't think I'll ever stop worrying. Calvino says, "Lightness for me goes with precision and determination, not with vagueness and the haphazard." And then to illustrate his point he quotes Paul Valéry, "*Il faut être léger* *comme l'oiseau, et non comme la plume."* One should be light like the bird and not like the feather. This is a challenge to me because in the 40 years of my pursuit of craft, half the time I was probably spinning my string, but in the other half one of the most important advances that I made was the discovery of the seemingly haphazard. I won't say anything about vagueness being powerful, although ambiguity of course certainly can be. This might be an essential difference in our methods—or it might be a mere difference in terminology. We may actually be talking about the same thing. But I have seen you wade into a seemingly final draft and—as nearly as I can determine—savage it, shape it, reverse it. But for myself that can be the quickest route to the destruction of the ephemeral spirit that constructs the fiction, that shows the connectedness of all that is so seemingly haphazard in life. I have had to learn to allow my mind to accept the words that are handed up to it from wherever it is they come from. Or as Beckett said, "It all happens between the hand and the page."

Frank: Is there anything Beckettesque about how you write, Duff?

Brenna: Basically he was a very deliberate craftsmen and he knew exactly what he wanted from his novels and from those who performed in his plays. "Less emotion, please. Play it flat, Billie," was something I heard him say in a profile on TV. I am perhaps as deliberate as Beckett in the revision process, I don't know. But the big difference is that he was a genius and he knew how to get the effect. I know the effect I want, but I'm never as sure of it as I'd like to be, never as sure my readers will see it the way I see it, and I often have to do what Tom does and just allow my mind to accept the words that are handed up.

Frank: Let's ask John Calder, Beckett's publisher and life-long friend if Beckett simply knew what he wanted or if he was also consumed by great doubt whether what he wanted and what he achieved were the same. Hold on, I'll call John in London right now... It's ringing.... John, it's David in Paris. We're in the middle of an interview with Tom Kennedy in Copenhagen and Duff Brenna in San Diego, and we have a question for you. You knew Beckett like few others did; help us understand if even the greatest of the greats, a Nobel Prize winner, was obsessed with self doubt as a writer.

John Calder: Of course he was. Every writer is. On the other hand, Beckett constantly worked gradually from doubt to resolution in his writing. 99% of everything Beckett wrote he threw away by revising and pruning down. What's important is that he knew what he wanted to say, but he had to work out how to say it. He once said to me "All I want to do is to put my head against the cliff wall and move it one millimeter." Beckett's greatest talent was to cut through all the beliefs that we have been told and to decide what he disbelieved and then cut through it. A good example is religious ceremony; we cling to it because it gives one security, but in the end it stops us from thinking. Beckett was certainly a craftsman, but one that was never satisfied.

Frank: Thanks John... Tom...

Kennedy: What a privilege to hear that! About a third of my hundred or so short stories, maybe more, and maybe the best of them, if I can say that, occurred in such a way that their structure was largely inviolable—if I started trying to pull bricks out it would topple. I think all the stories in *Unreal City* came that way and many of them in *Drive, Dive, Dance & Fight*. Sometimes I didn't understand the story at all, I only felt its rightness, and later, after it was published, I would discover the "meaning." Of course, I rewrote, polished, shifted sentences about, but the basic thing was basically as it came to me, and I learned how to judge this by ruining a few stories first with undue and unnecessary monkeying, trying to insert "reason" into what was essentially "wild."

Frank: Tom, you're an avid writing teacher. How do you teach aspiring fiction writers to trust what comes naturally while also insisting on a strict attention to craft?

Kennedy: For me, the hardest thing to teach, but one of the things that has occasionally seemed to work, is to advise the person struggling with a story to take a walk with its main character—or with its voice. To imagine the narrative persona strolling through a known or imagined landscape and seeing that landscape through the persona's sensibility and allowing language to crystallize around the thread of that movement. As often as not, I find my character or my voice will lead me to the heart of my fiction and reveal what the story is seeking.

Frank: Don't you often have your writing students shine flashlights into the dark corners of their childhood memories and other haunting exercises to see what really lurks within? I remember once in Amsterdam you completely freaked out a young writer by having her go down into the cellar of her house when she was five, or something like that.

Kennedy: Yes, I do a 'basement' exercise which I contributed to Pam Painter's book *What if?* which seems to have been useful to a number of workshop participants. The object is to find an unknown door by traveling through remembered sensations into the basement of your childhood home, by remembering the smell of your father, the sound of your mother's voice, etc. Once you find the door you open it and start to write, it is supposed to convey you from deep remembrance into an instant outflow of expression. Afterwards, those in the workshop who wish to are invited to read what they have written. Well, sometimes I have a feeling that some of the participants would like to be gently nudged to read their piece rather than push themselves

BRENNA: DON'T WRITE UNLESS YOU NEED TO.

forward, and in the case you refer to, I asked one of the women present if she would like to read, and she nearly burst into tears, whispering hoarsely, "You don't want to know what happened in the basement of my childhood home...." I was terrified that I may have called forth some serious difficulty for the poor woman and began to question my right to work with this exercise; however, that woman did come back to me later in the day to assure me that she had come through the terror and found something valuable in the experience. Still, it was a scary moment and I am reluctant to try again. Free association can be a dangerous game, and sometimes you can inadvertently put people into a near state of hypnosis.

Frank: Duff, you teach writing as well. What's the most important lesson you share with younger writers?

Brenna: Don't write unless you need to. A lot of people say they want to write. They have a book in them and someday they'll get to it and wow! Writing is hard, hard work. The rewards of writing are generally personal, occasionally maybe a cathartic release that might heal some mental wound you've been nursing half your life. Sometimes you actually make some money. Sometimes critics actually say nice things about your work. You might even get famous if that's what you want. But chances are none of those things are going to happen. Chances are you'll find mostly rejection and heartbreak, lots of it, and you'll become bitter and you'll quit. Unless you need to keep going. Wanting will not get you there. Needing will. But only if you've got talent and perseverance and you've really got something to say. Without that combination, you're dead. I also tell them about the great writers who were rejected and vilified, but who finally won out against all odds. I always use James Joyce as an example, the problems he had just getting *Dubliners* published and then the shark-feeding criticism about *Ulysses* and so on. I want my students to know that if they stay true to their vision and work like hell at their craft and don't crack up over how unappreciated they are (by parents, publishers and friends), they can beat the odds.

Kennedy: Joyce is mined for ideas by the critics, and surely there are ideas there, but I had to smile when I read in Richard Ellman's biography of Joyce, "To the French among whom he lived for 20 years, he lacks the refined rationalism which would prove him incontestably a man of letters." Dubus used to quote Zola as saying, "My books are full of ideas but none of them is mine." I wonder sometimes. The critics are so ingenious; they sometimes dazzle me with what they mine from a work, but often, maybe even usually, if I start thinking in that vein while I'm writing, even while I revise, I'm a dead man.

Frank: And yet the opposite is worse. What a perfect bridge we've built to cross over to a discussion of the publishing world. The battle for fiction writers to get reviewed at all is intense. Worrying about being misunderstood today, Tom, seems like a luxury in a world that gives so little attention to the work of unknown novelists, especially ones writing difficult and ambitious books. Readers are unaware that 60% of the books purchased in America's bookstores have been written by a grand total of ten authors! All the rest of us share the remaining 40%. Duff, are you bitter that it has taken so long before the publishing world has discovered your talent, or are you grateful that you are now at least being read? Tom, hold on, I can feel you chomping at the electronic bit. We'll let you have a shot at this one too.

Brenna: Believe me, I'm as grateful as I can be for all that's happened. It took four years to get my first novel published and those four years were the most despairing years of my writing life. I couldn't get anyone to read my manuscript, not agents, not publishers, no one. I was very frustrated then and filled with self-doubt. It was only a fluke that I sent the manuscript to the AWP competition. When I got the call a year later saying it won first prize, I was so astonished and overcome that I couldn't speak. I don't think I even told the caller thank you. I kept the news to myself for several days before I finally told my old friend and fellow writer Jerry Bumpus about it. It was like if I told anyone, I would jinx myself and the AWP would call back and say it had been a mistake. I'll always be grateful that the AWP exists and I'll always be especially grateful to Andrea Barrett and Toby Olson, who picked *Mamie*.

Frank: With a hundred published stories, Tom, you are either the most successful unknown writer or the least successful published writer in America. Which is it?

Kennedy: I guess it has to do with what one considers success. I can make a pretty fat bit of money writing speeches or other papers for professional leaders. Fortunately, I have never been called upon to write something I did not believe in so I can do that without prostituting myself. I am happy to exercise this facility, but it does not give me even a fraction of the sense of success I feel when I manage to create a piece of viable fiction for which I am paid a fraction of what I get for the speeches. This may sound like sour prunes and I am not saying I don't want to earn a cool million for my fiction, but I would not feel like a success if I became a millionaire writing stuff that did not nourish my own spirit. What I am trying to say is that success, to my mind, is in the writing, not in the size of the check you collect or even the number of readers you have. I want to be read, and I want to earn some money for what I write, but most of all I want to write as well as I can and to have it pub-

> **BRENNA: THE TERM "LITERARY" DOOMS A BOOK OVER HERE.**

lished. What comes beyond that is not a matter of success so much as a matter of fortune, I think.

Frank: Why is the market for literature—serious fiction—so paltry in the United States, and comparatively much larger in Europe. Either one of you can answer?

Kennedy: I'm not certain that's true. Every year I go on a reading tour for two to four or more weeks in the U.S., and everywhere I go I meet people who love serious fiction, who buy it and read it and go to readings and find it important and enjoyable. The small presses and literary magazines in the U.S.—thousands of them—are a national treasure. So the marketplace is different today from what it was in the first half of the 20th century. The commercial market for serious fiction has dwindled, but the less commercial market is stronger than ever before, and I am immensely satisfied about that. I want my books and stories and essays to be published, and the chances of that happening in today's American literary market are very good. Write something good, and it will see print more likely than not, but if you're in it for money, reconsider the options. There's more dough in underwriting.

> **KENNEDY: IF YOU'RE IN IT FOR MONEY, RECONSIDER THE OPTIONS. THERE'S MORE DOUGH IN UNDERWRITING.**

Brenna: *The Holy Book of the Beard* fell off a cliff in the U.S. But a German publishing company brought it out in translation and it did pretty well, even got into reprint paperback. I asked myself why the book did well over there but not here. For one thing, critics here were unanimous in their praise of *Beard*, but also unanimous in calling it "literary." "Highly literary," one called it. The term "literary" dooms a book over here. Maybe that isn't the case in Europe. It's only a guess on my part, but I think being called literary might be an asset over there. There are a lot of medieval allusions in *Beard* that the German education might be trained to see. *Beard* is a kind of *Quest for the Holy Grail* story, with subtextual (there's that word again) references to the works of medieval writers like Gottfried von Strassburg and Wolfram von Eschenbach. I may be crazy, but I think the Germans picked up on what I was doing and got a kick out of it. With few exceptions, American education doesn't prepare readers to enjoy literature on a holistic level. I mean a level that is not only emotional but intellectual as well. Americans generally get only half the pleasure out of a book that is available. If the book makes them laugh or cry or get scared or feel horny, then it's all they need from it. They want an emotional experience, period. I have the sense that Europeans are more hungry for the holistic possibilities of literature. Maybe I'm giving them too much credit, but I bet I'm not.

Frank: Duff, you've seen the seamy side of American life, prison, poverty. And Tom, you write from outside the US, with an expat point of view with a critical eye on contemporary American life. How do you both feel about being American? Or what does the United States mean to you today? Especially now that we have not only a new administration but a different mind-set and aesthetic in the saddle.

Kennedy: I love Americans—their big-heartedness, their generosity, their warmth, their "make room for one" more mentality—but I don't think much of America when I consider things like the employment of the death penalty and when people are invited, even encouraged, to witness executions, some of them standing outside and chanting taunts; I am sickened at the thought of our swollen, packed prisons, where even children are shackled and jailed, where there are still slums and greatly deprived persons. Where the first thing the new president does—one of the richest presidents in American history—is to grab an enormous amount of the so-called surplus (which is not really a surplus but money collected to invest in future social needs which will not be otherwise funded) and fling the bulk of it back to the richest one percent of the population. And I find the universal commercial blight of McDonalds, KFC, Burger King, Pizza Hut, 7-11 *et al* disgusting, embarrassing, poisonous, and dangerous not only to human beings but to the poor animals that are bred under dubious conditions. I mean goddammit! Remember Ibsen's *Enemy of the People* a hundred years ago? He was warning us about what was happening. In that play, people refrain from mentioning that the water supply at a profitable spa is poisoned and the man who speaks out against this criminal silence is referred to as an enemy of the people. Well the poisoned source of our contemporary lives are spreading all over the world, and I hate the fact that so much of it originates from America. Still there is no denying it is a wonderfully exuberant country, a land of enormous beauty, a country where people are full of life and hope even if they are cheated of a life of quality and charm.

Brenna: This is not my favorite subject, but since you've asked I'll tell you briefly that I'm one of those who believe that America's so-called potential for creating "The Great Society" is idealistic bullshit. No society has that potential and especially not a society whose mixture of Puritanism and Social Darwinism makes it both anti-intellectual and intolerant of dissension. Of the absurd outcome which "elects" a silver-spooned boy to the highest office in the land, all I can say is, he lost the popular vote by more than half a million and yet somehow he "won." How can that be? The only explanation is that we get the politicians we deserve.

LANGUAGE VS. FILM

Brenna: Can we talk about how film has impacted literature? I've been wondering if Tom ever writes with the movies in mind? It seems like one of the best ways to break out from the pack these days is to get a movie made of your story.

Kennedy: Right in the heart! I would be a big fat liar if I denied I would love to have a movie made out of something I've written. I kind of thought that my third novel, *The Book of Angels*, might make a good movie, but I never wrote it with that in mind. I've had several option queries on it, but so far no takers. The whole idea of waiting to get picked by Hollywood, or even by a noble independent, appealing as it maybe, is I think something of a sucker's game. Sure most of us want it, I guess, but what does it really entail? I know people who've gone through years of options finally to have the movie made—and maybe the movie is even good, like Gordon Weaver's *Count a Lonely Cadence* filmed as *Cadence* by Martin Sheen—but in some way or another they get railed out of the project, end up with a small handful of dollars and nothing much else because the thing is not released in theaters, but as a video with some unsatisfactory and unrecognizable title—they did that to Carolyn Chute when they filmed her *The Beans of Egypt, Maine*, a fine novel and a fine and faithful film, too, but the video people gave it the goddamned title of *Forbidden Desires*, to try to play up on the incest implications. Or you get a famous director and lead actors but are denied the right to make use of it with a tie-in publication. So what really comes of it other than a demonstration of what an insignificant shit a writer really is in the bean-counting world of the silver screen? Of course, these are problems most of us probably wouldn't mind having, but my point is that it can too easily come down to an expense of spirit in a waste of unfulfilled greed.

Brenna: Chute's experience reminds me of Irish director David Keating's movie called *The Last of High Kings*, which was re-titled *Summer Fling* when it came to the States. Or what about the film adaptation Stanley Kubrick did of Stephen King's *The Shining*? Do you know that story, Tom?

Kennedy: Actually, yes. Kubrick took large liberties with King's book, turned it into a kind of horror burlesque. Real camp. Most of the humanity that was in the novel disappears. King's book was about child abuse and the child abuser as victim of his own past.

Brenna: I've heard that King made his own version and it wasn't very good.

Frank: But remember Stephen King is not a filmmaker! Duff, you brought up the film thing; this must be bothering you. When *Too Cool* is released as celluloid you can be sure more people will see it than will have read it. How does that make you feel? Are writers in competition with the visual world, and if so, isn't the online world, electronic books, and the Internet a greater threat to—or potential replacement of—literature as we have known it for the last two centuries?

Brenna: IF it comes out, it will increase the likelihood that the sales of *Too Cool* will increase and that my other novels will get into paperback and more people will read them and maybe I'll even be able to turn to full-time writing one of these days. Yes, writers are in competition with the visual world and the Internet is a threat to literature as we know it. But the reality today is just what Tom said it is, and sometimes a movie can give a writer the break he or she needs. Publishers may publish you, but unless you've got a big name, they are not going to advertise you, they are not going to push your books, they are going to wait around like Wilkins Micawber and see if something turns up. Word of mouth is one of their favorite phrases for how a book becomes popular. They wait around to see if word of mouth does it.

Kennedy: I'm not worried. Yes, the Internet is changing things about writing just as papyrus, the printing press, the typewriter, and the word processor have. Television and film are important media, and I do notice that some workshop pieces I see in my writing classes in recent years read like film scripts, but trying to write like that is based on a misunderstanding you see often; young writers responding not to poetry or fiction but to film. I had a manuscript a while back that started something like, "Boston. I can't believe I'm back in fucking Boston." The writer explained it was a play on the opening lines of Coppola's *Apocalypse Now*—a great film, but you can't write a great fiction just by trying to call up images from a film. Film is not fiction. In *The ABC of Reading*, Ezra Pound points out that literature is made of words while drama is made of people speaking words and what is lacking in the words they speak can be made up for in the movement of bodies. Some people think they can see a film in their head and just write the dialogue down, but it doesn't work that way, not for me anyway. In a film script when you write "He walks across the room" it works because you've got a Harvey Keitel or a Robert Duvall or a James Earl Jones waiting to put the power of flesh to those words. If you write in fiction "He walks across the room" it is dead wood, pulls no weight, does nothing for the most part. Alec Guiness told about how he did not understand the character he was to portray in a film until he could literally walk as the character would. Sometimes he would go to the zoo and watch how the animals moved for a clue to human nature or walk down the street and study the movements of people. External movement for him was a channel to the inner life. The way fiction walks is based on

BRENNA: AM I BASHING FILM? MAYBE SO.

beats, each one symbolized by a letter of the alphabet.

Brenna: Yes, some of the hardest scenes to write in fiction are transition scenes from one room to another or from a chair to the kitchen, from a car to a porch. But as far as literature goes, what will happen to the language if it defaults to the movie screen, if people quit reading and make movies their literature? Wouldn't that be the true death of the language, not to mention the novel?

Kennedy: To my mind, language is the supreme medium, always was and always will be. I've been trying to read *Finnegan's Wake* again of late—a story as you know of a sleeping man dreaming the history of mankind. There is an interesting statement by Seamus Dean about it: he says that one of the book's implications is that the myth of the Fall can be understood as a fall into language, that language is secondary and not primary. We experience this whenever we try to "tell" a dream—the very act of casting the images, or whatever they are, into language changes them; nuances drop away by the scores with every word we select. The world and the word are two different things. As Dean puts it, "the priority of the dream over the language in which it is narrated cannot be established linguistically." Because language is secondary. But if language—which forms from the simple natural act of raising the words of thought on our breath—is secondary, then what is film? Film is made by groups of people and a complex of machines in an impossible and rarely spontaneous interaction; it is not even tertiary—it is reduced by a thousand-fold. Of course, if you take a shitty writer, you don't get the power of language either.

Frank: Hold on fellas, this film-bashing, whether rooted in truth or not, I think misses the mark. There are far more dangerous tendencies in contemporary life than our dependency on cinema as entertainment. Consider again the way the digital revolution is changing the way we access and distribute information and culture, let alone our reading habits, and look at how the roles of the writer and the publisher in society are being redefined. Do either of you feel threatened by this invasion of traditional relationships? Or do you feel challenged to participate, find your readers, and gain impact as writers? On a personal front, what we hope we are doing with this interview on both paper and on our web site reveals at least our thinking...and belief in concrete gains for literature and writers with a big L and W.

Brenna: First things first. Am I bashing film? Maybe so. Let me qualify what I think about film. I think I'm bashing the trite and the trivial in film, the lack of respect that some filmmakers have for their audience. But film can also be an enlightening experience. Film at its best, like literature at its best, might enlarge a person's perspective about life. I want film to understand and care about its power over us. I talked about good literature being a holistic experience and that's what I want film to be as well. Less special effects and more substance, please. As for being threatened by the electronic and digital explosion, I'm not particularly worried. I can only write the books I write and I don't have time or energy to devote to feeling challenged by the Internet or the technological revolution taking place. I have a feeling that the next generation of writers will find their way through the maze of cyberspace and set a precedent for those to come, and only the older writers will fret about it. The younger writers will wonder what all the fuss is about and they'll do just fine. In fact, they might end up with more readers than anyone ever imagined.

Kennedy: The only problem I have about publishing on the Net is the question of copyright, and I have yet to obtain a satisfactory response about the implications involved. When you publish a story in a print periodical you usually sell one-time rights, and if there is a press run of say 5,000 copies, that's it. Of course, the story continues to exist in each of those 5,000 copies, even as they are remaindered or tossed into second-hand bookshop bins, god bless 'em, or illegally photocopied for classroom use. But when you publish a story online it would appear that it is there forever, accessible to anyone with the necessary electronic equipment to click it forth. So one time rights suddenly means forever and everywhere in the world. I am very jealous of my copyrights. With one exception, I own every story I have ever written, and I like it that way. I know that wonderful things are happening on the Net in terms of literature—just take a look at Mike Neff's fabulous *Webdelsol* (www.webdelsol.com) for example with all its many many links and connections. Maybe the Internet will change the idea of ownership of what we write and make us all noncommercial in the end, return us to the sacred sense of language when the beginning was the word and the word was with god and the word was god. What's John Grisham gonna do then, huh?

Frank: Maybe we should ask him? I'm sending an email to him now. We'll see what comes back? There are lots of other models though to consider or invent, and some may be in the greater interest of literature and serious writers. Others, less so. Stephen King, whom we've already mentioned, recently sold chapters of a new book in progress for a buck a chapter, delivered as email. The idea is inviting. The problem is that King already has a huge readership and the ability to promote such innovations on the front page of daily newspapers, something that the rest of can't do. The result is that King ends up making lots more money by cutting out the publisher and the bookseller, and in the end, the mega author comes to resemble the huge chain or the corporate publisher, hardly friends to more literary work by lesser-known authors.

Kennedy: But the King project failed, didn't it? He had to close it down before the end of the book for lack of sufficient subscribers.

Brenna: Survival of the fittest. Social Darwinism, I tell you. Just kidding. Sort of.

REJECTION AND THE SPIRITUAL DISCIPLINE OF WRITING

Kennedy: It must have been a great lift to you, Duff, when Doubleday offered you a two-book contract. And winning the AP Prize must have done a lot to soothe the wound of those 46 rejections *The Book of Mamie* weathered. Nearly every one of my own dozen books has been published by a different small press, and I never know when I finish a book whether it will be published or not. It's almost always starting with square one in terms of the market.

Brenna: Does it bother you?

Kennedy: It's part of the experience.

Frank: Tom, answer the question!

Kennedy: After a while you get used to it. About 10 years ago I looked into the subject of rejection to try to get a handle on it. I researched and published an article on it in *Poets & Writers* (www.pw.org), and I found out how many outstanding writers have weathered monumental rejections and how few writers can actually live from their sales. Gordon Weaver sent one of his stories out something like 70 times, then sold it for a few hundred dollars to a magazine that published the next two or three he sent them. Andre Dubus—who recently died and who is recognized as one of the great contemporary story writers—sent one of his stories out 38 times before he found a little magazine that would take it. And it is a splendid story, a very short one titled "Waiting." Writing that article on rejection helped me realize it's not personal, it's part of the experience, you have to be the water that wears away the stone.

Frank: Duff, what do you have to add on the subject of rejection? It struck me that we at **Frank** should be thinking more about this subject; with 950 out of 1000 manuscripts being returned each year, there are far more negative messages going out than acceptances although rejection is often unrelated to quality or merit. And often it takes us months before we even say no. It's a lousy deal being the writer and laborious being the publisher.

Brenna: Tom said you have to be the water wearing away the stone. I'll go with that. But I'm wondering, do you ever feel like you're the stone, like you're the one being worn away? Have you ever thought of quitting?

Frank: Wait, Duff, you go first...

Brenna: I could say "Survival of the fittest" again. I don't mean by that that the best writers survive. I don't even want to think about the great writers who have killed themselves or have just given up in despair. But it's not enough to be good, you have to be tough as well. Survival is to a great extent what the writing life is about. I go back to what I said before about perseverance. Tom's water wearing away the stone. And it also helps if you've got a strong ego and get angry at rejection, rather than go weepy with self-pity.

Frank: Okay—but don't show that anger to us. Writers don't realize to what degree editing a literary magazine verges on masochism.

Kennedy: That's true. Writers should be grateful as hell to the small magazines and presses. I am. I've thought about quitting, but the next day I'd be back at my typewriter anyway. As Rainer Maria Rilke says in his wonderful little book *Letters to a Young Poet*—which I would recommend to every beginning writer—hell, to every writer—"Go into yourself and test the deeps in which your life takes rise; at its source you will find the answer to the question whether you must create... Perhaps it will turn out that you are called to be an artist. Then take that destiny upon yourself and bear it, its burden and its greatness, without ever asking what recompense might come from outside... Go into yourself. Ask yourself in the stillest hour of your night: 'must I write?'"

A writer produces a story in much the same way that an oyster produces a pearl—around some grain of irritant, through pain and worry and irritation. So you write a story and half the time you have trouble even giving the thing away. But you can't dwell on it. Your business is to write what you can, the best you can. To tell the truth, after that initial 20 years of frustration, every time I sell a story now I feel like a kid on Christmas Eve. Five hundred bucks and I feel terrific! Sometimes I get a nice fee for reading one of my stories, and to me, it is a small miracle that some college will pay me fifteen hundred dollars to read for half an hour to fifty or a hundred students and faculty. I feel truly privileged even just to get that much attention and recognition for doing something that I love to do and that makes it possible for me to live and be happy. In the end, that is our prime duty in life: to live and be happy. I feel sure of that.

> **KENNEDY:**
> **A WRITER PRODUCES A STORY MUCH THE SAME WAY THAT AN OYSTER PRODUCES A PEARL – AROUND SOME GRAIN OF IRRITANT**

Frank: And, it's easy to forget that. Personally, there are two levels of need, the act of creating and the satisfaction of publishing. If we are talking about being happy in this life, both the inner soul and the outer ego need nourishing. The knowledge that your art is connecting with readers who are reliving what you've created is pure joy. That's the publishing part.

Brenna: I've heard people say we have a duty to be happy, and I can't help but be puzzled by that. Actually, I don't know why we're here at all. It seems like evolution just got carried away and couldn't stop itself in time. We are predetermined to struggle and to both succeed and fail. Happiness in that "pure joy" category that you mentioned comes, but as you well know, it is evanescent, a minute, an hour, and then we're looking for what to do next. Writers live to write and they live to connect themselves to others through their work. We want to entertain and be admired, loved, appreciated. If all that happens, will we be happy? No, we'll be dissatisfied. We'll want more love, more appreciation. And we will want to prove ourselves over and over, so no one will think we're fakes. For me, the unfathomable experiences of life drive us to create our novels, poems, stories. It's a compulsion, a need to understand, a need to get control. It doesn't make me happy, really. Happiness at one end or the other doesn't have much to do with any of it.

Kennedy: For me the writing itself is its own reward. The rest is gravy. The writing and then, afterwards, as John O'Hara pointed out, the contemplation of the finished product. That part doesn't last as long, though. Really, the true joy of writing is experiencing that rush of well-being and creativity while you are in the process, feeling it happen, experiencing yourself as a tool of the craft, a medium of the story, an essential force binding together the scattered elements of an existence, it is a spiritual feeling really, a communion.

Brenna: You see it as spiritual?

Kennedy: Yes, writing can be as spiritual as any religious act I know. A communion with some force greater than yourself. A lot of writers don't like to talk about that. Maybe they feel that they are aggrandizing themselves or their work by calling the craft a spiritual pursuit, but it is that nonetheless in my opinion. It is the spiritual discipline I have been able to work out for myself, and I feel pretty sure that a lot of writers feel the same whether they will admit it or not. Look, I never heard you call it spiritual, but when I read some of your scenes in *The Holy Book of the Beard*—the scene where Mary's boy drowns and she saves herself, for instance—if you aren't in the heart of the spirit of existence with that, I don't know where you are. Was that not a holy moment for you, writing that?

Brenna: A holy moment? I suppose so. It was very...intense, very revealing.

Frank: Tom seems more adamant about this. Is it vulgar for a writer to talk about what it really means to be a writer? I get the sense, you think people should read the book and leave the writer alone.

Brenna: I don't mind talking to other writers about writing. But sometimes I do feel as if the words I use to describe it are absurdly inadequate. I think also that writers are essentially reclusive spirits and they often don't know what they're doing except that they're just writing out of some gnawing compulsion. Such writers are often shy and inarticulate. They only come alive intellectually when they are alone with the words. And yet these days they are asked to be celebrities, personalities, glib stars of the reading circuit. They are asked to stand up in front of audiences and entertain them. If you do a good job, you'll sell some books. If you don't do a good job, you might get a pity sale of one or two books and you'll go home feeling like a failure. Truth is, I put on my public mask and do the readings only because I have to; otherwise I wouldn't bother. I would say instead, "Please just read the work. The book is all there is about me that might be interesting or important." A writer named Judith Moore told me that when she reads she feels like a whore, like a prostitute selling herself. And that is what you do, you sell yourself and hope your book will benefit. Tom, I've seen you read several times and I'm always a little in awe of how well you do it and of how well you handle an audience. It's brilliant. But is it as easy for you as it looks? Do you ever feel like Judith Moore does? Do you ever feel whorish?

Kennedy: Well I guess I am a bit of a ham. I like to read aloud. My father used to read to us when we were kids, and he was great at it, and it always fascinated me how he could make the words come alive in his throat and mouth and by the use of the expressions on his face. Not fancy like an actor—that always seems overdone to me—but rough-edged and strong. I always wanted to do that myself. My mother used to read to us, too—she could recite poems by heart, even one in Spanish, and I can remember being fascinated by the rhythm of her voice even when I couldn't understand the Spanish words. So, no, I don't feel like a whore, but I do enjoy standing up and doing it like that. I always wanted to be able to sing, but I don't have much of a singing voice, but reading aloud is like singing. It feels good. Language is primarily a physical act; we store the words on the page like the notes in sheet music and then we bring them back to life with the instruments of our lungs and mouths and throats and that is a joy to do. Of course, it is not ONLY the words, but what the words in concert can evoke—symbols, metaphors, levels of meaning, the multilayers of the telling, but often these things too are brought to life on the tongue. It's really kind of magical. Of course not all prose aims to use language in that way—some, as Anthony Burgess pointed out, aim to invite the reader to look through the screen of the words at the motion picture behind them. He called that Type 2 writing and gave as examples of it "The American Irvings"—Irving Wallace and Irving Stone. And what about Jaspar Johns, Duff, the protagonist of your *Beard*? You identify him with Jesus, yet a Jesus who steals and lusts and who is not exceedingly selfless. Aren't you exploring religion there, digging in for a deeper grasp of the spiritual essence which provides the myths of one of the prime religions of the western world? And when you were writing it, weren't you in the grip of something? The Mary figure is not selfless either—she even chooses survival at a very crucial moment of her life, when her young son is drowning, yet this provides the source of spirituality for the remainder of her life. At the same time you give us Godot, the old patriarch, who ends up impotent, groping for the power of words. You give us a sense of Jesus, Mary, and God the Father—not merely weightily, but also playfully.

Brenna: I wouldn't want to see those symbols taken too literally. One needs to be careful of symbols, that they don't get in the way of telling a good story. The symbols a writer creates are often just guides for him to get a handle on his characters. To tell you the truth, the Jesus-God-Mary trinity didn't come until later, after the first or second draft, when I began to see that there were some associations there. But I hadn't purposely put them in the narrative. Once I saw what was going on, I changed their names (Mary was called Betty in the first draft; Godot was Samuel) and let the allusions fall where they may.

Kennedy: Recollected in tranquillity.

Brenna: Right. I see Mary as a cross between the mother who can't save her son (Mary couldn't save Jesus either) and the whore Mary Magdalene, who discovers the missing tomb: Mary Quick has her own "tomb" in the book. Both of these women are sustained by the "resurrected" Jesus, as is the Mary of *Beard*, if you slip in the sustaining Jesus figure. On this same level, Godot becomes the rejected Old Testament Yahweh, who has come to earth and is overthrown and finally tucked away in a garage, where he is searching for the old magic words, the formula, that once upon a time created an entire universe. He wants to start the whole thing over again. Who can blame him? But none of these symbols I've named dominate the story itself; at least I hope they don't. I wouldn't want that.

INNER MAN: BEHOLD YOUR INNER WOMAN

Kennedy: Not at all. Most readers would probably not even notice. I hardly did myself. It interests me, though, that old Yahweh—Godot rather—is impotent. The character is sexually impotent. This functions, I think, on a number of levels, but it also makes me think of your take on women, and particularly with regard to *The Book of Mamie*. It is at once wonderfully funny and mythical, and Mamie seems a kind of

KENNEDY: A WOMAN WITH NO FACE HELD UP A TABLET BEFORE ME ON WHICH WERE WRITTEN SOME WORDS.

spirit of American woman in all her innocence, toughness, hunger and force, even slyness and, beneath it all, cleverness, love, generosity—maybe even a spirit of America in general, though this time as a woman.

It fascinates me how the once two-dimensional view of women has been displaced. It really does seem to be a paradigm shift and it has emerged, not only through the conscious effort of intelligent women and men, but even through a subconscious or archetypal surfacing of a force to rectify an imbalance in our structures. Joyce, of course, was writing about this too in both *Ulysses* and *Finnegans Wake*, but in truth, how many people actually read those books? Your character of Mamie seems to me a part of this—she is an American giant. I understand that Mamie was modeled on a real person, but your choice of her as your main character—did it have to do with the sort of thing we are talking about?

Brenna: No, I simply chose Mamie because I was told a story about the actual Mamie Beaver of Golden Valley, Minnesota and I became fascinated with her power and her spirit, the joie de vivre of someone who had lived such a hellish childhood. In writing about her, I made surprising discoveries. That she was a savant, for instance. The world's greatest mimic, greatest actress, and that she was magical, a spiritual Earth Mother. I had none of that in mind when I started writing her story.

Kennedy: I find this in my own writing, too, where men are suddenly making surprising discoveries about women. This grew further over the past couple of years in the form of stories that came to me almost as dreams—in one case, literally as a dream, in which a woman with no face held up a tablet before me on which were written some words. I awoke, scribbled them down, saw them in the morning, and they seemed to be words in a foreign language. They were, in fact, a mixture of French and Italian, and so I emailed them to a woman I know in Rome. She immediately emailed back that the words—*donna della aube*—meant quite clearly "Mistress of the Sunrise." Around the same time I had that dream, I experienced an optical illusion by which I thought I saw in the window across the way from my apartment an illuminated statue of the Blessed Mother, with her arms opened out in embrace—it was only a lamp whose shape resembled that form, but my eyes, or my mind, read it that way. At a writer's conference where I was teaching, a group of women organized a goddess circle to go out on the countryside and welcome the full moon; to my surprise, they invited me to join them. I was the only man invited. A story came out of that, "Rafferty the Goddess." I know that I am by no means finished with this—or rather it is by no means finished with me.

Frank: Tom, trying to be as objective as possible, do experiences like these reinforce your belief in the spiritual, or do they reflect themes and issues that occupy or haunt your imagination? In other words, do dreams bring you closer to Truth or only to your personal version of truth?

Kennedy: Let me answer that this way. I am old enough to remember a time when women were generally not regarded in contemporary society as serious beings. Men laughed at them, mocked them—women couldn't think, women couldn't drive, 'Hey look! Girls! Let's snowball 'em!', etc. Women were literally enslaved, and as with all enslaved groups, they were assumed to be inferior by those who enslaved them. They were beaten and terrorized in other ways and denied the right of equal education. For Christ's sake women were not even allowed to vote! And even today many women continue to be paid less money for the same jobs that men do. It took me many years to understand that this very obvious situation was a fact. Most societies had enslaved half of the life force and confined sexuality as something shameful or worthy to be practiced or purchased in the dark. A whole generation of American men knew everything about the mechanics of the internal combustion engine and was ignorant of the existence of the clitoris (that's a quote from Steinbeck's *Travels with Charley*). Until the mid-twentieth century, the Christian tradition did not even have one single goddess—then finally Mary was given special status, but she was and remains a sexless goddess. Compare her with the Celtic hag goddess Sheela na Gig, holding open her vulva with a tilted smile. Or with Kali or Rangda devouring the earth. Or Diana the huntress. In the past decades startling changes have taken place, and it is now possible for a man to overcome the handicaps of the past and begin to see a woman's full and wonderful humanity, the true sacredness of her sexuality, her power, and to begin to become more of a human being himself as a result. Yes these things haunt this writer's imagination, and yes they reinforce my belief and trust in the spiritual. I am eager to try to explore this in my fiction to see what I can learn and discover. When Duff and I were in Dublin this past June to celebrate Bloomsday, we sat up drinking vodka (www.AbsolutVodka.com) and talking about women one night, and Duff suddenly looked at me with surprise and exclaimed, "You actually adore women, don't you?!" Guilty as charged! And what better accusation to suffer than during a celebration of the greatest woman adorer of the 20th century, Leopold Bloom!

Brenna: I have to admit that I'm more ambivalent about women than Tom, but I'm also very ambivalent about men. It balances out. I'm not picking on anybody. But Tom's adoration of women caught me by surprise because I've never felt that way about them. You talked about Mamie as embodying a kind of adoration of American women, and I answered, "Yes, at their best." Thinking of Mamie as solid and foundational, Earth-Mother if you will, helped me keep her in focus. I thought at one time that maybe I was being too obvious with her; but then one day I got a letter from a woman agent in San Francisco to whom I had sent the manuscript, and she said that for her to represent me, I would have to get rid of all the anti-feminist symbolism in my book. She didn't go into specifics. I was flabbergasted at first. But then I told her to send my manuscript back pronto. I always have to keep in mind what Blake said, "Every eye sees differently." What makes it so difficult to communicate clearly with one another is just that, the mind interpreting according to what's been stuffed into it. I do it, you do it, we all do it, but that agent was carrying too much feminist baggage and it was overloading her judgment, making her see her peculiar biases rather than what was really there.

As to Mamie's model, she was a woman who lived in Minnesota, a friend of my mother and my aunt and her real name was Mamie Beaver. She lost her parents at an early age, and she became a ward of the town, and they taught her to run the movie projector at the theater. She actually did fall in love with it, kiss it, hug it and get graphite on her fingers and face. She called the projector Powers, which was the brand name printed on the side, and would say to my mother, "It's that Powers, he loves me so." From that anecdote told to me years ago, I wrote a short story and it just kept going, until it became a novel. It was the mystery of a girl falling in love with a movie projector that propelled the writing. I wanted to find out why she fell in love with this mechanical thing that couldn't really love her in return. I guess much of the book was an attempt to find an answer.

Frank: Which you obviously did.

Brenna: Yes, it was something to do with what I just said about communication, how difficult it is to truly reach one another, to sweep life's baggage aside and get down to the heart of things. You might have noticed in the book how difficult it is for anyone to "teach" Mamie, or even to have a conversation with her. But *not* for Powers, not for the machine, which opens up the world to her, shows her things she never dreamed existed. Powers has the power to teach her. He is able to bring out her hidden gifts, her perfect pitch for voices, her ability to mimic anyone she sees on the screen, her acting talents. No wonder she loves him so. Actually, what happened to Mamie is happening all over this country right now. The computers, TVs, video games, the movies, and we learn much more from them now than we learn from anything else. This can be bad or good of course, depending on what's inside the machine. In Mamie's case it was a good thing at first, but ultimately it had tragic consequences. That's the story of knowledge, a mixed bag.

WRITING TOOLS

Frank: Let's reach into that bag. Do you write on a computer? Does the keyboard and screen bring out any hidden gifts. In an interview we published in the late 80s Robert Coover mentioned that the cool dead space inside his computer, especially at night, helped free up for him a world of boundless invention.

Brenna: It varies now. I used to write with a pencil on legal pads. I still do that, but I also find myself composing directly on the computer. Eventually I expect the computer will completely take over. It has for many writers. What about you, Tom?

Kennedy: Ballpoint pen on lined white pads when I have them. Otherwise whatever paper presents itself. The novel I'm working on now I had five hundred handwritten pages before I decided to go to the computer as a way of reviewing what I had. I write in a mixture of long hand and short hand—Gregg method, which I learned in the army. Very useful. Makes it possible to write as fast as I think. How often do you write and at what time of day? My own favorite time is early morning, but as time grows scarce and other pressures mount, I will take any unit of time I can get my hands on and wherever it might be—I like to write on planes for example. No one to bother you—except the drink trolley which is no bother at all.

Frank: Thank you Tom for lifting the lid off that kettle. Let's banter a bit on drink for a moment. A fair amount of your characters drink in your stories, and alcohol, although not the subject or source of conflict, does either soothe the pain of living or helps these people confront their issues. Curiously, both of you refer to vodka in your excerpts. Aside from commenting on how your characters use alcohol, say something on what effect drinking has on the writer and the act of creating?

Kennedy: Well, the first chapter of *Beneath the Neon Egg* is called "The Sacrament of Vodka." Drink can serve to fuel the spirit and the body in what I would consider an almost sacramental manner, but too much of it can ruin you. How sad it was to read in the journals of the great John Cheever that toward the end his days had become a struggle to put off taking his first gin until noon—a struggle he increasingly lost. You've got to keep your substances under control or they will control you, and that is not good. But alcohol for me is definitely one of life's pleasures, consolations, and means of insight. Amen.

Frank: Duff?

Brenna: When I'm working on a novel I work seven days a week, usually in the morning, but lately I've been writing late at night, in the weird zone—night writing is more dreamy, less controlled for me—because my school schedule is so hectic.

Kennedy: How much do you get done on a good day?

Brenna: On a good day I can average three or four pages. I've gotten up to 10 on rare fire-in-the-mind occasions. But there are equally as many days I've spent on one page or even one paragraph, diddling with it and wondering where *le mot juste* is hiding.

Kennedy: I guess I do about the same. Do you drink or smoke anything while you write?

Brenna: No. I can't drink and write. My mind is too mucked up as it is without adding liquor or drugs to it. I tried writing under the influence a few times, vodka logic, grass wisdom. It was all shit the next day.

Kennedy: I always start dry, maybe with a glass of juice or club soda and will write as long as I can, but I do find if I am going strong but near exhaustion, a drink can carry me a little further, even two or, rarely, three, but then the next day it is hard to read my short hand. Sometimes I like the stuff that comes out that way though. It breaks patterns, breaks up the line. Sometimes of course it is just silly though, but it can be silly dry too. It's like the joke Gordon Weaver tells about the preacher who keeps a pitcher of vodka on his pulpit shelf and finds that a little sip every once in a while helps him wax eloquent, but one day he takes a few sips too many and finds himself telling how Samson kicked the motherfucking Philistines asses!

Brenna: Now there's a possible story, Tom, a preacher who talked that way one day in front of his parishioners. What would happen next? What would the congregation do? To what stunning heights would the preacher's "eloquence" soar?

Frank: Let's invite our readers to take up the challenge and see what grows! (www.ReadFrank.com/vodka)

To communicate with Tom, Duff or **Frank** *or to know more about our sponsors (Absolut Vodka), connect to www.ReadFrank.com/conference18.*

DUFF BRENNA

"I, George,"

from
The Altar of the Body, part one:
Many a Lecherous Lay

The first time I see her she is steering a Lincoln Continental through the neighborhood. Slow as vodka logic she comes, looking left and right, searching for something. Tree leaves reflect fractal patterns off her windshield, smearing her image, bringing her in and out of focus.

I'm on the porch, sweaty from working in the Minnesota heat, my shirt clinging to my back, my toes steaming inside my shoes. I'm smoking my pipe and drinking a can of Grain Belt and watching the Lincoln, the bumper low, sniffing the asphalt. It's an old car, a four-door boater, champagne-colored, with rust patches showing through the wheel-wells, roof dented in the center looking like a little birdbath or a holster for a cannonball. The tires suck at the hot pavement. The engine is idling. A valve-lifter ticks beneath the hood.

When she gets closer I see platinum hair, bushy, like a dandelion gone to seed. Her hair shines in the sun for a second, then darkens as the car enters shade, then it shines again. When the car comes parallel, she spots me. The passenger window is open and she is leaning toward it, keeping one hand on the wheel. Her pale skin and pale hair make me think of Icelandic girls with hard cheekbones and translucent skin and eyes bold as glaciers.

The rest of the car eases forward and I can see a man pushing it, a big man with big shoulders, his huge hands splayed across the trunk. His head is down, his back bull-like bulges, his legs churn in slow-motion. He glances at me and I see heavy-lidded eyes. Strands of hair cling to his forehead. His breath is harsh, sobbing with effort.

Eyes as big as June-bugs

The woman pulls the car to the curb and the man leans his forearms on the lid for a second, then he straightens and pulls his shoulders back, rolls them and groans. I don't know if I've ever seen a chest so big, nor shoulders so wide or a neck so thick. He puts his hands on his hips and grins lopsided and says, "She's a heavy hussy, man."

I point my pipe at the old Lincoln. "Lincolns," I say.

"Freeway floaters," says the man, "but hell to push when they break down." He winks at me. There is something familiar about him, but I can't place it. Eyes big as June-bugs. I've seen those eyes, I tell myself. I've seen that jutting chin, that tic of a dimple in it.

Sunlight through the trees shimmies over him. A gold stud in his earlobe sparkles. He glances back at the woman in the car. She is looking at herself in the mirror, fussing with her hair.

And then he says, "Hey, I'm looking for George McLeod. Does that bugger still live here?"

I stand up and cram the can of beer into my shirt pocket. "That's me. I'm that bugger," I tell him.

"Hey, George, that really you?"

"Yessir. What can I do for you?"

"What happened to your hair, George?" I finger the top of my head where a few hairs still mark a path down the middle. He smiles and I notice that his upper lip has a fleshy hook pushing it slightly over the front teeth. And that's when it hits me who he is—big eyes, olive skin, the hook-lip grin. "Mikey?" I say. "That you, Mikey?"

"It's me, George."

"No way."

"Yeah way."

I laugh and say, "How the hell you get so big, Mikey? Jesus, you look like . . . like a Sequoia."

"Pecs, abs and gluteus to the max," he sings, shifting his butt sideways and patting it. "I growed. I'm not Mikey no more, George. I'm Buck Root. "

"Buck Root?"

"It's my stage name, my show name."

"Buck Root," I say, savoring the sound of it. "So where you been all these years, Buck Root?"

He says he's been everywhere—east coast, west coast, midwest, down south and up north and down Minneapolis at a competition there: Mr. Minnesota. And he says he thought he might as well come by Medicine Lake and see if I'm still kicking.

"Still kicking," I say. "Older, fat as a toad and damn near bald, but still kicking, yhah."

Above him the leaves move. The tip of a leaf brushes his hair and he swats at it. "Thought it was a bee," he says, staring at the tree as if it has done a whimsical thing. I'm thinking he's a woman's dream of what a man should be, nose heroic, velvet-lips, and eyes that say bedroom-bedroom.

"So, George, you got a hug for me?" he asks.

I stick my hand out to shake. He grabs it and jerks me in and nearly crushes me. I smell beef on his breath, hamburger-beef. He kisses my cheek and roughs me up, then lets go and steps back and looks around. "Hey, I'm glad to know you're still in the same place," he says. "Things haven't changed so much as I thought they would. I expected there would be some shopping mall here, you know. Or maybe some big resort and old ladies in bikinis trying to get laid. But it's still the same. Trees, houses, lawns, the lake. I remember that tree there." He points at the spruce in the front yard. "That bugger got tall. What is it now, sixty feet? Seventy?" A wistful look glides over his face. "Lot of wind gone through those needles," he says. "Time flies. That's what happens."

The woman kills the engine. She has kept primping in the mirror, touching her hair, painting her lips, but now she's ready. The door protests like old doors do when they're never oiled, *kaareak, ba-wham!* as she flings it closed. She moves toward us and I'm watching her hips moving in a sheath of leather skirt and I'm whispering, "Oh wow," and she catches what I say and she puts on a look like she's the home-coming queen and she says, "I'm Joy Faust."

I take her hand. She has a large hand for a woman. The touch of it makes me feel giddy. She's as tall as me, very thin, with arms pale as taproots. A gold earring drilled through a flap of skin in her navel flashes beneath a blue tanktop that has *IMAGINE* written on it in silver letters, Gothic style. She has fine-firm boobs. The nipples look like bullets pressing against the cloth.

fat as a toad and damn near as bald

"This is him," says Buck to her. "This is cousin George."

"Cousin George," she says.

I feel my ears burning. A feel my lips quivering, smiling. I make a helpless gesture toward the apartments and say hoarsely, "I live here." She lets go of my hand. My palm is moist. It feels swollen.

"This is the address all right," she says. "We almost didn't get here." She chucks her chin toward the Lincoln. She looks at me with crinkling, smiling eyes. Her eyes are blue with flecks of gray beneath lashes thick enough to float a toothpick. She has a delicate jaw, a rounded chin, a small nose with a tiny, ball-tipped end, a tempting mouth, the lower lip large and chewy, the upper lip slightly thinner.

Buck is beside her and even though she is tall for a woman, she looks petite next to him.

"Buck and Joy," I say. Sunlight shines around them. "You guys look like moviestars," I say.

Buck's eyes glitter with pleasure. "Quite a change, hey, George? What's it been, twenty years since you last saw me?"

I think on it for a second and say, "It was not long after Dad died when you left. So what's that? I was fifteen. Now I'm forty-four. Twenty-nine years, can it be that long? Twenty-nine years?"

Buck says to Joy, "We all lived right here in these apartments. Both our families. Us upstairs, them downstairs."

"I know," says Joy.

"Buck was so skinny back then he had to stand up twice to make a shadow," I say to her. "But look at him now."

"I growed and growed," he says. And he raises his arm, shows a massive biceps. "I'm Buck Root: Mr. Los Angeles, Mr. Philadelphia, Mr. Chicago, Mr. Mount Olympus."

"And Mr. Baja Peninsula and Mr. Minneapolis Thighs," adds Joy.

"That name Buck Root," I tell him. "It rings a bell. I feel like I heard it somewhere."

"Where?"

"Don't know." I concentrate on his name, trying to remember.

"Talking about me," says the weightlifter, glancing at Joy. "Everywhere I go, people have heard of the Root. It's a catchy name, once you hear it, you don't forget it. Hey, a word to the wise. Fame is in the *name*. If you know what I mean. Hey, Marion Morrison a.k.a John Wayne; Archibald Leach a.k.a. Cary Grant; Bernard Schwartz a.k.a. Tony Curtis. Get the picture, George?"

"Norma Jean Baker a.k.a. Marilyn Monroe," I answer.

Buck looks at Joy. "Told you my cousin was cool."

"I think I saw you doing some kind of advertisement," I tell him. "Some kind of thing on TV?"

"The Tubeflex!" he says. "Hey, you saw my Tubeflex commercial: *Maximum Buff*!"

"I didn't know it was you.

> "Buck was so skinny back then he had to stand up twice to make a shadow"

Hey, you got a good memory there, George." He looks at Joy. "George always had a good memory."

"Buck's was better," I say. "He memorized *Alice Through the Looking Glass*. You remember that, Buck?"

"Sort of do, yeah."

"My mother. She got you into it. You two seeing who could memorize most. Mom loved you, you know. She said you had the mind of an artist."

"Hear that, Joy? Mind of an artist."

I turn to Joy and say, "But mostly he was shy as a mouse, hardly said a word. Mikey Mouse, we called him."

> **"Fame is in the name. If you know what I mean. Hey, Marion Morrison a.k.a John Wayne; Archibald Leach a.k.a. Cary Grant; Bernard Schwartz a.k.a. Tony Curtis. Get the picture, George?"**

"Not my Bucky no way," says Joy, looking at him as if seeing him new.

"That was then and this is now," says Buck. He puts his fists into his waist, sticks out his chest and in an announcer's voice he says, *"Be Buff! Get Maximum Buff!"*

"Buck's posed in magazines," says Joy.

"*Pumping Iron*, I was in that about two years ago. Hey, I've been in *Bodybuilders*, and *Steel Body*. In *Body Sculptors*, I was a big article in there. They called me the dean of bodybuilders."

"Little Mike, the dean of bodybuilders," I say.

"That's right."

"We won Mr. Minneapolis Thighs this morning," says Joy. We all pause to look at Buck's thighs. He is wearing faded jeans and his thighs put a strain on the fabric.

"In Minneapolis . . . Mr. Thighs," adds Joy, her words drifting. Then she points at the lake and says, "You get to live on a lake. Lucky you."

"That's Medicine Lake," says Buck. We all look toward the curve at the end of the street, where the lake shows silver threads visible through some trees. "Used to swim right off there, me and George, hey, George?"

"Kids still do," I tell him. "It's kid-paradise."

A car goes by on the road. A bearded figure waves. It is our cousin Ronnie.

"George!" he shouts.

"Ronnie!" I shout.

He honks and keeps going.

"Is that cousin Ronnie?" says Buck.

"That's him," I say.

"Another one of my cousins," says Buck. "How about cousin Larry? Is he still around?"

"Larry's a Golden Valley cop."

"A cop! Holy shit, a cop."

"And Ronnie owns a bar over at Foggy Meadow Lake. He's got topless dancers."

"Ronnie owns a topless bar." Buck shakes his head. He looks at me as if I'm sprinkling wonders all over the place.

"I've heard all about you crazy kids," Joy tells me. She touches my arm. "Crazy kids," she says again.

I wonder what Buck could have told her that was crazy about us. I recall summer days swimming with my cousins and friends, Mikey hanging at the edges sometimes, but mostly staying indoors, reading, watching TV, eating pretzels and drinking Cokes. Sometimes he would sit for my mother and she would paint him and he would tell her jokes. Buck was a joke collector, kept them on three by five cards in a shoebox. He clung to my mother, took her over for a while and made me jealous. His mother, my aunt, was a depressive, stupefied on pills. She couldn't cope with him. I'd hear her yelling at him, calling him a little bastard, telling him to get out of her sight. My uncle had given up on her, had taken off, disappeared and she cut her wrists then and Mikey stayed with us for months, until my aunt got out of the hospital and took him away, she and Buck going west with some pipefitter she met.

"Hey, our car won't go when you put it in gear," Buck says. "Tromp on the gas and the engine roars and nothing happens. What you think is wrong with her?" He is looking at me the same way he did when we were boys and he'd bring his math over. Smart as he was, he never caught on to math. Said it made his head hurt.

I chew my pipe and study the car. "Transmission be my guess. The bands."

"The bands," he repeats.

"Or maybe the fluid's low."

"The fluid."

"Something like that."

"How much to fix it?"

"Hard to say. Something like that can be tricky, it'd be a wad. You remember Joe Cuff? He can tell you. He's got a garage over at Crystal Lake."

"Joe Cuff? He still around? I hated that sonofabitch. He was always kicking my ass. One time he told me I couldn't go past that telephone pole—that one right there. He said on the other side of that pole was *his* territory and if I wanted to go through his territory I had to pay a quarter." Buck starts chuckling, and he tells us how he would sprint past the telephone pole and buy his mother her cigarettes at the store and sprint back, but sometimes Joe Cuff would catch him and beat on him and take his change.

"He's the same," I say. "Still likes to fight. He was in Vietnam. Couldn't wait to get there, afraid the war would be over before he got old enough. Only seventeen and he went over there and won metals—a Bronze Star and a Purple Heart. Shot in the kidney. He's only got one now. A big ole scar where the other one was. That's Joe Cuff for you. No fear."

"Hated that sonofabitch big time," grumbles Buck. He cocks a serious eyebrow at me. "You see these fists?" he says. His fists look hard as stones, the knuckles volcanic. "Next time we meet, I'll be taking *his* quarters, you watch."

I look at the car and feel pity for it. Old and decrepit and starting to cause trouble, the Lincoln is a candidate for the bone yard, get rid of it. Everything about it is sagging. Tires are curb-chewed, bits of body rusting away, showing a dozen rusty red holes, like steel termites are living in it. I run my hand over the dent in the roof and think about taking a bathroom plunger and sucking the dent out. "How'd this happen?" I ask. "Somebody shoot a cannonball at you?"

"That's his fist," says Joy. "Hammered it that way. Just one blow. Bam! The day we lost Mr. Reno. Buck was mad. Boom!" She makes a fist and brings it down on the roof to show how he made the dent. "Boom! like that," she says and the roof reverberates.

"Hey!" yells a voice inside the car. "Quit poundin on my head, goddammit!"

I hadn't noticed anyone in the back seat, but then I see her and she is hardly bigger than a monkey, a hoop of a lady bent over, her head hiding between her shoulders. I nod at her and say, "I didn't see you there."

"I seen you," she says, her tone crabby. She has violent red hair and a face seamed like a walnut. She has a yellow and black-striped afghan across her shoulders. On her lap is a paperback book and next to her is a pug-faced, black and white dog. The dog raises its head, looks at me with foggy eyes, opens its mouth to bark, thinks better of it, lowers its chin on its paws again.

I glance at the title of the book: *West Of The Pecos*. A narrow-eyed, dark-skinned cowboy is looking at me and drawing a gun from a holster.

"That's my mom," says Joy. "And that's Ho Tep."

"Ho Tep," I say.

"Chinese god of happiness," says Joy. "Or maybe it was Egypt. I can't remember. Mom, is Ho Tep Chinese or Egyptian god of happiness?"

"What you askin me for? You named him, didn't you?"

"I wouldn't be asking if I had." Joy whispers, "She's getting forgetful."

"Ho Tep," I repeat. The name makes me smile. "The god of happiness, huh?"

"He's seventy-seven in dog years." Joy leans her head in the window and shouts, "Mom, this is him, this is Buck's cousin, this is George McLeod!"

The old lady puts her hands over her ears. "Am I deeef?" she says.

"You are when you wanna be," mutters Joy.

The old lady snorts. Then she looks at me and works up a bloodless smile and she says, "Pleased to meet you. I'm Livia Miles."

"Pleased to meet you, ma'am."

"He says ma'am," says the old lady. She has slightly crossed eyes and I don't know which one to look at. "I'm thirsty," she says, pointing to the top of the can sticking out of my shirt pocket. I slip the beer out and offer it to her and she snatches it, finishes it off in a few swallows.

"Good beer," she says and burps politely behind her fingers.

Stepping over to the trash can at the curb, I drop the bottle inside and a mess of flies fly out and swizzle around my head. One flicks off my chin and I swat at it and watch it zip over to the Lincoln and land on the back window and feel its way around a nickel-sized hole in the glass. The hole has a web of fine lines circling it. I go over and wiggle my pinky through the hole, feel the edges tugging at me. Joy and Buck are watching.

"Big hole," I say.

"Big gun," says Buck.

"It went off," says Joy.

She and Buck look at one another. I am puzzled over the hole, wondering if the bullet came from inside or outside, wondering who was shooting at whom. I wait a second for the story, but no one says anything. Joy takes hold of the hem of her skirt, gives it a shake, then waves at a mosquito.

"Minnesota's sticky," she says, shaking her skirt again.

I'm downwind. A not unpleasant scent of female body drifts my way and I think how long it's been since I smelled Connie Hawkins. It's been awhile, a couple months since we were in her van.

Joy pinches her nostrils and says, "I'm ripe. I need a shower."

I check inside the car and see the bent lady holding the book, turning a page, her lips forming words. The dog sleeps with the tip of his tongue sticking out. His lower canines thrusting up on each side full of tartar. A cross-breeze runs through the open windows and pecks at the old lady's hair and I see patches of scalp. She doesn't seem to feel the heat. The afghan over her shoulders hangs like furled butterfly wings.

I tell Buck and Joy that they might as well come in and use the phone. Joe Cuff has a tow truck that can haul the car down to his garage.

"That's a plan," says Buck, looking at Joy.

"Them too?" I ask, pointing at Livia and the dog.

"Let them stay for now," says Joy. "They won't even know we're gone."

I lead the way up the walk to the porch and stand to the side, motioning Joy and Buck to go first. The wooden stairs, dimpled with age, sag under Buck. His body fills the entrance, his head dipping as he goes through into the hall.

"Same place. You know where it is," I tell him.

To read more of Duff Brenna, visit www.ReadFrank.com/conference18

THOMAS E. KENNEDY
THE SACRAMENT OF VODKA

from
Beneath the Neon Egg

What is time, he wonders. A work-week is never so long. Neither is a weekend. A bottle of vodka is not so deep, a drink is shallow. But as he steps out of the shower, towels himself dry with Getz's "Sweet Rain" on the CD, splashes on aftershave, steps into clean shorts, undershirt, shirt, ties a double windsor in his old silk favorite, steps into his britches, pulls on a sweater and his old sheepskin, the world is so new again and full of hope. It always starts again with hope.

Friday, blessed Friday. Time to open the gates of the world hidden behind the veil of matter. With the purist of elixirs. An allergologist revealed this secret to him once when he was suffering from a bout of rhinitis. If you must drink, drink vodka. The purest of drinks. Her face rapt as she told him, her elephantine face like Lord Geneash, remover of obstacles. There have been cases of patients with acute, near fatal asthma attacks cured by vodka, one woman who had to drink six wine glasses of chilled vodka every hour to keep her lungs functioning under a drastic attack. Think about it.

Bluett thinks about it: Absolut. Icebreaker. Leningrad Cowboy. Kremlyskaya. Smirnoff Red. Smirnoff Blue, hundred proof. Smirnoff Black Mellow Russian. Irish Boru, nice. Danish Danzka. Polish Siwucha, lovely but more like brandy than vodka. Moskovskaya. Soul of the Bubble King.

Ynkologi, he thinks and grunts like a pig, letting himself out the door, wondering what Sam is up to tonight. There is only one god and one vodka: Stolichnaya. Yes.

Bluett descends the wooden staircase from his apartment and enters the freezing afternoon. A thief's start on l'heure bleu: red sun still hangs on the smokey horizon of the frozen lake. He waits a few respectful moments, watching his breath, watching the red glare from the edge of St. John's, the old leper colony, stain

> THERE IS ONLY ONE GOD AND ONE VODKA

the ice of Black Dam Lake.

In medieval times, Copenhagen stopped here, where he stands. No one was allowed to live beyond the lakes, only the lepers or a few tinkers whose shacks were razed under threat of invasion. Now it is the city center, this side of the lakes, and a million people live on the other side, the leper colony has been shut down, and St. John, their patron, has joined the long line of dead saints.

The red ball of light sinks into the ice. Bluett waits for a taxi to pass, then crosses the blue road beneath the bare chestnut trees and steps out onto the ice. A lone skater makes lazy loops out in the center, gliding through the steepening dark, and Bluett trudges across the ice, his heart, his mouth, his brain yearning for the holy sacrament of vodka, his first drink of the week, of the weekend. He experiences this moment as worthy of a frieze on a Grecian urn. Drunk Stolis are sweet, those undrunk are sweeter yet.

To his right, across Fredensbro—the Peace Bridge—stands the tall white graffitied monolith titled Fredensport—the Peace Gate—slanting up phosphorescent into the dusk, a keyhole cut into the middle of its flank. Like modern society itself, it appears always about to fall, but never falls, frozen perhaps in a seeming interminable collapse.

Above the dark buildings behind it, Rigshospitalet—the State Hospital—looms like a beast of prey. And to the left, his favorite neon chicken, mounted five stories up on the top floor of an apartment building, lays neon eggs. The light sequence gives movement: first the chicken appears, yellow in the dusk, with a red head and feet, then a large red egg drops, hangs at an angle on the wall, a smaller blue one drops on top of that and finally a tiny white one atop the heap. The great red egg hangs suspended above the frozen lake, reflected in the cold black surface; the chicken's red head turns to view its art before, in the wink of an eye, egg and chicken both disappear into darkness. Then the process begins again with a neon explanatory note of praise for the eggs of Irma's Supermarket.

Bluett steers his course between the two cherished artifacts, monolith and egg, around the frozen island, toward the Front Page Café on the opposite embankment.

Chill seeps up from the ice through the leather soles of his shoes, penetrates his socks. He pictures thin ice cracking beneath his feet, the icy plunge, black grimey water in his eyes, his sheepskin coat dragging him down as he claws toward the dark surface and all the ghosts of the dead lovers and lepers, drunks and killers, bankrupt and disgraced who took their lives here in Black Dam Lake reach up to his feet, his ankles, drawing him down to their encampment in the black cold watery room beneath the ice.

Tightening the fur collar around his throat, he whispers aloud in Danish, "...*gaar ud til sortedamsoe*, a Danish proverb of sorts—I'll go out to Black Dam Lake, something like Goodbye, cruel world, down the flusher.

He steps up onto the embankment, tries to stamp warmth back into his soles, crosses to the Front Page Café, nearly empty at this hour. L'heure bleu comes charitably early at this parallel in winter. Eyeglasses steaming and nose running in the sudden heat, he strips off his coat and scarf and gloves and Kangru, mops nose and lenses with his handkerchief, and goes to the bar.

An indifferent barmaid, heartbreakingly slender, looks at him without speaking.

"Double Stolichnaya on the rocks," he says in Danish. "No fruit." She squints. He points at the bottle. She scoops ice into a glass with her slender red fingers, pours the vodka into a pewter measure, once, twice. Four centiliters, hardly enough to fill his hollow tooth.

He says, "*Introibo ad altare dei.*"

She squints at him so he wonders if she needs eyeglasses. "*Hvad?*" she says. "What for something?"

He shakes his head with a smile, pays, takes a bamboo-mounted newspaper from the rack and sits by the window where he can watch the street, the lake and the interior of the café all at once. He raises his drink, relishing the chill damp glass against his palm and fingers.

"To god," he mutters (the place is empty), sips, sighs. "The joy of my youth." Another taste of the creature and he sets the glass down.

Then he turns to the paper, *B.T.*, a late morning Copenhagen tabloid, the less flamboyant of the two available. He leafs through it at a leisurely pace. The front page story is about a seventeen-year-old Russian boy, son of an immigrant family, who killed his father with an axe while the man sat in his chair and watched television. The boy's two younger brothers stood by with knives prepared to intervene in case the coup should fail and three sisters and the mother huddled in the kitchen. The boy was found guilty but received no sentence because the father, it appeared, had been a mad sadist who had tormented his family for all their lives. In the mornings they were compelled to rise in silence, bathe, dress, and sit silently in their assigned places at the breakfast table until the father sat and gave the nod that they could begin to eat and speak. Sometimes he made them wait on his pleasure for an hour. If they did not comply, they were whipped, punched, kicked, threatened with death. It seems the father was a jovial man in public. All this occurred in secret, within the family walls.

Bluett turns the page, tastes his vodka, orders peanuts which the gloomy barmaid delivers without a word, takes his ten crown coin silently.

HIS FAVORITE NEON CHICKEN, MOUNTED FIVE STORIES UP ON THE TOP FLOOR OF AN APARTMENT BUILDING, LAYS NEON EGGS

He reads an item about a pig farmer who is suing the state because he has lost more than fifty-percent of his hearing from the constant pig screams. He is a state contractor, so feels the state must compensate him.

Another draught of spirits and he proceeds to an article about a freak hailstorm in Dublin. The article includes background research on hail. "Like tumors," it says, "hailstorms come in standard sizes: the size of a pea, a walnut, a golf ball, a pool ball, a baseball, a grapefruit. There are even cases on record of cars totaled by hailstones, of light aircraft whose fabric was torn to rags, of cattle killed out on the open range, leaking their bespattered brains into the ground." Bluett rereads the last sentence to be certain it actually says that; it does. The Dublin hail had decimated a flock of pigeons on O'Connell Street—a dozen dead birds were found outside the post office.

On the next page he reads an article about the Hale-Bopp Comet accompanied by a map with flow arrows showing where it will be visible when. He makes a note that it should soon be clearly displayed in the northern sky above the lake here.

He drains his glass. The slushy ice chills his teeth. He calls to the barmaid for another just as the door opens and his friend Sam Finglas floats in.

"Sam!"

The man halts and looks about with his startled blue eyes. He has a dreamy look about him. Then, with a visible reluctance that wounds Bluett, "Hey, Blue," he says mildly.

"You been over to Christiania smoking some of that hippy hay or something? You look spaced."

Sam chuckles, and Bluett notices his clothes: an expensive looking heavy black leather coat he hasn't seen before, black shirt and splashy silk tie under a sharp-looking bottle-green sweater. The waitress delivers Bluett's vodka and waits to be paid, eyeing Sam's coat.

"Join me in the sacrament," Bluett says to his friend.

"Can't, Blue. Got an appointment."

"An appointment? You dog. Is that who you're all dressed up for?"

Sam grins self-deprecatingly.

"That's a delicious coat," the barmaid says, and Bluett is jealous. He tips her, gets no thanks, says to Sam as she disappears, "Well what in the hell are you here for if you're not drinking?"

"Just a quick one, then." He goes to the

THE SECOND LAW OF BLUETT: WHEN A MAN HAS ONE WOMAN, OTHERS WANT HIM AS WELL.

bar, and Bluett watches him chatting with the girl there. She smiles brilliantly as she takes his money, and he returns with a bottle of snow beer. Bluett says, "My feel-good shield has suffered a few blows."

Sean's startled eyes show lack of comprehension. Bluett drops it, but can't help but wonder. "So tell me about this appointment." They raise their glasses, say, "*Skaal, slanté, kipis*," sip. Bluett adds, "*Tjerviseks*," an Estonian toast, in honor of the madman who accosted him in Vesterbro last week, preparing to tell his friend about it.

"Just an appointment," Sam says over a self-loving smile.

"You dog. You've gotten lucky. What do you have that I don't? Other than that fantastic coat? Be careful. Your brothers'll hit you on the head and throw you in a ditch."

Sam takes a long draft of his beer while Bluett sits watching the white snowflakes on the blue label of the bottle, deciding not to go into the story of the Estonian. Sam lowers his glass, sighs. "Tell you, Blue, this woman rings the bell. Never thought this would happen again. Again? Hell, never happened before. Never wanted it to. But here it is. Happening. It's like... you hold back, you hold back, and suddenly..." He shakes his head, baffled.

"You surrender."

The startled eyes. "What do you mean?"

"You surrender. You give in to the, uh, the calling of love."

"Yeah," Sam breathes. "Yeah, that's it."

Bluett laughs. "You got bit bad, my friend!"

The startled eyes flash, blue glass. "You got something better going?"

Bluett raises his hands. "Hey, no offense, I'm nowhere. I'm jealous." And the eyes are earnest again. "Listen. You live a life that is all, like, broken up. Compartmentalized. I don't mean you, I mean people. Like the Brits say: One. It don't have to be that way." Sam sighs, abandoning the enormity of explaining himself.

"You gonna marry the chick or pay her off?"

The eyes flash again, then damp down. "No. Don't know. Hardly really know her to say it true." He burps discretely behind his fist. Bluett thinks maybe this explains why the barmaid was drawn in. The second law of Bluett: When a man has one woman, others want him as well. The first law is: No woman wants a womanless man.

Sam leans closer across the table, speaks softly. "She is wild. She wants to do it all. She really wants it. And she's fun. And beautiful."

I'll be the judge of that, Bluett thinks. "Who is she?"

"She's Russian. A blond blond Russian. Funny, I used to read Russian lit in college, loved it. Jesus. Dostoevski. 'White Nights.' Turgenev. Tolstoy. And of course Nabokov. Hell, it's like this was ordained, awaiting me somehow. Look, I'm older than you, Blue. My age, never thought it could be this."

"So why don't you marry her?"

He shrugs. "When Karine and I split. All that, that, that mess, no. Don't want it no more. See people get divorced, then marry again, come on, get real, you know? You been through it now too, you must know what I mean. But you know, when I want to be with her, I call, she says, come on over. Visit her..." He hesitates, looks embarrassed to say what he is about to say, but is clearly too eager to share it. "...I go over, she lets me in..." His voice lowers. "She kneels down and takes off my fuckin shoes, mine! I mean this woman is beautiful, and she's young, and she kneels down and takes off my shoes, mine! And..." He wants to tell more, Bluett can see, but drinks some beer instead, starts again and Bluett can see that he is not going to get the rest of it. "She understands me. She's a genius," he adds suddenly. "She knows me, the only one..." He stops, as though he has suddenly heard himself gushing and feels embarrassed.

"Is she bright?"

"Wisdom of the pussy, Blue," he says and looks surprised at himself for saying it, but goes on. "Wish I could crawl in, die there. I would light a candle to her cunt and worship it."

"Is this love or a hard-on?"

"Don't know man. She just knows me."

"Sounds like maybe she's in love with you, Sam. Isn't she gonna want more?"

"That's the thing. She says, however I want it. She wants it that way, too."

Bluett fills his mouth with vodka, lets it chill his tongue before he swallows. "I've made a lot of mistakes in my life, but I've also learned a couple things. One is when a woman wants to give me that much it's because, regardless what she says, she either loves me, with all the implications and expectations that involves, or she wants something out of me. Or both. Maybe one and the same." Bluett tries to think a little more about what he was trying to say, but what started seeming very clear suddenly blurs in his mind. He sips his vodka, decides to turn it all into a joke. "It's like the old Japanese proverb, Sam. If you want to keep a woman, make her pay. A woman will never leave you while you owe her something."

Sam just nods, lost in his own thoughts. He says, "I met her at a party." He lowers his voice again. "Dancing with her, right? We just met, talked a little. Clearly fucking hitting it off, right? So I ask her to dance a slow one, Smokey Robinson, and her lips are up against my ear, warm breath, and whispers... He looks right and left, behind him, leans closer, and with pursed lips whispers the act in Russian.

"Hey, take it easy, I'm gettin hard. Slow down, no, you dog, she got a sister? Where do you find parties where you meet women like that, huh? Where?"

Sam is chuckling as he lifts his glass, drains off the rest of his beer. "Woman ever say a thing like that to you?"

"Yeah, a hooker." He sees Sam's eyes get hard so he hastens to add, "No, seriously, Sam, so when do I get to meet her?"

Sam's smile slips away. He stares off a little. "This is kind of separate like. Separate part of my life, you know? For now."

"Scared of the competition, huh?"

> MAN, WHITE, ADVANCED YOUTH, DIVORCED, CHILDREN, HAS NO IDEA WHAT HE WANTS, SEEKS GREAT-LOOKING, BRIGHT, LIKE-MINDED WOMAN.

The distant eyes turn to Bluett, slowly refocus in a grin. "Eat your liver, boy!" He tips back his glass to let the last drops of beer slide into his mouth, sets it down with a clack. "Got to go."

"Hey, watch out for the old ticker, huh?" Bluett says. "And watch you don't use up all your orgasms. Limited number coming to us, you know."

Sam is at the door, buttoning his fancy leather coat, a merry smile beneath his startled blue eyes. He lifts his hand like Hitler, and cold air sweeps in as he departs.

Bluett watches him move quickly up to Queen Louise's Bridge, toward the city center. Then he sits looking at the white snow flakes on the blue label of the empty beer bottle. He looks into his glass. The ice is slush, a finger left. He glances out at the lake again, glimpses Sam's head bobbing along above the bridge wall, looks across the dark sweep of ice to the lights on the other side.

Behind the bar, the girl leans on her elbow, staring at a glass of water.

"Dead tonight," he says.

She lifts her eyes to him, lifts her brow, says nothing.

Would a kind word kill ya? Bluett spills the rest of the vodka down his throat, goes to the gents. He studies himself in the mirror over the sink. His once grand lamb's skin coat has gone a bit shabby, scuffed up, missing a button, some loose threads hanging from the seam. He looks at his shirt and tie and sweater, at his winter-grey face, wonders what he wants, considers taking on some more translation jobs, maybe buy some new clothes, attend some translator conferences, meet some new people. Maybe he should put an ad in the papers, personal. Saying what?

Man, white, advanced youth, divorced, children, has no idea what he wants, seeks great-looking, bright, like-minded woman, object unknown.

He considers going home, read a book, rent a video, shakes his head. He winks at himself in the mirror, polishes his glasses, steps out, crosses to the door, raising his arm to the barmaid. "*Hej hej,*" he calls out.

"*Hej hej,*" she replies, but somehow it sounds more like Fuck off, jerk.

At Krut's Karport, he eats a bowl of chili with a glass of wine, and he feels okay, studies the green row of absinthe bottles behind the bar, 120 proof, scourge of nineteenth century Paris, resists the urge. He looks into a local newspaper to avoid looking at the tables full of beery youngsters in sweaters and leather jeans, grinning and pawing each other.

Fortified, he has another glass of wine, tips the charming young waitress who rewards him with a smile meant for him only. He pastes it to his feel-good shield and sets off past Soelvtorv to Noerreport, down Fiolstraede, past the university, the cathedral, behind which people queue at a yellow-lit sausage wagon on the dark street to eat fried *poelser* with their chilly red fingers. Through Joerck's Passage, he takes a left on Stroeget, looks into Café Rex, Pilegaarden, continues down to the Palae Bar, stands on the dark street looking in to the bright window at the crowded tables, decides to save that for later, doubles back for a peek into the Bobi Bar.

Across the half-filled bar room, he spots a familiar face at the back table, two familiar faces. An American translator and Irish book salesman. The Irishman waves him over. Dermot Grady with a face full of whisky veins, map of Ireland on his nose. Bluett notes they are drinking Black Gold beer and Gammel Dansk bitters, orders a round and three hard-boiled eggs on his way back to them. Dermot has channeled a series of lucrative contracts his way in the past couple of years and Bluett feels he owes him.

Watching their fingers fumble at the brown bits of eggshell, Bluett sees they are a few rounds up on him, reminds himself Dermot has supplied half his business in the last year. He wonders if the American, a Southern Californian who jumped ship in Sweden during the sixties, resents Dermot's generosity to Bluett. But the American—Milt Sever—is listening raptly to the story Dermot is telling about a Danish novelist who has just returned from Thailand where, Dermot reports, the novelist has reported to him in considerable detail about the children he has paid to misuse.

Bluett cracks his egg on the edge of the table and rolls it between his palms, peels away the shell in one crackling sheet, pinches on finger salt from a stone bowl on the table.

"You wouldn't actually consider such a thing yourself, would you, Dermot?" he hears himself ask and regrets being there.

Dermot blushes, clearly surprised. "I but tell the tale that I heard told," he says and looks at Milt Sever. "What about yourself, Milt? Would you ever consider such a thing?"

Milt's smile is buttery. He is a tall, broad-shouldered, dark-haired man. He clearly enjoys looking at Bluett in light of what he is about to say. "Well, now, I'm sure I would hate myself in the morning." He shrugs serenely. Bluett finds himself contemplating taking a swing, realizes he would probably miss or be blocked, realizes he is in danger of screwing himself out of money, a lot of money, hears himself say, "Well I think a man ought to burn in hell for a thing like that," holds his breath.

"You're an honorable fellow," says Dermot, and Bluett starts calculating an exit that might cut his losses.

Milt is not finished with him. "Have you seen Tim Kimball's new novel?" Kimball is another American translator living in Denmark, a novelist who makes his living delivering mail and translating. Bluett has read the first chapter of the man's new novel in some literary journal. It is about the heyday of child pornography in

Denmark in the early seventies and it includes a terrible scene in which an adult man penetrates a ten-year-old. The scene had inspired Bluett to write a letter expressing his ardent distaste to *Politiken*, the leading Danish daily, where he could be sure it would be seen by all concerned. The letter had evoked a surprising response from people who called upon the immortal beauty of Nabokov, Genet, and others in defense of Tim Kimball, all of which made Bluett realize he had walked into a trap here.

He shrugs, raises his Gammel Dansk, says, "Gentlemen. I drink to your very good health," swallows, chases it with Carlsburg draft, and as he retreats from the Bobi Bar, wonders whether he has ruined his economic stability.

His slow steps moving him toward Kongens Nytorv, he refuses to think about these people, takes a long loop behind the Royal Theater to see if there are any attractive joints back there. He notices a door, just across from the New Scene, on the edge of the square, a scooped away corner with a red door on which is mounted a brass plate that says, Satin Club. Ring Bell. 10:00 P.M. to 4:00 A.M.

He stares, wondering, crosses the square, past the French Embassy to Nyhavn. Your problem, he thinks, as he climbs down the steps into The Mermaid Bar, is a classic one. Forget these provincial fools. Have fun.

In The Mermaid, he orders a shot of Stoli and continues with beer, orders a pint of draft lager and sits on a stool at one of the high drum tables. The place is filling up. A fiftyish Scot in the middle of the room strums a guitar and sings "The Streets of London," as Bluett surveys the joint. No familiar faces.

The Scot takes a break, and an Italian kid comes on who is much smoother. He sings some Simon and Garfunkel, Elton John. The first pint goes down fast, and halfway through his second, the bar continues to fill nicely. The pleasure of a crowded bar is that it forces contact. Three women join him at his drum table. Look like office girls maybe. He likes the blond. They chat a bit in Danish. She asks him about his accent, asks how an American speaks such good Danish. He tells her she's too kind, explains his ex-wife was Danish, the key word being ex, his ringless fingers resting on the table. He buys a round. More people come in, forcing them closer together. She lights a cigarette. "Is it okay?"

"Sure," he says, wishing he were up-wind.

The Italian kid is singing "Nothing's Gonna Change My World" and doing a fair job of it. Bluett studies the blond woman's face. She is maybe thirty-two, full-lipped with a bright smile and light eyes. They talk about films, music. She buys a round. Nice. She lives in Albertslund. Shit. She glances at her watch. He guesses that she's thinking about the train. Her girlfriends have moved to another table. Her name is Birgitte. The last time he looked at his watch it was nearly eleven. Their glasses are full again, and he is shoulder to shoulder with her, the wall behind them, staring into her light bright eyes. He kisses her, tastes her tongue. Then she kisses him. Kisses and smiles in the dim smokey light, hands touching. Her soft lips. The Italian kid takes a break and the Scot comes on again with "The Streets of London." The girlfriends are back, and Birgitte has to go, to get the train. She writes her phone number on a coaster which he slips into his pocket, gives him a last quick tongue kiss, stands for a moment pressing her breasts against his arm, smiling at him, then she waves goodbye.

Bluett sits there watching a snow beer poster above the taps. The white flakes really seem to be falling down the night blue background. He watches, hypnotized, realizes he is getting sloshed and likes it. It occurs to him that love is a chemical. His beer is nearly empty. The Scot seems to believe that he is the vicar of Roger Whittaker in Copenhagen.

He takes the coaster out of his pocket, reads the name and number she has printed there. Birgitte Moerck. *Moerck* means dark in Danish, he thinks. Ironic for such a light, bright face. She told him she is a bookkeeper at the electric works near Noerreport. She has a two-year old daughter named Astrid. Sweet name. A little girl. Albertslund.

> ...YOUNG WOMAN WANTED TO PUT HER TONGUE IN MY MOUTH. MINE.

Bluett has been to Albertslund two times in his life, the first and the last. Middle of nowhere. If hell was absence, as Thomas Aquinas or some such philosopher suggested, Albertslund was a good candidate. Nothing. Nowhere. He suggested she stay the night with him, here, which was possibly some kind of somewhere, a lesser hell at least, and she smiled, as if to consider it for a moment, then said, "Call me."

Nice answer.

But I will never visit you in Albertslund. Ever.

The Scot sings "The Streets of London" yet again. Bluett wonders if the man is having a nervous breakdown. Two American women sit at the table beside his, drinking dark beer.

"It's so rich and creamy!" the one exclaims as though she is in the grips of ecstasy, not of a pharmaceutical sort. He empties his beer and climbs out to the street, the cold clean air along the frozen canal. He looks down into it. The old sailing boats moored there are frozen into the ice. He sees an empty wine bottle frozen at the surface, upside down, the husk of a left-over New Year's Eve rocket.

There are many people on the street. Nearly midnight. He begins to walk, feeling good, past Tatoo Jack's, hears a singer from a bardoor singing, "Kiss my neck! Watch me ride!" He passes Skipperkroen, Pakhus, Faergekroen, Gilleleje, all packed and noisy, some in the cellar, some up the steps, these harbor streets which years ago were the sailor's district, now sequestered by the bourgeoisie.

He climbs the steps of one lively joint where a crowd is gathered around three guitarists in the smokey back. The singer is doing "My Darling You Look Wonderful Tonight," as Bluett orders a beer, looks around at the men and women in the smokey light, thinks The night life ain't no good life but it's my life, savoring the moment, the image of a slender woman standing there alone swaying to the music. The beer is very cold and tastes wonderful.

Perhaps it is the next or the one after that, but suddenly it begins to taste acidic. The musicians do a last number, then a last encore, an absolute last one, "The House of the Rising Sun," and Bluett gets up to let himself out while the music is still going rather than have to leave a dead place, but before he gets to the door the music stops and the juke goes on, someone singing, "Kiss My Neck..." Must be some new hit.

The streets are still full of people. He stands outside for a moment watching them, pleasantly buzzed, charged by Birgitte's kisses. That was really something, young woman wanted to put her tongue in my mouth. Mine. Still a little attraction value in the old fart. But I'll never visit her in Albertslund. Never.

Twenty yards up the Canal, something catches his eye. A fancy leather coat. Sam Finglas.

Bluett opens his mouth to call out, then notices Finglas is walking with someone, a woman. An incredibly beautiful woman, pale, hair long, white as gold, high cheekbones, slightly Asian cast to her face. The Russian woman Sam talked about. He stands there on the step, open-mouthed, breathing steam. They are coming sideways toward him before they turn toward Kongens Nytorv, and Bluett catches a full view of her. She is as tall as Sam and slender. She moves like a song, and her eyes are blue as ice, her skin white, her mouth wide, lips soft as a plum.

Bluett closes his mouth and follows at a distance. Sam has his arm around her shoulder, and her head is tipped onto his. They cross the square toward the Royal Theater, past the statue of the mounted king in the center, and on the other side, they stop in front of a door. She rings the bell. A moment later the door opens, and they enter.

Bluett stands on the opposite sidewalk, feeling like a voyeur, staring through a keyhole at a door: The Satin Club.

He considers following them in, ring the bell. Then he peers down beneath his fog of drink at the muddy brown toes of his shoes and sees he should not, walks home along the teeming Copenhagen streets.

It is a thirty minute walk to the lakes. Good exercise. Past groups of people, couples, the scattered lone wolf staggering. Two a.m. Some big-faced kid yells at him, his stomach plunges, he keeps moving.

Along the lakes, the street is deserted and dark, the frozen water streaked silver in the moonlight, most of the windows on the other side dark. Just the neon chicken, the neon eggs dropping, the red neon chicken head turning to see the product of its work, then nothing again.

A taxi flies past, green dome light lit. He finds himself thinking about his kids, when they were little, when they were a family. How he misses those years. Family. A point in time is all. There and gone. He is proud of them, both off to university, doing well. Maudlin thoughts assail him there, thinking of his wife and how he never managed to make her happy, even as much as he wanted to, as much as he tried, even if she would not agree with him that he had tried.

Suddenly he misses his father, aware of the burden of fatherhood, wishes he were here so he could tell him he understood that it had been hard for him, that he had not understood that before.

He thinks of all the years in Denmark, speaking a foreign tongue which to him is like wandering through a misty landscape never quite sure where you are, never quite at home here, never quite at home in the States anymore either. He thinks of a book he read as a kid, *The Man Without a Country*, a man torn between the U.S. and England in the early years; he recalls it ending with the man on a raft out in the ocean by himself, not allowed in either place anymore. The image is very sharp in his memory. Then he remembers that is because in fact he did not read the book, he read the Classic Comic and that was one of the drawings.

He crosses Queen Louise's Bridge, pauses in the shadows and the sweep of the moonlit ice finds his heart. He mocks himself for a self-pitying fool. This is a beautiful place. He has nothing to regret. All he has to do is translate five pages a day and he can survive. Simple enough. What a deal. No boss. No annoying office intrigues. He has it made. He thinks fleetingly of Dermot Grady and wonders if he has fucked himself out of a flow of work, thinks, Ah fuck it, fuck it all.

He blows his nose, moves on, remembering how when he was a kid, fifteen, eighteen, in his twenties, he yearned for a woman, desperate to be complete. Missing a girl and trying to make it real, to make it mean something, excite him, but he was only exciting himself. He is not quite certain what he means with that thought, thinking again of kissing Birgitte Moerck in the bar, the healing touch of her mouth, her fingertips on his cheek, in the close-cut hair at the base of his skull.

All my life, he thinks, decade after decade, I ask myself is it really true, am I deluded, can this be a fact? But decade after decade, my eye, my heart, my body tell me the most beautiful in this world is to see a woman walk, to see a woman. What I am to do with her and what it is all about I do not know. I used to think it was sex, to fuck, but it is not really that at all. It is to touch, share an instant. He remembers moments with his wife all their years together and feels unreal to think they are apart, that their life together failed.

At his house he pushes through the blue port, climbs the stairs to his first floor apartment, glances across the hall at Sam Finglas's door. He'll get married, you watch. They'll move. That apartment is not big enough for a couple. Who could resist a woman who looks like that if she is all the things he spoke about. Sam is his closest friend in Denmark. Another departure.

He lets himself in to his apartment and sits in the armchair without taking off his coat. He feels that his vision is dimming, his stomach hurts. He feels he is dying.

Fuck that.

He rises, sheds his coat, pours a glass of vodka on three rocks, and turns a straightback chair to the window, straddles the seat and looks out across the lake. A lone couple is walking, arm in arm, across the silver-lit ice, silhouettes moving on the frozen water.

Sometimes when he thinks about the fact that this life might be all we have, nothing but a growing accumulation of memories that will end in the wall of death and vanish, sometimes when he thinks that this is all there is and all that will be, that it will all be over just like that, the life of his childhood, his parents, his own children's childhood all over, he feels he is locked in a small windowless room and that he must break out, must try to break out and that he must do everything, anything, yet that too, all of it is doomed to the same end, vanishing, and all the while, every minute trickles away, the sun burns consuming itself, and we are without power, alone, kissing in some smokey room listening to some cheap music before we die...

He raises his glass, looks through it at the neon chicken, the neon egg that seems to drop, its red reflection smeared across the silver-black ice of the lake, and he thinks of all the lovers down there beneath the surface in their freezing black room.

F

To read more of Thomas E. Kennedy,
visit www.ReadFrank.com/conference18

poetry

From the mail bag, the stratosphere, and hidden keyboards everywhere, poems that slither into your grasp.

ALAIN CAMPOS - UNTITLED DRAWING

to e-mail **Frank** poets, connect to www.ReadFrank.com/poetry

Chris Agee
Dark Hay

June grasses had burgeoned to monumental hay: slabs and beds
Printed in eights by the baler's sledge following its green coil
Of concentric windrows like stone spirals at New Grange or Radmilja

To a last comma near the midpoint of the O
Where those eight dolmens stand at Giant's Ring. Then stacked
Into stooks "like lambdas" they darkened

To outlines of Mayan temples gathering shadow
In the late light breaking
Low from floes and plateaux, dark quadrilaterals

On the lit immaculate nap of shaven stubble
That reminded me that art is dark
For all its shining genesis. Seeing in stone

The image of hay, I saw too the vision polarized to God's glyph
Vanishing midpoint into nothing
(Swan-necked, double-helix, bull's eyes) on stellae swimming

In grass at the limestone necropolis on the road to Stolac
That passes the dumps of its razed mosques. Then, pausing to smoke,
Two men stood waiting to upend the last bales of an evening's work.

VIRGIL SUAREZ

Poem for My Uncle Emilio, the Last Horseshoe Blacksmith in Las Villas, Cuba

Between the hammer and the anvil
and his hands, a crow with gnarled claws,

an echo of metal giving way, malleable
like human life. Since the triumph

of the revolution, he worked the same
job, this artistry of horseshoes, red-hot

metal, a plink-plink of the hammer
keeping rhythm with the cicada's mate

call. He was a young man when he started,
now his back aches and is stiff as a *cavilla*,

each iron rod he shoves into the kiln
to soften it, to make it speak this history

of what a man chooses to do with his hands,
the horses, they walk better into the fields,

this land behind his back, rising, greening.

ALAIN CAMPOS, DETAIL
FROM "HISTOIRES DE
PIERRES" ACRYLIC ON
CANVAS, 1998

Louis Armand
Jacques Cousteau est mort
(July 25, 1997)

warned against the expectations of plot & dénouement we nevertheless
    attended our commiserating in the public library & at the feet
    of the national monument
& as the day passed on it seemed the flags on the flagpoles had entered
    a humid phase of indifference
a child in a blue hat waves down from a tram window as the tram
    pushes against the tide of pedestrians
it was agreed, there was no longer space in which to perceive ourselves
    alighting there in that sea of gregarious well-wishers
voices in voice-balloons floating above the shapeless mass
this in accordance with the programme: a note, insisting on pure
    spectacle: "so much happening & nothing taking place"
we retrace our steps & attempt a crossing from the opposite direction
                                                               repeat
at 12.00 take a break catch up with the gossip, clues on the outcome of
    unheard-of events
after, to pay our respects at the dead-letter office (in hope of intercepting
    misdirected correspondence)
& drink coffee at a stand
& scan the headlines of a newspaper on a newspaper rack: "change
    predicted ..." thinking about where i'm supposed to be next,
    never in the one place or "there" as they say
quietly adrift in the gaze of passing strangers two three four, waiting in
    line ahead to pay "so much poverty is an eyesore" says the
    woman in the patent leather boots & the billboard says vote x
    for more y less z
the pigeons do their thinking under eves in the blue twilight cooing
& suddenly, as it always seems, you don't want to be alone again,
    tonight, climbing the stairs that lead one after another upwards
    to the surface & air
but like the doors in dreams it has no handle

Fred Johnson

To The Horizon

for Mike and Petra

By a simple act of grasping
The dry harvested earth, stalk ends
Yellowing and sharp and brittle,
You go into the earth in a way you
Wouldn't think, where all the horizon
Comes to is a barely brushstroked line
Of rising dust and machines wider
Than a country road come white-eyed
Out of the quick night, reptilian,
Unmannerly and forcing you over
To the unditched dry verge.

This is where you are, driving
In the swelter and endlessness,
Crawling round a hot corner of
A village of red tiled roofs, seeing not one
Other soul whose country face might break
The day into the part before and after
You saw him, giving you two imprecise
But orderable halves by which time,
Which passed on here before you arrived,
Can be recounted.

Wyn Cooper

Postcard of Saxton's River, Vermont, 1910

for Jack Peters

Five men strike poses in front of the general store. In the middle distance, the snow is as tall as the woman who walks toward them. The men wear coats of their own sheeps' wool, befitting the season but not the day. They sweat beneath their hats. The woman thought it warmer than it was, and chose something springy, which according to the men was just right, her dress swaying in the March wind, the opposite direction of the trees. Three of them look as if they'd just been caught watching her walk. One looks straight ahead, his hands in his lap. The final man, closest to the camera, his face open to the moment's movement, smiles broadly at the woman walking, it appears, his way.

POSTCARD OF MAIN STREET, SAXTON'S RIVER, VERMONT, C. 1910.

WYN COOPER

Postcard Looking at a Postcard of Le Château de Picasso, Vauvenargues, France

Just what I need: 30 rooms of stone, cool in summer, cooler in winter than I am in Vermont. Six satellite dishes, not visible in this photo, make the roof a fortress of news, bringing figures from Sotheby's, weather from Spain, images of women from everywhere. He's buried here.

The day I stole onto the grounds the back way, down Mont Saint Victoire, the building, too big to call home, five hundred years old, rose like an animal above the forest of scrub trees. The rust-colored shutters were mostly closed, the massive front doors bolted shut.

Its north and southwestern corners, which face down the canyon to Aix, are reinforced turrets that combine the sexes, their cylindrical towers capped with sun-seeking breasts, like some work of the former owner. I sent the postcard to my own address, to prove to myself I was there.

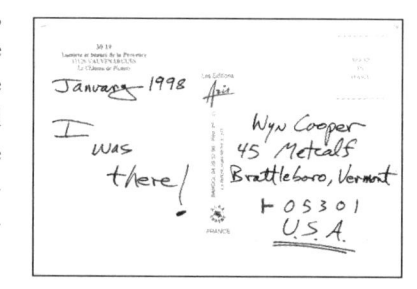

Jennifer Dick

Rain

In the fall perhaps a dream hand rested, called out my wanting to the mattress. Back dreaming of dark. Her voice the edge of where time was on my doorknob. Named her for touch. On my floor Zinnaida Gippius. Hurt. I held something reversed—her and her voice. Once I answered: "Pull her into where I lay Tsvetaeva." Just taste all married now. Her garden a belt of man and the pregnancy. Weeds water-careful, her name in that foreignness. The small grows tight chastity—only body breaking, roots not to spill in my mouth. But she has squared about her like men, this only against her thin soil. Then one drop.

Ruins

for J.B.

Dusk before us, red and swollen. Your scraped ankle, my wrist against your thigh in the car. You drove upwards, leaving a past that wasn't ours, hieroglyph-like etchings, clay walls, chipped shards of pottery. I picked a small, dried leaf from your brown hair, let it sail beyond the window. We would take nothing with us. Your sketches only a grey blur, so unlike the red earth, the strange angle of tree fallen to later become an oval key, orange and blue, yellow and green, peering out from each of the paintings you'd do. Unrecognized. But then, as the car groaned against your insistent foot, I closed my eyes, tracing a map along the inside of your thigh, some memory or labyrinth winding back to where these people, too, lay together in the night, pressing their warm flesh one against the other in the cold.

Robert Gibbons
Match Point

So much light, 2,000 meteors an hour reported over the Canary Islands last night. There's nothing extraterrestrial about walking the earth with your sin at your side in the dream. We sat down on the grass to watch a tennis match. The chain-link fence turned to see-thru mirrors. Much to my surprise my sin turned over on her back. Rocks watch stars.

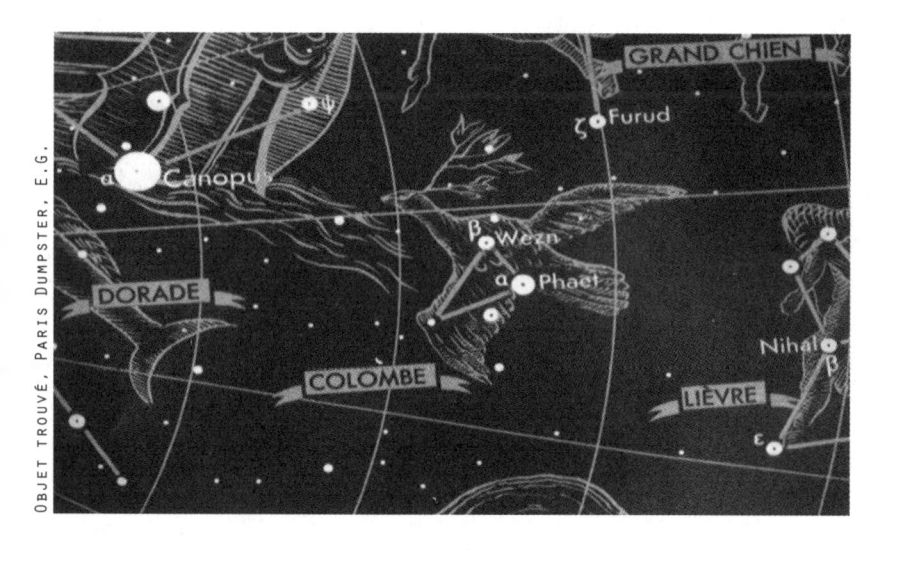

OBJET TROUVÉ, PARIS DUMPSTER, E.G.

Jill Alexander Essbaum
A History Lesson

No, the sky was not unique
with stars and an arbitrary moon.
It was bright August, an afternoon,
and I had only just learned to speak

of grief and solitude with the command
of full or proper sentences. *That
was how it was.* Remember when we met?
You smiled and I turned soot and sand,

useless as an undiscovered well.
Then, drunk on the drowse of summer
sleep, I crumbled into you, a tipsy lover.
No, no, no—the air was not sick with chill

and rain, and there were no witnesses
to catch us feebly grinding bone to bone
in that unchaste pastime of romp and groan,
only the screaming jays and random birches

looking on. Oh, you got it wrong, my dove,
my drone, *all wrong*. Nothing you recall is up to par.
And since your disremembering seems an increment art,
won't you soon forget that it was me you loved?

JILL ALEXANDER ESSBAUM
Disengaged

The angels, in their own unkind and thoughtless way,
have given up on us, have left our lips for good, for better.
Before you know it, we'll have frozen to our underthings,
and soon enough, the shiver of our thighs won't seem so grave
a malady. I've already caught myself mid-marvel, thinking
what's the difference, really? The last I heard, you'd taken up
kite-flying and divination. As for those angels, why just last night
I caught them sneaking out my back door, with some books,
the radio, a string of pearls, and a bed sheet tucked up under
their wing-folds, taking as much of me as they could carry.

Michael J. Dennison

From Sky

When I said your skin was perfect sky
I also meant it was too distant.
Forever you are just beyond the door,
and I hear you gliding toward the next.

Tonight, angry, I searched for matches
And in a drawer found the opal
You brought me years ago from Kowloon.
Outside of its silk pouch it glows
Like milk on fire. In its hard veins
Are all the colors of Burmese sky.

I put the stone back in darkness to shine,
Nest for the egg of a ghost.
The Chinese say opals bring bad luck,
Worn close to the skin they confuse
The mind with delusions. At night
They draw lying dreams from moonlight.

Rick Mulkey

Theoretically Speaking

My father writes to say the seven year locusts have hatched.
All night the whirring and clicking
in the maple and fir have kept him up. "Oh," he writes,
"how I hate that haunting voice." Hunter, not yet five,
decided last night he wanted to sleep with me.
He'd heard something outside, a monster he thought,
and though I've tried to explain about monsters
last night I accepted that fear has no explanation.
It arrives when it wishes, clicking just outside the glow
of the night light at 3:00 a.m. Yet, I admit
I'm at home with the ghosts. They accept me,
and I accept them in all their late night forms.
There's one in my cousin's three piece gray suit, another regular
in my aunt's poodle skirt; there's Steve, childhood friend
who'd lived up the hill, whose father claimed Jesus came to him at night,
sat upon his Italian leather sofa and offered business advice;
Steve, the preppy, even now dressed in khaki slacks,
striped oxford and blazer, and not a single scar to show
what guardrails and cars can do. My mother tells me that
Elvis, the only spirit she'll claim, exists at the center
of a considerable debate between those who've spied him
sporting 1950's chinos and those who've seen 1970's sequins.
I no longer doubt any of this, or the psychics,
or that one day my fortune cookie numbers will win the lotto.
Besides, wasn't it Wittgenstein or some other reasoning German
who said go ahead and believe, what harm can it do?
On the other hand, my friend Carol believes in one thing,
her fear of bridges. Carol has decided she could never
belong to any of the dark age's religions in which the soul
had to cross a thin, thread-like bridge to find paradise. Fall off
and you're lost forever. Take Carol across the bay from Tampa
to St. Pete, or across the Cooper River Bridge into Charleston,
and you'd might as well ask her to cut off her arms.
It isn't the idea of falling or even dying—it's the bridge itself,

as if it represents the worst kind of modern haunting,
the technological prowess of steel and concrete a living
marvel of torture, atoms exploding beneath those Firestone tires.
And why not? Even quantum mechanics, that newest of religions,
believes that reality is not only a product of the external world,
but is bound up with our perceptions of it. Still, Carol's no Hart Crane
and I want to help, so I explain how in mythology, bridges
have almost always represented new life, good fortune,
that the Milky Way itself was once known as "The Bridge of Souls."
"No thanks," she says. "I'd rather go to hell
than cross a bridge to get to heaven."
In the face of that theory, how can I argue?
Though there are, of course, other theories. One described
by Thiselton Byer of Lancashire, that children born during twilight
have the peculiar ability to see places, events and people hidden to others.
Or the modern physics theory that "alternative worlds are not
always completely disconnected from our own: they overlap
our perceived universe." Or my personal favorite offered up
by Leonora Galigai, a convicted 17th century witch,
who, when asked by her judge how she had enchanted her victim,
replied "My spell was the power of a strong mind over a weak one."
Still I'm not sure how any of this can help my father
up past midnight listening to voices, dealing with memories,
real or perceived, that he'll never reveal.
Or Hunter, awakened to a world of unrecognizable sounds and sights.
Or even me. I lied when I said I was o.k. with the ghosts.
There was one I never understood, never wanted to believe in.
He stood at the edge of my room, just days after I'd found him
dead outside his bath, his heart twisted into a knot,
my grandfather over my childhood bed, staring.
I'm not sure why I woke, or how long he stood there, silent,
or even why I didn't say anything to him, or call out
down the hall where the phantom glow of the t.v. flickered.
I was a grown man with my own child before I ever confessed
this, my first real fear, my first connection to another world,
to my father. When I did he looked away, nodded
then sighed and nothing more was said. We sat on the back porch,
late August, and watched a meteor shower. We understood
the how's and why's of each falling star, the theories behind

interplanetary bodies, but we preferred the mystery,
the old wives' tale of how each represented a death.
One of us, I don't remember which, lit a candle. Then I slept
under that sky, and when I woke it was morning and the world,
so bright and clear, was beyond my knowing.

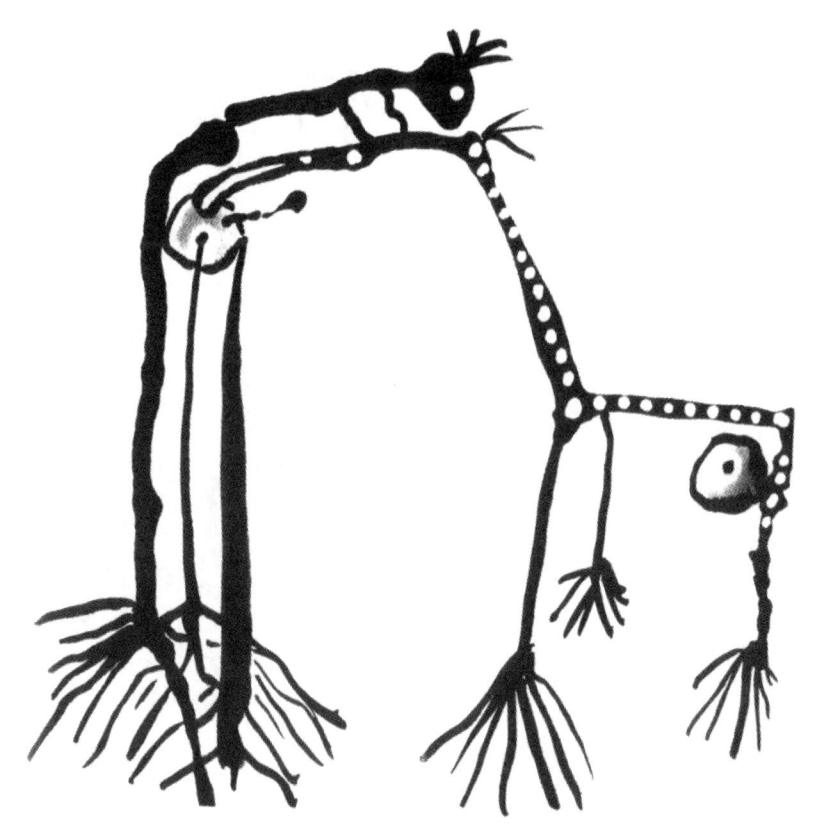

BONO - UNTITLED DRAWING FROM *EQUILIBRE* - 2000

Raphael Dagold

Dirt Heart

Sometimes there is a shape to them,
the blackbirds—an arc or swirl, a wave,

the air like water following
itself around a rock.

And sometimes the air bursts
with the black specks

suddenly like fall leaves
gusted ahead of storm clouds

before the rain has come
to batter them out of the sky,

a great crowd of leaves
like a startled flock before it's a shape.

The road goes down to the river
and the crowd is there in a startle

from the field's edge
low across the dirt,

the air full with it,
almost swollen, so large, right there,

as if the sky is in front of my face,
something to rush towards and be in it,

like a building half-demolished
before an excavation for a new one—

exposed rooms and hallways,
floors with wall-to-wall carpet

dripping from a lip jumbled with plumbing
and chunks of concrete hanging on rebar

making it more present
than in its life of still composure:

to be in it, eye mesmerized,
no scale anymore, to rush in

and through it, this bird one way,
that one another, all of them

a tumbling swarm from one side
of the road to the other

before they're a flock and turn
their wingtips thin to the horizon

so for a moment disappear,
then settle into the field.

The dirt at the field's edge is dry, and light.
Tiny stones float on the fine layer.

It's soft and in the shade it's cool,
in the sun it's hot to the hand.

Here where the blackbirds have added
and taken, where my fingers press

and their impression stays—
my hand, the heel, the palm,

the hand can lift and leave itself,
its fingers filled with air,

here where the birds have passed.
Where the body has just come back.

Where the blackbirds have
broken and made their shape.

CAROL V. HAMILTON
A Revelation

The bruised gardenia, drunk on its own sweetness,
lies in a bowl of water, listening
to the Ravel Concerto in G, slow movement,

as a patent-leather darkness covers
the french windows, and unexpectedly
a nail clipping of a moon appears.

It's a revelation!

All this time we had believed in time,
in progress, the ballot box, vitamin supplements, and yet

there were black balloons flying at half-mast,
dreams of ineffable sadness,

bungy-jumpers bouncing off bridges
while playing the viola da gamba,

and those dark, disconsolate strangers
loitering on street corners
as if transfixed by desire and grief.

In the cerebellum's folds that sweetness lingers
a time-bomb with white petals

to detonate this dull existence
with its sitcoms and fire escapes.

Let us decamp.
The landlord won't pursue us.
Some irate neighbor will have the car towed.

Music will spill like water from a sluice
and we will discover the difference between
money and justice, daylight and knowledge,

suicide and hope.

MICHAEL MORSE
Mercury, Slickered

Quo, with the rain in his head and starch in his heart,
his feet bone-soaked with the rain that won't stop.
He's out in the crowded streets backpedaling, he's singing a song
where lyrics wander back and forth, winter, fall, fall, winter.
It's a two-step out among the gray and navy men,
the Burberry's and the Brooks Brothers,
when out of the what's-not-blue comes a small girl
out of the great gray cloud of men a girl, a yellow slicker.

My name is Quo and I'm talking about the kind of coats we wear
when we walk down a block and can't quite feel our feet on pavement.
I'm talking about the times when there's something *in between,*
something slight and soft, ephemeral, small, and tragic,
like my lip between my teeth when I think of a girl in Cambridge.
And here's this girl in her yellow coat, impermeable.
I'm Quo. She's yellow. It's a joust or a sign to clear the streets—
I run, I'm Quo come in out of the rain, yellow slicker to my eye
a stain, an awl to isinglass; I murmur my plants on the sill,
now, my ficus, my little spider plant, my esmerelda,

now we'll have a god run among us in the streets,
someone come down like Mercury as a girl in a yellow slicker
but a god nonetheless with his wings on her back,
a little salt in his blood and his desire down here—
like Quo thinking of his girl in Cambridge and he's *there,*
like a god coming down to run an empty street just to feel his feet on
 something firm,
Mercury, his head in his heart and his heart in his head, living in-between,
yellow, his sandals hitting water, two-stepping the lumen down
under the lamplight, stomping and dancing, the gray coats long gone—
Oh Mercury, you little girl in gold, welcome back.

Billy Collins
Tree

Ink strokes on rice paper—
a wooden bridge
over a river,

mountains in the distance,
and in the foreground
a wind-blown tree—

I rotate the book on the table
so the tree
is tilted toward your village.

Sergey Gandlevsky

"Obedient to a gypsy itch..."

Translated from the Russian by Philip Metres

Obedient to a gypsy itch,
Someday we'll cram our suitcase full.
Someday we'll stand on platforms
In strange and deafening lands.

We'll make our circuitous way
Like a daring February snowstorm,
And someday above Kelny city
We'll light the table lamps.

The smoky nights drag on.
Goodbye, *do svidanya*, adieu.
As a hunted animal runs
From death, humans run from life.

Nearing old age, with a tourist trunk,
I'll head off—shaking before my time—
With a flawlessly Austrian face,
And, let's say, a Turkish wife.

Depressively choosing his words,
An intelligent student will show us
The sights of some boundless place:
Baikal, Leningrad, Tashkent.

The vast Russian land,
A trunk in an old man's hand.
What will I ask my heart then,
And in what language?

Sandor Kanyadi

Sigh
(Sohaly)

Translated from the Hungarian by P. Sohar

oh would that it were my
home and homeland that
airplane with foreign markings
hovering
almost standing still
above the ice floes
of the ocean somewhere
between canada and iceland

Sigh
(Sohaj)

how I wish that plane with
the foreign markings hovering
almost standing still
above the ice floes of the frozen ocean
somewhere between
canada and iceland
could be my home and homeland

Sandor Kanyadi

Should be Abolished
(El kellene)

Translated from the Hungarian P. Sohar

not only punctuation marks
but capital letters basking
in class distinction
should be abolished
words should be stripped
naked just like
those deported

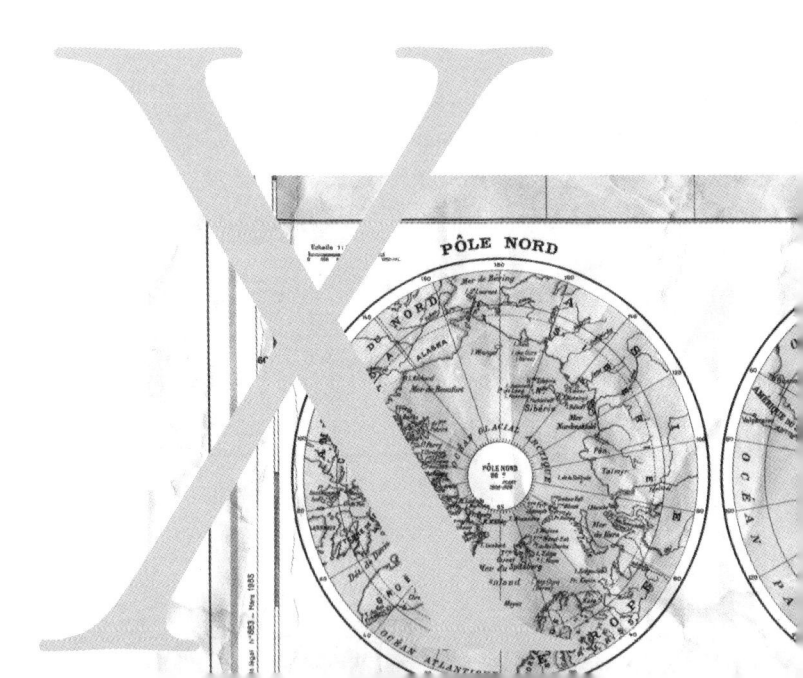

FRANÇOIS TRÉMOLIÈRES
The Oracle

Translated from the French by Peter Skelton

for Luc Ferreira

You remember that café beside the station
one woman alone behind the *comptoir*
made us draw a tree
on a pad of coarse paper with the wine merchant's logo
not far away, a man who must have been her husband
almost incapable of uttering a word

her son was sitting exams for a job
a fly lad
let me tell you my son
she intoned in her rich soprano voice
don't think too much about your roots
you're too afraid of moving away from home

no this was no chance comment
after all what could be more important
customers could wait
and leave, accompanied by a strange guffaw
we went back several times,
but aren't sure she knew us anymore.

FRANÇOIS TRÉMOLIÈRES

The Son of Abraham
or Mad Love

Translated from the French by Peter Skelton

Early one morning
my father packed the car
and normally so taciturn
warned me that journey would be long

along the empty roads we sped
past all the girly billboards
three days and three nights
with heavy hearts on leashes

we opened and shut the motel doors
he never stopped talking of his land and his love
and of the trash in the tabloids
and children found dead on beaches

but it's too easy to escape into death
to fling oneself off the cliff to smash one's body into smithereens
and blend one's blood with the breakers

I recall
climbing up the mountain tracks
I was loved
like the calf fattened for the slaughter

> I dreamt
> of a huge conflagration
> up on the peak,
> the blinding flash
> all white
> I was struck down by lightening

consumed by death through a kiss from the Lord
beneath the awesome countenance of Abraham my father
racked with pain I thought God wanted me to die
and suddenly happy I found faith
in the sublime sacrifice and thought
I could see more clearly than he with his tearful eyes
his arm old but invested with incredible strength
which I was incapable of resisting
my only hope of escaping lay
in uniting in the incandescent love in his heart

but then the heavens remained grey like a day without rain
and I found myself tossed onto the bush by a strong swell
breathless, my kidneys punctured
then
above me
my father looking dumbfounded

after the knife under its own weight had averted his hand
he wiped his brow, and with renewed vigour
he slayed the calf
drunk with the fumes of flesh and blood
then turning his back
he signalled me to follow
down to the town

> we know not why we live
> amidst such indifference

and you standing half naked on the beach
in sun and shadow so secretely soft
you walk
like a cloud in the sky
filling up the emptiness

and with your finger you caress my skin, kindling hope
marking the spot for the knife to strike
pressing your lips on my neck

Deborah Reich
Coffee & Tits

This morning I made coffee
    with milk & two sugars—
took it back to bed, lay down with it. Klutz.
Spilled it.
    And that was the last clean shirt—
    It's laundry day anyway—

Took the shirt off, threw it on the pile,
went back to the kitchen,
made myself another coffee
    one sugar, this time—
    it's grocery day too—
carried it to the open window;

I'm a perfect height—
when I stand next to the window
my tits lie sweetly on the sill
sticking their little noses out.

There's nothing finer than a spring breeze
on your tits.

in other words

Please do not touch the works of art.

PHOTO WITHIN PHOTO: D.A., "FOUND POEM," (WITH HAND OF E.G.) SCAN 2000.

Documents, personal essays, letters, misfit scribbles, and serious ideas.

Bogdan Korczowski
"The Only Way Out Against Nothingness"*

*Poland, its Jewish past, Technocracy, Painting, and the Logic of War...
Selected moments from a long talk with David Applefield, soon to be a book.*

Bogdan Korczowski is a painter from Krakow who has lived in Paris for twenty years. His grandfather, Wilhelm Korczowski, a political prisoner, died in the concentration camp Mauthausen on January 14, 1941.

The incredible part about violence created by humanity is that it doesn't come out of nowhere. It always comes from advanced thinking, from cutting edge technology. The burning of books in early Nazi Germany first required a "knowledge" of literature. To determine that a book was "rotten," one had to know what was in it. This was the work of Cultural Commissions, appointed experts, careful deliberation. The recent war in Kosovo began with the elimination of Albanian literature ten years earlier, the ousting of professors, the closing of libraries, the censorship of newspapers, the shutting down of television stations. The same in South Africa, Cambodia, and elsewhere. It always starts with the repression of writing. Culture always originates with the written word. And totalitarianism and fascism always depend on the professional destruction of culture.

The threat isn't the cultural object itself. What is really art? Look at the recently-found watercolors of Adolph Hitler himself. You can always invent a scenario to attack the content. But, the freedom of creating a work of art is already a threat to most totalitarian regimes. The Nazis removed paintings from museums; the paintings themselves were innocent—Cubism and small abstract paintings. It was the mere idea of having the freedom to create abstract paintings that was threatening. Remember, they didn't select anti-Nazi works specifically, they destroyed the writing of poetry, paintings and books by writers who wrote about love, and that had nothing at all to do with politics. They

PHOTO: D.A.

BOGDAN KORCZOWSKI

burned books precisely to show that the only volumes that were "good" were the ones that celebrated themselves. And it worked very well. The schools of fine arts and institutes of music flourished at the same time. This barbarism wasn't the work of tribalistic mobs who destroyed at random. The modern barbarism lay in the hands of great minds, top engineers, architects, city planners...First, they burned books, then paintings, then entire peoples, to show the superiority of others. Achievements. The horrible logic of the time, we must remember, occurred in the most civilized country in Europe in the 1930s. Even now, the butchery in Rwanda was carefully planned by some of that country's most talented managers.

The logic of war is the end of the world, the end of civilization.

BOGDAN KORCZOWSKI - *THE ONLY WAY OUT AGAINST NOTHINGNESS (WITKACY)* - PAINTING, 1999

* from the painting by Witkacy (1885-1939) who committed suicide in 1939.

The moment that the first warrior in time built his first weapon marks the beginning of "high-tech." The F-16 is a Roman chariot.

That there are no more Jews in Poland today is a tragedy. We don't speak of the same war history in Krakow as in Paris or elsewhere in the world. In France, how many *tens of thousands* of Jews perished in the Second World War? In Poland, we speak of *millions*, of *hundreds* of villages, of *entire* neighborhoods. Not just the people on *one* street or in a *particular* building. War erased an *entire* civilization.

The historical questions we tend to ask ourselves here, today, in Paris or New York tend to be absurd. We shouldn't forget that in Paris during the war, the theaters remained open, Picasso was building his career and successfully selling his paintings, Jean-Paul Sartre was writing and staging his plays. Life continued to exist in Paris. In Poland, Bruno Schulz, the greatest artist of his generation, a Polish-Jew, was shot in the head in the street like a dog. Culture ceased to exist. Houses were burned. We're talking about annihilation. Poland lost everything. What was recovered? Ruins. Look at Warsaw after the war. Warsaw in 1945 was a field of ruins. Paris was always Paris. The Germans came to Paris to visit the Eiffel Tower and the Louvre. Germans didn't come to Poland to visit the museums.

Hate, you mention? No, not hate. I'm far from being consumed by hate. For me all that matters is to understand. It's not a question of turning the page, of getting on with it. It's a question of looking reality in the face. That's why I say that today, Germany is a country like any other in the European Union.

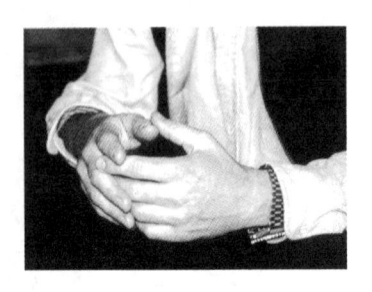

I went to see the Holocaust Museum in Washington, D.C. At the end of the exhibition, it was very very painful for me, as a Pole, to revisit the Pogroms of 1946. I admit, it was a real blow, it was not the Poland I wanted to believe, but it was the truth. The museum is excellent because it depicts for future generations history as it was. The danger of story-telling always comes from the confusion and manipulation of interpretation. This is what concerns me. Even a powerful vehicle like the Internet today, where one can state anything to anyone and reach hundreds of thousands, ridicule or exaggerate anything with convincing credibility, reinforced with technology and design, requires our constant concern. The tool is miraculous, but the use of human suffering to manipulate fact and distort understanding, is a crime. The way we remember and the way we tolerate and form opinions must be our primary concern.

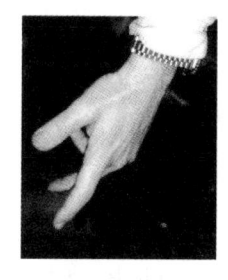

There is something innate in humanity that requires us to be vigilant. We need to assume the reflex of a watchdog. We've seen genocide. We know that atrocities originate with a thought-process. We know what Pol Pot succeeded in doing in Cambodia, we saw what happened in Rwanda, we witnessed the bestiality in Yugoslavia. Violence, on this planet, thrives. I don't want to over-philosophize on the origins of violence – being human simply means that, being human – but we need to perpetually keep watch. The challenge is to know how to keep watch? Through education. If we tell the truth in our museums, our paintings, our newspapers, our exhibitions, if we tell how humanity arrived at Auschwitz, maybe we can create a generation of people with a different logic. If we say that Auschwitz was just a story somewhere in Poland, it's all over. We need to be constantly reminded that truth is vulnerable. It can be manipulated. The tools of technology and engineering always pose the same dangers. I can't imagine sitting behind a screen and clicking on what Yahoo serves up for gas chambers. The tools for composing truth can be terrifying because they permit us to simply fall upon information that is right, and with equal speed and ease, information that is wrong. The means to manipulate are seamless. The lines between right and wrong are drawn by whom and for what reasons? Our only defense is to repeat and repeat. We need to repeat, repeat, and repeat again. How do things happen? How did this happen? Not *why*, but *how* have things happened? Correct the small details, the minor distortions, the little lies before they become huge and irrepressible. It is in the *how* that we discover extraordinary things. The links, the complicity, the interconnectedness between industry and special interests that results in totalitarianism.

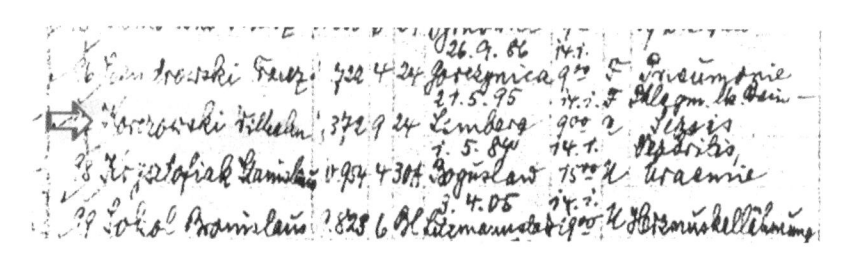

DETAIL FROM PAGE 47 OF THE ORIGINAL
TOTENBUCH GUSEN ZI. 3.501/4580-III/12MH/00,
AMTSGERICHT MAUTHAUSEN, JANUARY 21, 1941

José María Mendiluce

Leila

Translated from the Spanish by J.P. Glutting

When you looked at me from the rubble of what had been your house, Leila, your enormous blue eyes, made bigger by horror and incomprehension, were not asking for food for that week. You were not asking for more months of useless negotiation, you were not thanking me for the enormous efforts of my colleagues. You could not and did not have to understand what it had cost so that, for at least a few weeks, you had been able to eat. You never knew what it had cost to prevent them from killing you by starvation, what it had cost to open the airport to a humanitarian airlift.

All to find you there, under that damned beam, in that rubble that held you trapped and which, bit by bit but inexorably, Sarajevo was becoming.

Your eyes were simply asking what I was doing there, at your side, as helpless as you to stop the bombardments, the death, your death, the systematic and prolonged destruction that we lived through and died through for so many months.

You were not even old enough to add a reproach to your incredulity when you saw the man that you recognized from the television. That man who came on day after day to talk about peace and coexistence without achieving anything. The man you had in front of you, crying from rage and pity before your broken body, bleeding and trapped, that man to whom you had offered candy at the end of Ramadan.

I could only say—I'm sorry, I'm sorry—repeated, painful, useless. I tried to snatch you back from death by moving your body, pushing the beam—and I was left with your arm in my hands. You went out without a flicker, abandoning your gaze behind you.

And I have it with me still, following me day and night, reminding me that I have no right to be quiet or to forget the reflection of you in so many other children that continue to die in our arms, while we continue without making them stop the artillery and the bullets and the machetes, stop the land mines from exploding. And you continue to die in innocence. In Bosnia and in so many other places…

I stepped out on the street and saw the body of your father on the corner, with a bloody loaf of bread, bread made from the wheat that we were able to bring to Sarajevo. Bread cooked with the fuel that we were able to bring into Sarajevo; wheat and bread that had cost me weeks of negotiations and your father, in the form of bread, his life. Bread as an excuse for those who wanted to ease their consciences by sending it, at the risk of your lives and ours. Bread from the heroic and besieged bakery. Bread from the bread line, corpses are our daily bread, and do not give us ours today, but give us peace.

Impossible peace the politicians said, and lied, while they used us as shields, giving you Bosnians more bread. Leila did not want more bread—she only wanted to live. Leila loved her father, and her brother, who was at the front. And her mother, who is no one knows where, perhaps with her little brother, who has also been missing from home since the start of the bombardments.

VERÓNICA FRÜHBRODT - NIÑITA ARREPENTIDA NIÑITA QUE NO QUIERE VER (DIPTYCH) - OIL ON CANVAS, 1999

A typical family, concrete expression of the horrors of that massacre they called a war, that we abandoned for so many months so they could continue slaughtering you. Because the West has lost its values, has forgotten its role, because nobody, almost, has the time to waste on you. Even the images of your broken bodies, insisting every day, began to get tiresome. New bodies and new graves, like yours, Leila which will go unnoticed among so many others, from the very moment that it joins the fifteen thousand in the cemeteries of Sarajevo.

Your resistance to extermination made you Bosnians unpopular among those that would have preferred a quick, inevitable genocide. That would have bet on the victory of those that wanted it so badly, those that needed the dead bodies of so many

Leilas, of all of their parents, of all the families of all the Leilas. Qualifying that genocide as a conflict, talking about the "conflicting sides," reducing you Bosniansexpression of human dignity—to the same level as the genocidal let them feel better, let them avoid any commitment, perhaps smothered their unreliable consciences.

It was irrelevant that the facts and the constant efforts of the barbarians showed what they were. There was always an Owen to explain it away and even things out. It almost seemed, listening to some illustrious cynics, passively or actively complicit in the genocide, that you Bosnians had made some type of collective suicide pact in order to accuse Karadzic's poor Serbs.

But you knew, Leila, as your father knew, as we all knew, who was killing, why they were killing and what they were trying to do. They never hid that from anyone. They trumpeted it.

Only a few deaf people who did not want to listen. But they will have to, I swear to you, Leila, that they will have to listen. And when we excavate all the hidden mass graves, from Prijedor to Srebrenica, when the bodies from Vukovar and from the banks of the Drina appear, when we find the orders that were given, when we give a name to each corpse, then we will pass the bill to those that said so many lies and so much bullshit, snake oil salesmen, liars without borders, rabble without limits, accomplices—whether due to stupidity or cowardice or for unconfessable interests—of an unfinished genocide. Because you Bosnians did not let them finish you, which was very irritating for the UN and its generals, who wanted to wrap up their mission as soon as possible, as you know: it was more comfortable at home during Christmas and, furthermore, there are no budget problems.

Your gaze, Leila, that follows me as a permanent reminder of my commitments, together with those of so many others, making it impossible to forget, demanding justice, so that there will not be vengeance. Telling the truth about your massacre, so that no one dares to rewrite your history. I promise this to you with the same rage that I felt that day when I tried to wrestle you back from death, probably hastening it. With the same determination that accompanied me, transmitted by you Bosnians, during the two long years that we survived, some of us, together.

With the determination of someone who has seen more than he can stomach and remain detached, and terrorized by deaths like yours, Leila, and who also knows the guilty parties personally. I don't have—and even if I did I wouldn't exercise it—the right to forget any of you. And you, Leila, least of all.

Until love triumphs and I can visit your grave in that immense Olympic cemetery of Sarajevo. Because I have always been sure that pure hate cannot triumph. Although it contaminates our souls, since contact with it is contagious, and we all are going to need healing and rest to clean ourselves of its filth and temptation.

And if love does not win, I assure you that hate will not triumph. Because, delayed and with shame, with dignity and great effort, love was able to arm itself. And that is why Sarajevo stayed alive, sick and isolated, destroyed and abandoned by many of you, but alive. And therefore able to be reconstructed by love and diversity.

And that cursed general, that execrable general named Mladic, who, with his customary and haughty already-passed arrogance, invited me to visit him (the last time that I had the misfortune of meeting him) "next summer in Zadar, where I have a summer house," which is to say, on the Croatian Adriatic coast ... convinced that no one would stop his tanks of hate, that damned general will have to hide for the rest of his days or sit on the bench to be condemned by justice and spend what is left of his life where he belongs.

And if he escapes justice, he will regret the day that vengeance hunts him down. That is why justice is so important, to help you Bosnians escape the lasting contamination of hate. That is why Serbian and Croatian criminals must sit and answer for what they have done, so that a peaceful vengeance is possible for a love that resisted death and will grow again, in all its splendor, one day.

A day that we will have to come together so that triumphant love flowers as soon as possible over the ruins of Bosnia. So that your death and your dead, Leila, will not have been in vain. So that you all can feel that you have contributed to halting the barbarity, hateful and expansive, that threatens other Leilas in so many other places on the planet.

VERÓNICA FRÜHBRODT - *EL VESTIDO* - MIXED MEDIA, 1999

ROBERT FAGAN

Musée de l'Homme

The ad said there were countless exotic exhibits in the museum, including dioramas, panoramas, and virtual realities. So I made the long and tedious journey with great expectations—even with hopes of finally resolving some of my doubts about humanity. But I was completely disillusioned. The museum was merely an attic with a few index cards pasted on hideously stained walls. The ancient attendant, sitting behind a sagging desk engrossed in a Superman comic, did not even look up when I expressed my dissatisfaction. But having come so far, I did copy down the contents of some of the cards.

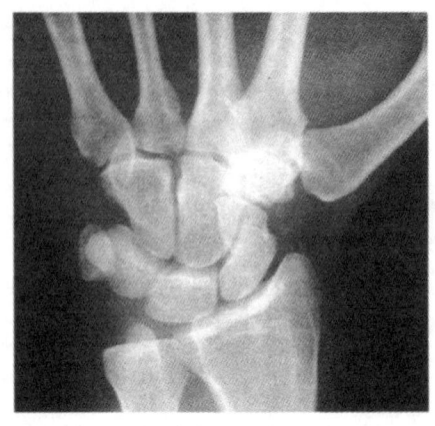

Une radiographie de la main droite d'un homme.

The beginning of time fell upon the entrance of the night preceding the 23rd day of October in the year before Our Lord of four thousand and four.
 —Bishop Ussher

An Important Anthropological Discovery After an arduous descent through caves and a scientific sifting through bones, an expedition led by Richard Leakey excavated deeper and found our earliest ancestral remains, five partial proconsul skeletons. Two of them were adults who probably weighed 20 to 25 pounds and were about 18 inches high.

Man is a featherless biped.
 —Aristotle

The shrubs moved closer. The giant birds ruffled and started up and ran in circles. They stopped to listen to the whistle of a hen in the shrubs. They moved closer. Above the shrubs, feathers waved. The birds moved even closer. He let the feathers fall and reached down for the spear he had been dragging between his toes. This animal he could eat. It was not his own flesh, but the flesh of his cousin. He was kangaroo, not emu.

>The use of God in the singular is racist.
>—Toto Demos

If it rained any more there would be no reason even to walk into the field. There would be no harvest. There would be no field. And the world must be given back to Noah. Yet there was a solution. One could climb the bell tower and down into the chapel. There would be no priest—he was always in town drinking or whoring. But in the chapel was the Lady of Mercy. One could kiss her painted wooden toes. She would answer any prayer. The rain would stop. Or he would steal her. He could sell her to the heathen across the border.

The entrances to villages and longhouses are particularly vulnerable to supernatural attack. Shamans place ferocious reptilian carved figures to guard them. Beads of all types are also valued. In former times, single examples of the most sought-after varieties could be exchanged for a human slave. Most valued of all are the enemy skulls displayed in the longhouse gallery. In sufficient quantities, they ensure the fertility of the fields.

>Down rivers bearing wine.
>Heart-breaking women
>trapped in my palm.
>Wake. Ten years lost,
>a drifter in the brothels.
>—Tu Mu

When Bridget left service, it was only because her belly was big. She had been a very good maid. When Bridget left Jocko, it was only because her skin was covered with scars and red splotches. She had been a very good whore. When Bridget left the poorhouse, it was only because her body was thin as a matchstick. She had been very good and quiet and she didn't cost much wood.

When the soldiers raped him, he said to himself, "Some day I will have many women." When he was buggered by the great poet, he said to himself, "Some day I will have many poems." When he left Europe, he said to himself, "Some day I will have a lot of money." When he took three wives from three different tribes, he said to himself, "Some day I will know enough languages." When he tried to return to the East, with his swollen stump and paralyzed arm, he said, "Lord! Will I ever find a stone to put my head on?" When he died in Marseilles and the news reached Paris, they said, "We hear his body smelled awful."

At the UN today Mrs. Kirkpatrick said, "Their economy is weak, and we can help them with some training for their police."

Miguel didn't know where to put them. Finally, instead of putting one in each hole, he put four or five in, depending on their size. It helped that they were new and still unrigid, and battered or broken. They could be squeezed small like babies before birth. But he was worried that he would get in trouble for bad bookkeeping. When he asked for names, the sergeant punched him. When he asked for occupations, the lieutenant said: troublemakers, possible terrorists, faggot intellectuals, unwomenly women, godless commies, and punk kids. So he had no names. But he tried at least to mark the multiple graves with small stones. Otherwise, when there was so little room, what excuse could he give prospective customers? These newcomers—packed in tight, their bodies embracing, one bunch almost touching the next—were forming an underground community, and taking the land away from respectable people.

To the left and right of this card, along the walls here and elsewhere, is a labyrinth pattern that attempts to contain all the lacerations of the human condition. Please affix your thumb print anywhere. It will be added to the pattern.

JEAN LAMORE

Fragment from

WOVOKO

A novel in progress

It comes down to the river at four a.m., approaching cautiously, then ever more boldly towards the morning mist rising.

Very close now, I can see that pieces are missing. A woman it is, with half a face, a quarter face. Neither amputation nor anatomical imperfection. The vacuity is moving, jumping and shifting over the body; now a leg gone like my own, then an entire section of the torso. The leg comes back perfectly. The effect of a migraine mirage that punches swirling holes into vision but here I know that I'm striving to see what isn't there anymore.

During the interminable wait I've remained perfectly immobile, ticks, leaches and other small hemophagic creatures patiently make their way up my body to gorge themselves and swell in silence.

She laps up the river water like a dog, furtively turning her head to either side as she drinks. She sees things I have never seen before. Structures and beings that surely lie between us, rising from the river, bearing perfume and murmur but invisible to me.

ANONYMOUS - "HARP" - HUMAN SKULL, WOOD AND BRONZE, 21ST CENTURY

Goes on drinking, her body momentarily intact, kneeling in the mud.

When I advance the entire body vanishes, leaving only the trace of her genuflexion in this place.

And yet there is a scent here as if she had left behind lingerie with her odor lingering, into which I could bury my face smelling all of her. Know where it was she had come from, what she has eaten and that which she drank, the trace of her sweat bears

the message of extreme effort.
I am sure now where from she comes, together we once were there^ and partook of the same fare, our arms enlaced, strange brew drew us down.
Rhythmic clanging comes from across the river. The iron thieves wielding their small hammers to the melody of Rhinegold *niebuling*. They've taken now all but the feet of the Eiffel Tower that thrust stumpily into the air.
Alone I hop in the mud.
Thud, my single foot goes deep with each leap. I am naked, turquoise testicles swinging freely to one side before slapping against the only remaining thigh as I climb the bank.
There is no measure of time, no way of knowing when last she came to drink, nor when again she shall return. Only space, such a vast quantity of it. The position that the planet was in then, where it now lies and where it shall be when she returns. Perhaps not yet an entire revolution around the galaxy but certainly a broad arc half about.
Will she sense that we crossed paths?
— I have seen parts of her again! It is. These are. Fragments that I shall..., I mutter in the morning air, steam rolling from my nostrils.
Without them the study of life's end becomes an imperious necessity. Intensive care unit in broken down hospital where life timidly trembles upon artificially sustained meat; dusty wards echoing with the complaints and groans of the dying.
Ruby dragon flies arise with the sun, their blazing thoraxes winking in the dawn while dog-birds bark as they pass over the river with heavy wing beat blowing mist into slowly spiraling columns.
Scrape the parasites from my skin and put on the cloths I had left by the cold torch and empty hypodermic. No satin pajamas but a crude outfit made of blue dyed jute that makes me itch.
There is time again and I'm very late. A rubber car awaits me where I had left an equian mount, the interior littered with incomprehensible notes, the delicate bones of some kind of fowl, gnarled clean and a thermos of fermented cuttlefish ink.
I gulp black.
— Don't look back! says a voice coming from behind.
Turning around, nothing there I find. A flash of heat in my mind?
Light within is dim, coming through thick glass ports of reduced diameter, capable of resisting the deepest ocean pressure, imbedded in the heavy rubber body, grayish and flaky on the surface from aging and UV exposure. Rubbing in oil with soft cloth is recommended, especially before immersion.
Massive, squat and almost perfectly round it has long whiskers. Speedy and very silent in progression were it not for the sound of constant collision, plowing over banana tree trunks and ficus roots that obstruct the streets. This is rue de Rivoli. Sometimes fluid from something of living splatters the small windows. It is a brutal ride.

Suddenly a mouth is next to me, only this, hanging in the air. The lips are so well formed, the teeth and tongue too. It can only be hers. But my vision now blurs. How many things it had said to me, this buccal chef-d'oeuvre? Merely the timbre of her voice would send tremors surging through me. No need to comprehend the meaning of what she was saying. Whether she spoke to me of emerald snakes pushing through high grass or the darker hue of a new lipstick, it was all the same. Verbal viagra.

How often had I crushed my own lips against these? How many times had I been in the mouth? The touch, taste and scent of it.

Zanda!

— For once listen to the meaning of what I say! Don't just hear but try to understand, comes the voice through the lips perfectly parting over the teeth.

— I need a cigarette, she continues.

— They no longer exist...

— That, if nothing else, is reason enough to leave this place!

— Is it you who laps water from the river?

— It's only the second time I have returned since this part of the sky has turned halfway around. The atmosphere, the air you breath, light itself, will never be the same again. You can sense this change when you look at old photos. There's a different glint in people's eyes, the glow of light on reflective surfaces is far more radiant. It forms halos.

SPEEDY AND VERY SILENT IN PROGRESSION WERE IT NOT FOR THE SOUND OF CONSTANT COLLISION, PLOWING OVER BANANA TREES AND FICUS ROOTS THAT OBSTRUCT THE STREETS THIS IS RUE DE RIVOLI.

— You're speaking of technical tricks photographers used to make their work appear more luminous...

— You've been misled. Light was altogether different back then. The way it fell on objects, enveloping them; we paid attention to it, remember all of the chrome, how vehicles were angular and always shining, not like this blistered black mess you now drive.

The mouth, with its perfection, is making me uneasy. It's clear to me that she no longer remembers. I shall begin all over again.

— Why here? I could have missed you. The first time I didn't even realize that it was you down by the river.

— The bridge that lies there in a heap, it once rose over the river and that's exactly where I threw down a cigarette, the one you picked up and put to your mouth. The Pont d'Arcole which you crossed daily, bringing me food when I was heavy with Urulu, your daughter.

Be it then she knows who I am?

— I like the feel of the mud, the silence of the city asleep.
— Don't leave!
The streets are slimy, they smell of mint.
— About anything. You must speak!
I know it's the only way to keep her with me momentarily. Perchance she will begin to remember, other parts will then join the mouth.
— On war then. They had, and this in itself is a paradox, been right when they claimed that there would no longer be any great world wars. Only limited conflicts of the Rwanda, Congo or Kosovo type.

But there had been so many of these local wars, cumulating and finally concomitant, that the effect was globally more devastating than any full blown world war ever would have been.
And at last, had not the nuclear arsenal which never served directly,

TO BE ROBBED OF ONE'S DREAMS IS PERHAPS WORSE THAN SUFFERING THE AMPUTATION OF A LIMB. AN INSECT THE SIZE OF A COCONUT SPLATTERS ON THE WINDOW REDUCING VISIBILITY TO NIL.

proven infinitely more dangerous when abandoned, releasing its lethal contamination at a time when man's memory no longer retained? But you, tell me of friends we knew.
— Hubert? Remember him digging in the sand to hide his wallet on the beach? The long walks we then took together across the tide flats, seaweed and fish skeletons popping beneath our feet. The perils of his homosexuality in Africa; going from one administrative job to another, constantly changing countries. Falling into the same dangerous traps wherever he was. First in Bangui he befriends a young boy, really falls in love with him only to be blackmailed by his protector, a taxi driver, thoroughly mean type that makes his life impossible with constant threats. You're the one who had warned him against these situations you knew so well.
An ear develops, small and finely formed, just behind the mouth. Hers without a doubt.
— The protector threatens to go to the French embassy and divulge everything. Hubert pays up. He's in love, oblivious to the danger or rather he quite revels in it. The ambassador summons him, tells him that he must leave. There's too much at risk. He moves to Abidjan where he quickly falls in love with another boy. This time it's the police chief who blackmails him for an altogether different sum. Things are a lot more evolved here. A wealthy French coiffeur, the young boy's last lover, just died in prison while being held on the grounds of a rumor. A well-known journalist, another acquaintance, was thrown out of the window of his twelfth floor flat. "Yes we have high enough buildings here!" the television announced. The police chief confiscated all of his belongings.

Hubert never really realized the danger he was in. One day his family in Brittany received a neat little package, his testicles wrapped in manioc leaves, confirming the deep racism that they had always felt towards those of the Dark Continent and the loathing of their son's sexual life.
— A white man who attempts to penetrate African society inevitably encounters peril; only the degree is variable.
— When you first saw me...
— Everyone told me to beware of you. 'He'll do white things to you. Force you to make love with his dog,' the mouth and ear very dark.
— I had no dog.
— Just the same they had warned me that you would spend all of your time licking and eating me as whites are known to do.
— This has proven to be true.
— Now I remember you. Together we left footprints faraway. Beyond the horizon where I remain, only returning when thirst brings me here.
I scream in the car, utterly alone. To be robbed of one's dreams is perhaps worse than suffering the amputation of a limb.
An insect the size of a coconut splatters on the window, reducing visibility to nil. Now that she's gone there's no more thrill.
— On the banks I shall pray to thee. Forever, there I'll wait.
Erect a small altar with offerings, cigarettes that I somehow find, little bananas, the ones from the West Indies that she loves, the last photo of Urulu that I have always kept by my heart. It's a small fly-through in the blue hues.

Water. Again and again at the river's edge.
I have a well-developed crest on my head. It isn't blunt or primitive-looking but high and fine, like the keel of a racing schooner only inverted. It gives me a fierce look. A noble hallmark! Yet I must beware lest a sudden gust catch this small sail and twist my neck. However, and because of it, I have become keenly aware of wind direction. This in turn has developed my sense of scent, greatly improving my hunting capabilities.
No longer are there street lights nor publicity panels to illuminate the night. It is black, and those who venture out are assassins, running naked through clouds of mosquitoes.
None bear those scarifications of light that are mine. Blazing poison put there by the daughter of the solar flare. A toxin best not share.
Some, they are rare, smear luciferin and firefly purée upon their skin to mime those patterns of light that are mine.

Clinical observations: "Dull flickering flames occasionally seen to erupt along the forearms, more rarely on the forehead well above the eyebrows, close to the receding hairline. We suspect that the subject pours slender trails of tar over his body and then proceeds to set them on fire. Thin spirals of thick smoke tend to confirm the use of unrefined petroleum products. Subject sustains considerable damage to cutaneous tissues, confined to overlapping bands in the afore-described regions. The display of scarifications is symptomatic of pervasive pattern of grandiosity."

Yon a glimmer wan.
'Tis the lamp I had thought?
Scales beneath the moon full shining?
Merely some damp thing caught.
Rather a predator here dining.
A vapor, a carrion feeder's breath, scent of beast gorged on things foul.

In the black deep unfurls the necklace of heaven's pearls.
So dark is the night that those keen-eyed can clearly see the great nebula, the one that's face-on in Triangulum. Yes, here from the heart of the city.
— Where does it lie? Easy! Find Cassiope, an M or a W depending on whether you run on your hands or your feet, its shape hasn't that much changed, only broader. Midway between there and Mirach spreads the brilliant swath of M31 which has drawn much closer, coming in on a straight tangent towards us. Some claim that a bridge of gas already joins us. This is mating, not collision. Now down to the left, just as far again, you can see M33, it too growing much larger. Easy to find, I told you.
A woman runs past bearing a torch. She pitches it blazing into the water, hides beneath a porch, raising the fringe of her skirt. High up her thigh, she plants a syringe.
Her bottom half is bare. I cannot help but stare. It's all that's visible as if it had been abandoned there. I am sure that with practice she has learned to plant the needle directly into the femoral artery. Perhaps she was a doctor with considerable experience in performing angiography.
Deep pain in my chest. Plugged coronaries. Sleep, rain are the best. Just the preliminaries before the obituaries.
This river has many tributaries.
Should I have hugged her, slugged her? At least covered her with a vest, lest others in quest, reap what is jest.
These assassins do not fear you.
They will come in very near you.
Quickly now, it is day. A Negro faced fire finch grazes the water, his flight composed of flickers and festoons.˜
Culex and anopheles bring fierce new diseases that make malaria seem merely passing indisposition.
It is here that, striding lightly, I best favor contemplating the sky, captured an instant by the very water it has vomited down upon the land. Deep pools form slick sheets, perfect mirrors surrounded by the baroque frames of ripple brown water. Delicate

bamboo bridges have been put up overnight, spanning the river like the work of some great nocturnal spider.
The air is laced with long tongues of electricity knocking down dead clutches of roosting birds from their perches. Steeples have fallen; hardly a spire remains standing on the churches.
Storms dump oceans of water that crush buildings and gouge broad craters into the ground. Nature is much stronger than it was, once again taking claim to that which man had thought to tame.
Vegetal palaces.
Elephants and rhinos once kept as pets have bred to form small herds that wander through the steaming wreckage. Some still have keepers. At the break of day they come to drink.
The river is at its lowest, hardly more than a sluggish current in the mainstream that carries along slowly spinning rafts of drifting water lotus. Most all of the city's twelve bridges have collapsed except for the Pont Neuf which is said to be the oldest, built when stone cutters knew well there trade. It stands alone in the middle of the river, useless to those who wish to cross. The waters have washed away the banks to either side leaving the structure stranded in the torrents, strange monument awash with the debris of past floods. Other bridges have formed heaps in the river that with time have become islands covered with reeds and rushes where crocodiles pile vegetal matter to incubate their eggs.
But the Seine no longer is the docile thing it once was. Upriver, dams have long burst leaving it free to suddenly rage with the tropical storms which are frequent even during the dry season. Brown walls of water roar down its bed sweeping away fishermen's shacks and dugouts, drowning entire families caught slumbering or smoking the day's catch along the banks.
Whirlpools then develop, sucking down wreckage with ferocious appetite, spitting up debris with such force that it emerges from water like a breaching whale.
Alone I fish amongst the rocks, turning them over when I can or slipping my hands beneath the bigger ones, fingers churning the murky mud beneath. On the bank I lay my catch, spreading it over a plastic sheet. Coins bearing the effigy of a flaming head, the remains of a refrigerator, a motorcycle frame; here a statuette, much older, perhaps Roman. Hadn't I done this very same thing along the Tiber? But then I had been much more adroit, never soiling the fine clothes that I wore.
— Wovoko! yells a woman from the opposite bank. She's Chinese, one of the ten I keep.
— That Russian man, Illitch. He wants you to start his car again.
This is my latest temporary profession, starting the vehicles of those whose lives are really threatened. If a bomb there were, it would be for me. I am incapable of being philosophical about it; each time I shut my eyes while I turn the key, sweating and convulsing so hard that the muscles tetanize.
— He shall have to wait.

Mboulou, the dry season is upon the land. In the early hours the jungle surrounding the city belches thick fog that mixes with smoke rising from wood fires and floating red dust to form dense orange cover that masks the sun. The thicker the matinal veil, the hotter it shall be as the day goes on. It's the greenhouse effect that once prevailed on Venus. I refuse to work before the sun has burned through. If I am to die, it shall be a double blaze.

My home is a high arch of long curved branches covered with broad phrynium and banana leaves that so well repel the downpours. Once within, one feels as if he were in a vast green tunnel. It has the shape and dimension of the Azande palaces that were once to be found between the Uèlé and the Mbomou rivers, tributaries of the Oubangui. The women tend small fires upon which they smoke pangolin and little monkeys, the night's catch. The vegetal palace is set in what used to be a neighborhood park next to the tour Saint-Jacques which shows you clearly how the Seine has nibbled its banks over the centuries. The tower still stands, its base partially covered by the green walls of my home.

When besieged by packs of feral dogs or the more dangerous lycaons and hyenas that roam the city, I withdraw to the top of the tower where a peaceful gray light filters through the original glass windows bathing those objects which I treasure the most. These are not artifacts hauled up from the river. They are things which inexplicably fell from the sky one day, landing in front of the main entrance of my lodge. Huge polished bones, a stuffed blue polar bear and a most masterful painting depicting a landscape which nowhere below exists, yet somehow in memory persists. It is a world of flame, akin to early attempts to portray the sun's coronal bursts; extraordinary form where one can let fancy run wildly. The colors are subdued, deep reds and purples with the most transparent of blues. It is the work of someone who had spent much time contemplating fire, knew it intimately. There are no garish hues. Only a suspicion of brilliancy, yet heat is keenly felt by whomever lays eyes on this painting. The word Gogodola appears, barely decipherable along the upper edge. I am convinced that it has nothing to do with a signature.

Had come with these things, a monkey whistle, nets made of vines and a small hand-confectioned cross-bow. These implements I use regularly to call the owl-faced mangabey from the lair he affections high up on the Haussmanian rooftops from which I knock him off with darts fashioned from rolled tins. With the nets I catch the little forest pigs that invade the city at nightfall.

Their flesh is excellent, the carcass is separated, basted with the black city honey, wrapped in broad leaves of certain tropical plants that have become indigenous, and buried upon a bed of hot stones. Once cooked, the meat can be preserved for weeks by placing it atop a small frame over a smoking fire. The ceiling being low in the apartments where I personally take in charge the preparation of the pig, I'm obliged to walk on all fours. Wearing knee pads is a necessity.

Damir Uzunovic
The Quick and the Dead

Translated from the Bosnian by Maja Starcevic

Bare Cemetery, Sarajevo

It is March. Fragrant wisps of smoke rise from the houses on Mare's Head, mingling with the spring breeze like coffee-drinking women with all the time in the world, confiding to one another about the Bairam delicacies they have been making in their kitchens all morning. Colorful as bright Latin American flags a few men, wary of the Bairam ceasefire, are hurrying down the road leading to Bare, a Sarajevo cemetery.

I raise my binoculars. It makes no difference if I track a hawk's flight, a coil of clouds, a flick of a horse's tail, or the district of Mare's Head (which is at its loveliest in those foggy days when it seems to be fading away—when rooftiles and bricks bleed their color into the earth and all that moves flies toward the fog in the sky)—all these seem a series of deepening layers. Every visible object—be it a flying bird, a pear tree, a discarded shovel, a stream, a hill, or a sweaty man in the field—has its own plane, in and of itself. The sum of their solitudes becomes the world visible to the naked eye.

I look at the cemetery. There may be more living than dead there. Making the most of the Bairam ceasefire both the Catholics and the Orthodox are scuttling around. Everyone is truly confused because the graveyard looks the same everywhere now that the birches and weeping willows, poplars and pines, even benches have been cut down and used as kindling, and without such pointers all graves look alike. The people would like to stop one another and ask, "Excuse me, do you know where I...." or "How do I get to...," but who would think of other people's dead, when you can't even find your own.

But what draws my father to the grave of his mother and father, and which memory, what sort of sign will point his way to his brother's grave, now that the beautiful weeping willow, whose stump had for years shown him the way to their graves, is gone? He has never approached them any other way. There he is, reading: Hasan Uzunoviæ (1892-1960) and Hasmeta Uzunoviæ, born Softiæ (1906-1968).

He takes off his jacket. After hanging it on his father's tombstone, he bends and begins to tidy up the grave, thinking about who knows what. Perhaps about his father who is not really buried where it says he is, but on the other hill at the Bakije Cemetery, his grave unrecognizable by now. Every so often he pauses in his work, as if Hasmeta was talking to him from down below, "Not like that, son! Like this!" Hasmeta—when she walked the earth she had named me Damir instead of the family-favored Hasan, which means "beautiful", while Damir means nothing at all, though I sometimes jokingly translate it into English as "Yespeace." In the year she gave birth to her elder son Vahid she'd announced he would become a poet because Rilke had died the same year. From her son Fadil, who perished in 1966 in his thirty-sixth year suffocated by exhaust fumes in the garage and now buried close by, she took a name, as if picking a beautiful flower, and gave it to a newly born grandson, who was later killed by a grenade that turned his heart into a piece of shrapnel in June of 1992. For a long time now, the Uzunoviæ family will be without a Fadila—a name that means "industrious."

I leave my father, brought closer and made larger by the binoculars, and search the Bare cemetery for a silver pine. Not the pine, actually, but my Nana, my mother's mother, Nura Telegrafèiæ, born Muftiæ (1905-1971). Had I had more than the few six years I'd shared with her, I could picture her more vividly now. As it is, all I can remember is her goodness, great as the world, descending on me like an eiderdown, and me running under the bed, peeking out at her. But instead of the silver pine, who do I see but Dobrila. She takes a Muslim prayerbook from her handbag, puts on a kerchief, sits and reads out loud, moving her lips as she does when praying at mass in the Catholic church on Sundays. Born in Vrisnik, a Dalmatian village above Jelsa on the island of Hvar, she will for some reason love Nura for as long as she lives, and not a single Bairam goes by without Dobrila coming to pray for Nura, always bringing her a white rose.

That rose comes and goes, its thorns disappear with its flowers, but the rose on the grave of Nura's son from her first marriage, Sulejman Gabela—who died of leukemia a year after Nura—that particular rose is all thorns in bloom, bursting from the grave like a flame. Every time I tried to trim it and calm its frenzy, it would sting my thumb, though perhaps going straight for the heart. Days went by before the thorn would come out. All that time I'd dream of the empty diamond-shaped flower bed in the gravel on his grave, the bed that was the source of the rose's frenzy. I won't say anything else about Sulejman, except that his clamp, which I've been using for years, sometimes pinches me.

Most of his carpentry tools are at his brother's house, a certain Derviš Gabela, who was buried in January of 1992, somewhere near the very top of the cemetery, where not even binoculars can reach. We used to think he was rich. I can't remember why anymore.

Suddenly, several rounds of machine-gun fire hits the cemetery. The Bairam ceasefire is shattered. People start and duck behind statues, crosses, headstones. The living are taking cover behind the dead. "Even though he's dead, he takes good care of me," said one soldier's mother upon receiving state benefits.

The shooting soon stops. People revive and come out from behind their covers as if peace had suddenly returned. No one ever thinks about peacetime; people just go on, trying to disengage themselves and forget. One man spits on two fingers and irons the crease in his trousers, others shake off the dust from their sleeves. Beautiful bouquets wrapped in celophane glitter in the sun.

In Other Words

And there they are—stopping each other again, pointing, very likely showing where the departed birches, weeping willows, and poplars had been; they keep turning around, noting this and that, and looking in vain for their dead. Many of them are disappointed, feeling so disoriented for the first time in their lives, and are leaving the cemetery, placing their glittering bouquets randomly on graves entirely alien to them. When visiting their dead and remembering them, they had in fact been thinking of the birches, weeping willows, pines, and poplars now gone from the Bare cemetery.

On almost every house in Mare's Head, a chimney is smoking.

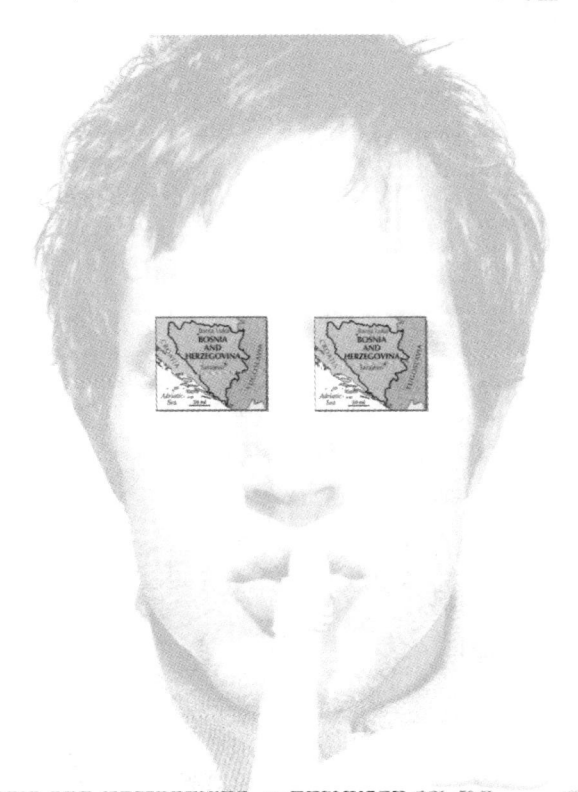

E.G. COLLAGE *H&M MAN*, 2001

See **Bosnia and Herzegovina**. —**Bos′ni•an** *adj. & n.*
Bosnia and Herzegovina or **Bos•ni•a-Her•ze•go•vi•na** or **Bos•ni•a-Her•ce•go•vi•na** (bŏz′nē-ə-hĕrt′sə-gō-vē-nə, -gō-vē′-, hûrt′-) Commonly known as **Bosnia**. A country of the northwest Balkan Peninsula. It was a constituent republic of Yugoslavia from 1946 to 1991, when it declared its independence. In 1992 the country erupted in war among Serb, Croat, and Muslim factions. A peace agreement was reached in November 1995 by Balkan leaders in Dayton, Ohio, which called for the creation of two substates, a Muslim-Croat federation to govern one half of the country and a Bosnian Serb republic to constitute the other half, united under a newly created national presidency, assembly, court, and central bank. Population: 3,527,000.
bos•om (bŏŏz′əm, bōō′zəm) *n.* **1a.** The chest of a human: *He held the sleepy child to his bosom.* **b.** A woman's breast or breasts. **2.** The part of a garment covering the chest or breasts. **3.** The security and closeness

François Lamore
Poem in Progress

Today I feel very weak, I know that if I were in battle I would surely die, But I am in civilization, and civilization permits the weak to recover.
    It was cold
    I built an igloo
    of frozen caribou
    and waited in
        center as
    the polar bears
    began to devour
        walls
They had captured a *wild* pig and were going to kill it
its mouth dry and white_was still alive , gasping for air,
the only thing it still could live
It terribly wanted to live
Why should we condemn one another forever

For more on François Lamore's poetry and art,
visit www.ReadFrank.com/inotherwords

FRANÇOIS LAMORE - UNTITLED - PRINT - 1995

Frank PRESIDENTIAL INTERVIEW SERIES

Interview with President Alpha Oumar Konaré of Mali

May, 2000 Bamako

In the spirit of expanding the territorial reach of the "literary journal," **Frank** *opened its pages to one of contemporary Africa's most impressive and creative leaders, Alpha Oumar Konaré, President of Mali and the West African Economic Community. An accomplished writer of anthropological works, a prolific journalist, and a fierce defender of pluralism, Konaré sees creativity as the intersection of politics, development, and culture. The talks between President Konaré and* **Frank** *took place at the Presidential Palace in Koulouba, Bamako on two separate occasions, in May 2000 during a conference on media and corruption, and in June 2001 during the visit of Député/Maire Jean-Pierre Brard's Delegation from Montreuil.*

ALPHA OUMAR KONARÉ WITH DAVID APPLEFIELD

Frank: President Konaré, thank you for agreeing to talk to **Frank**. It's late in the evening and you're scheduled to fly to Asia in a few hours. You're working intensively on helping to broker peace in a tumultuous neighbor of Sierra Leone. It's an unusual honor for a literary journal to talk to the president of a country about culture and society. But as an author, academic, and highest official of the country, you've made a name for yourself as a champion of democratic principles and your support of a free, independent press.

Konaré: A vibrant, independent press, media and publishing scene is of utmost importance. It's also important for a society to have competent people in privately-owned television and, as you know, there isn't yet much of this in this part of the world. But an independent press must express true pluralism and diversity of opinion based on an ethic of morals and professionalism. Newspapers nourish democracy, but democracy also is the foundation of pluralism in the expression of opinions.

Frank: Our readers should be reminded that in Mali, as elsewhere in Africa, the ability to write and publish freely is a relatively young institution and the role of a free press is in its adolescence, a period of development filled with experimentation, risk, and sometimes irresponsibility.

Konaré: If the ethical code is not respected and a high level of professionalism is not enforced, then a society may go astray. I can say that there have been numerous errors committed by our young press, but if the government insists on resolving these quickly by use of official sanctions, legal restraints and the courts, as we sometimes witness in other countries, we risk obstructing the elan of a free press. We must permit this elan to express itself and have confidence that with time the rigor of a professional press will take hold. Professional journalists will ultimately understand that their survival lies with their own professionalism and they'll flourish as a result of their own ethic.

Frank: It is difficult for readers in North America and Europe, where press and media is primarily a commercial product, to appreciate the fine line you are walking and to even contemplate the role of an "official state-run media." In Mali, the largest newspaper is government-run, as is the one television station. So the emergence of private press organs is crucial here.

Konaré: This is fundamental. I believe that state-run media can even support the development of an independent press. This will only happen when the state media affirms itself more as a public service than as a means of serving a political class. We have journalists of great quality in the state-run press but their reflexes are different as long as the radio, television, and print press continue to belong to one ruling hand, the State. It's difficult to express yourself fully when your mandate is official.

One way to evolve and reform a state media would be to open up the capital of these organisms to the employees, to a collective. We *can* evolve and improve. As the state media is the property of the government, we need to find other owners. This, to me, is very important. Let's face it, radio covers the entire country, television has no borders. So as long as there is state domination, our future is limited. But, as we evolve, I'm certain there will be a fantastic flourishing of an independent press.

Frank: That's an extraordinary message coming from the president of the country. Few leaders in the developing world are talking this way. It's interesting to note that in countries like Mali the real competition to freedom of expression is not the government, but the 80% of the population that either can't read or doesn't yet have the reflex or ability to buy a daily newspaper.

Konaré: This too is my deep conviction.

Frank: One of the most challenging obstacles you've faced has been your battle against corruption in bringing about reform in all aspects of intellectual and social life. How do you describe this challenge?

Konaré: Our greatest difficulty comes from the fragility we had with the democratic system. In the beginning our greatest concern was for the State to exist, especially a State ruled by law. When there is no State you can hardly engage in a battle against corruption, because you're immediately blocked. In 1992 there was no administration. We didn't even have the means to set up a police force. We had very few magistrates. These were the remains of a system we defeated but could not easily dismantle. We've witnessed a lot here in Mali. In the early nineties, we found there were many citizens who had been extorting public funds. Many of the biggest names in Bamako were involved. If everyone had been arrested, the entire society would have rebelled against the government. All the parties would have been against us. And, with the birth of many new parties, controlled by financially influential people with resources, this would have been problematic.

You have to remember that often there is one person in Bamako, the capital, who controls the votes in 20 or 30 villages, and who is responsible for the re-distribution of resources there. When an individual re-distributes money, regardless if the money has been illegally acquired, to normal citizens in these villages, he is a "good" person. It's hard to understand how someone who feeds you can or should be sanctioned or punished.

Frank: It's true that corruption takes on a whole different meaning in the cultural context of need.

Konaré: Our first reflex was to work with the Chamber of Commerce to set up reimbursement plans for extorted public funds. The most important thing for us was to ensure that extortion would not continue. Only if the money wasn't paid back would we take criminal action. But several weeks later, there were large demonstrations designed to destabilize this plan, supported even by associations and groups who were behind our democracy movement, many of whom ultimately had a very limited conception of democracy and were ready to muddy anyone's image if it weakened the government.
The genesis of political parties is often a question of self-interests. And that weakens the state. So you're obliged to make huge compromises with lots of groups and political parties to maintain stability. And once you've settled in to this logic of compromise, you're obliged to slow down on much of what you hope to achieve.

In Other Words

MALIAN PRESIDENT ALPHA OUMAR KONARÉ

Frank: It's for that reason that your battle against corruption is perceived by some, paradoxically, as a means of increasing poverty instead of the opposite.

Konaré: Of course. So when we arrest someone, people cry, "That person is good because he shares his money!" Even the notion of a good person has to be managed.

Frank: Much of being a president is waging this war of perception.

Konaré: Absolutely. In our society like we have in Mali, as soon as you start arresting people you have two problems. If you arrest militants who are political opponents, people accuse you of targeting their party. If you arrest members of the majority party, people ask why they are chosen and why not others. The other obstacle is the fragility of the instruments of control. We inherited the tools of a single-party system that went bankrupt. Thus, the system of control is fragile. Justice is fragile. If a trial doesn't occur quickly, people say there is no justice. When you arrest people and the courts release them provisionally, they may remain free for years. We don't have enough competent judges that specialize in economic and financial law. Often it's the same judge that handles all cases.

The irony is that the public, the workers, know what's going on better than the officials who are supposed to enforce the law. The people know. But when there is a lack of professionalism and the legal cases are incompetently prepared, the corrupt go free.

Frank: This is where journalists, media people, and intellectuals play a key role.

Konaré: It's necessary that journalists talk to the people, the public, and not rely on official versions of the truth. The people know who has what, who does what, the rules of the game. The role of an investigative press is very important. If the press refuses to be investigative, it becomes a fragile press because it can be easily manipulated. It becomes a press of sensationalism. Or it becomes an obstacle to the battle against corruption. If politicians give you money to write what they want, you've lost your credibility. So, the first challenge is to inform journalists, and encourage the press to police its own corps. There should be industry-wide guidelines that ensure the salaries and work conditions of journalists. There is no stability in the profession today; without security, journalists are vulnerable.

Frank: With an average salary in Mali of 35,000 CFA ($50 US per month), it's easy to be vulnerable. Another problem many journalists I've encountered complain of is a lack of access to information. Knowing your committment to greater freedom, what would you think of a presidential press conference every month open to all accredited journalists? At least no one could complain of lack of access to the country's head of state. Thirty minutes a month...

Konaré: I like that idea. I'm going to try it.

Frank: Due to your colonial history of West Africa, Mali is better known among the French than to others; however, the country is regrettably little known in much of the English-speaking world. What would you like the international community to know about your country?

Konaré: I'd like Mali to be thought of as a country of tolerance and peace. Malians are a people who want to live from the efforts of their work; they want to live by the expression of their solidarity with humility and, thirdly, a sense of responsibility. Mali lives by the conscience that with work, good management, and solidarity, there is no reason not to go far.

Malians are convinced that there is no future without our African neighbors. You know today I'm president of the Confederation of West African States (CEAO). The region is six thousand kilometers large with 220 million inhabitants. In this area, we have everything. We have the best earth for producing food. We have land for raising livestock. We have two great rivers which provide an abundance of fish. We have rich fishing coasts. We have immense mineral and energy resources. Gas. Oil. Diamonds. Gold. Manganese. Bauxite. Uranium. Iron. We have a tremendous supply of fruits and vegetables. The appeal for tourism is fantastic. We have countries with a common history and social foundation. We have an immensity of human resources in West

Africa. Do you understand the potential? All we're missing is communication. If we think of ourselves as a region, instead of individual countries, we will exist. In a West African context, we can produce and we can sell. In a West African context, we can be industrialized nations because we have the market to support that. Mali could be producing a lot of rice and cereal but there must be money to invest in these sectors. There must be a local market. We hear "privatization, privatization!" but that often means liquidation. We are moving toward globalization, but if we cannot afford to be buyers as well as sellers, we are condemned. Our future is our regional strength.

Frank: President Konaré, your mandate runs only until 2002...

Konaré: In 2002 Mali will have a new president. It will no longer be me. After a smooth and free transition of power occurs, great possibilities are open for our democracy. But I must prepare the conditions for others who may think like me, who share the same values, can continue with what I can't do. There are things I can do today that I may not be able to do later. I'm not tempted to stay on longer. No, what I can't do, someone else will have to do. I must help that someone else to arrive on the scene and continue. What I want for Mali is to continue this huge effort to build a democracy, to create real choice. This is very important.

Frank: The intellectual and political values you hold are clearly evidenced in your work, both as a writer and as a president. What has influenced you? Who are some of the writers and thinkers who have impacted you most?

Konaré: You know I read a lot. I read a bit of everything. In Malian and African literature there are a lot of writers I read for different reasons. But what strikes in the works of our national writers is their quality of solidarity. That's what strikes me. And their acceptance of responsibility. The re-discovery of my country. To re-discover that we have the fortune of living on this earth—in our daily language and daily battles. You know for me it is a great fortune and a great honor to find myself as the spokesman of my country.

For more on Mali, see www.ReadFRank.com/inotherwords

Down to the *Kemik*:
Bedri Baykam and *The Bone*

As Turkey struggles to find its place in the European family, famed Turkish painter and cultural *provacateur* Bedri Baykam launches his most audacious coup to date: a deeply personal retrospective of a half century of art and action echoing the political and social turmoil of his country. A record 3000 people turn out for the grand opening in the Atatürk Kültür Merkezi in central Istanbul.

Turkey's contradictions between economic sophistication and blatant poverty, democratic aspirations and human rights record, and worldly intellectuals amongst virulent fundamentalists, baffle many Western analysts ready to accept Turkey as a European equal. At worst, Turkey's external image remains stymied by unfortunate cultural stereotypes—belly dancers, Gästearbeiters, Midnight Express, Byzantine exoticism—the very things that Baykam and his three decades of abstract expressionism, multimedia performance art, and politicized conceptual installations have attempted to dismantle. "If we don't represent an economic advantage to Western museums and galleries we're as valuable as monkeys in a zoo," the painter states.

Son of the late Suphie Baykam, a high official in the PH opposition party and elected member of Parliament, Bedri lives in a sprawling but cluttered modern apartment overlooking the Bosphors with his journalist wife, Sibel, their three year old Suphi, and Baykam's mother. Amidst unruly stacks of old *Millyiet* and *Cumhuriyet*, Turkey's leading left-leaning dailies, books, files, toys, a battery of computers, modems, and scanner, a 6-foot home entertainment screen on which the Turkish football matches are watched religiously, the painter-activist plans and plots. Baykam's work incorporates objects, political news, old love letters, cut-outs of glossy porn stars and photographs of himself, and thus nothing can be tossed until the artist combs the print with scissors. It all becomes art and statement.

One wonders if it isn't obsessiveness that ultimately cements an artist's place in the history books. Driven by a passion to prove to the Western art establishment that

BEDRI BAYKAM *CALVARY* CHINA INK ON PAPER, 1963 (AGE 6)

talent and innovation are universal—in 1987 he installed a public ballot box and asked viewers to vote on the question "Do Monkeys Have a Right to Paint?" With 93% answering yes, he decided to keep painting. Part of Baykam's genius is his seemingly non-depletable energy to both create and self-promote, which he does with an unabashed bravado, often converting simple fans into adoring believers. His greatest accomplishment may be the way he has activated sponsors, banks, city government, Turkish Airlines, and a major industrial holding company, to publicly back art that openly affronts the values and traditions of its own culture.

Parts of Istanbul today feel like San Francisco, Milan, or Frankfurt with mosques. Traffic is dense and late-model BMWs and Mercedes are plentiful. Young Istanbulers speed around with cell phones, packs of Marlboros, and palm pilots. It is said that there are more cell phones in Istanbul per capita than anywhere in the world but Helsinki, the home of Nokia. Fewer and few Turks have time or patience for the old Turkey. One young taxi driver couldn't even find the Blue Mosque, Istanbul's most celebrated Islamic venue.

Three large rooms are filled with paintings, drawings, documents, objects and letters spanning the artist's life achievements beginning at the age of 2, when his first drawings were touted as those of a child prodigy and written about as early as 1964 when the *Washington Post* featured him. A total of 240 works, plainly hung and at times overly crowded, steer viewers from Baykam's early line drawings of cowboys and Indians through his recent layered paintings of cars, naked women, computer screens, weapons of mass destruction and Third World revolutionaries.

EIFFEL TOWER CHINA INK ON PAPER, 1973

Likened to the status of Andy Warhol in this country of 65 million, Baykam released a silver-cased 500 page bi-lingual monograph with an embedded DVD video documentary on his life and work, a publishing first for a mid-career artist anywhere, he claims. A household name in Turkey, his limited fame in Paris, London, Milan, and New York speaks directly to his *raison d'etre* as spokesperson for high culture from "the rest of the world."

Continuing to test the boundaries and public tolerance of art and intellectual freedom, Bedri self-published in 2001 a controversial best-seller called *Kemik* (*The Bone*) which, after sales of over 9500 legal copies and another 20000 pirated copies, has officially been banned by the Turkish government. A special committee attached to the Office of the Prime Minister cited on April 13, 2001 that the work of fiction was "obscene, indecent, and dangerous to the healthy development of minors and society at large." The legality of censorship is being weighed by the Turkish courts, as Bedri has taken his case to the Turkish Writers Syndicate and the Turkish Publishers Association. Aside from explicit description of sexual organs, acts, and aberrations, in the world of *The Bone*, JFK is alive and married to Marilyn Monroe, who has aged poorly. Jackie Kennedy died in the crossfire on November 22, 1963. Che lives but Fidel is gone. Turkey is one of the most socially and technologically developed countries on earth and its government is run by women. Here is a first taste in English of Baykam's racy and now illegal novel, *The Bone.—Marie Doezema*

Fuat was the first to stand and start to dress. With quick and calm moves he put on his pants and shirt. Selim's case had been opened but the contents had not been scattered. He was lying on Elif like a trunk. The exhaustion caused by the threesome struggle had been added to the sweet weariness of the after sex. Elif was left with her white shirt only. All the other clothes and stuff had been scattered around. While standing, Selim looked down to the girl whose eyes were still closed and who kept moaning. Elif's face was wet with the drying salty, glucose fluid. She opened her eyes to see Selim dressing right above her. He gently gave her a hand to stand up and helped her collect her stuff. The hook of Elif's bra had been broken. Her stockings were laddered and her panties were torn. Her skirt had been badly wrinkled. Her shirt lacked the middle button but her jacket was all right and it would save the day if it would be buttoned up. The stuff on the cabin floor was quickly collected and squeezed in her bag. It was as if they were preparing a damage report, without speaking a single word. Elif stood up and took her coat from the floor. She was glad when she found her glasses in the right pocket of the coat, unharmed. She put on her coat and looked at the guys. They all were ready now. Without exchanging any word, they all gave their "go" signal and Fuat pressed the "stop" button once more to let the elevator move towards the lobby. The cabin had to stop before it gained speed. They were now on the lobby floor. While waiting for the three seconds for the doors to open, Elif was standing in front.

REVOLUTION-THIS HAS BEEN DONE BEFORE,
MIXED MEDIA ON CANVAS, 1998

Almost unintentionally, as if he was bidding farewell to this anonymous dream, reaching in the girl's skirt, Selim moved his fingers over the butt. The elevator door finally opened and they got out. It was pitch-black outside.

The streets of Esentepe were in their normal state for 10 p.m. Monday night. November had brought along the cold weather too early. Selim called out: "Hey, we can give you a ride, if you want." Elif declined, saying that the subway was direct and brought her right in front of her house. She waved, and was lost in the dark night. Two men headed for the car. Fuat pressed the button on his remote. The car unlocked, the lights turned on, the engine started, and the vehicle automatically pulled up in front of them and stopped. They got in and drove away. They resumed the same subject that they were talking about earlier when they mounted the elevator. "Where shall we eat?" Selim asked. "Don't know," said Fuat.

for more on Bedri, visit www.readfrank.com/inotherwords

Interview with Deepak Chopra
Knowing God in Paris

Frank: As one of the most widely read and influential spiritual thinkers in the world today, doesn't the speed in which technology has overcome human life, at least in developed countries, frighten you?

Deepak Chopra: Science and technology are unstoppable. It's part of the evolution of the human role. Science and technology are neutral. What we do with them has to do with our psychological and spiritual development. If we look at the Genome Project, in the next decade we'll be able to replace any organ we want to with the cells of our own body. On the other hand, if we're immature and adolescent about it, we'll create monsters and we'll have genetic and germ warfare and we'll wipe out the human race. It's the same thing with nuclear technology. We could have done wondrous things but we made bombs. And the same thing with information technology. We can and will have information wars. If people are not psychologically stable there will be wars like we've never seen before—energy and information wars that will be horrendous. Done correctly, that same technology has the hope of wiping out racism, ethnocentrism, bigotry, nationalism. Personally, I think nationalism is a form of tribalism. We take so much pride in our nationalism, we're no better than being a tribal people. Information technology can do what religion and other things could never do, but it all depends on how we educate our children. Having said that, I'm neither optimistic nor pessimistic. I see possibilities on both sides. Personally, I would like to see an information technology society move to a knowledge-based society and ultimately a wisdom-based society. In my mind, I see hunters and gatherers to begin with, then the age of agriculture, age of industry, and the age of information, followed by knowledge-based and wisdom-based. And a wisdom-based society has to take information and knowledge and nurture the eco-system and the biosphere, because we are part of it. Information technology taken to the level I'm talking about can eliminate poverty in the world. In fact I've developed a plan for it, but I'm not going to tell it just now.

Frank: That sounds kind of utopian. Do you believe in immortality?

Chopra: No, we would all be doomed to eternal senility and boredom. Death is a creative response of our souls. It's a creative act. Without death there would be no magic in our lives.

Frank: Much of your work consists of sharing ideas on spirituality with people around the world. What differences have you observed in the receptivity of individuals from different cultures?

Chopra: The British and Scandinavians are the most receptive to spiritual thinking. India and the Eastern countries are the least receptive because they are so obsessed right now with Western success and the seductive way it has been marketed. California is up there. The rest of Europe is catching on. Eastern Europe and Asia are way behind. I find India, which is supposed to be spiritual, the most material country in the world, as well as China, which has such great traditions. Things go in cycles. I'll tell you a short story...I used to lecture in the Soviet Union to a group called The Knowledge Society, which I later discovered was a euphemistic term for the KGB. They were very interested in the so-called para-normal and extrasensory perception and all that stuff. Then, the Soviet Union came down and I stopped getting invited to these conferences. About two years ago I was in London and I suddenly recognized the voice of this fellow who used to come to my lectures, a top KGB official. He was now in the export-import business, of course. He and some East Germans were all saying what brought down the Soviet Union was not Star Wars technology, not Western military power, but a soap opera called *Dallas*. They were serious, not facetious. According to KGB statistics, when a critical mass of people in the Eastern bloc countries started watching *Dallas*—JR and the car he was driving and the woman in the beautiful dress—they didn't want communism anymore. So, what the West couldn't do with all their military power, they did through Hollywood. Right now, America controls the world, including all of Asia, through its music, Hollywood productions, and soap operas. You can go to the remotest parts of India where you don't have clean water but you can watch *Baywatch* and *The Bold and the Beautiful*. On the one hand, it's terrible what America is doing to the world— and no wonder countries resent this—no wonder the Middle East resents being invaded and not being able to do anything about it. But on the other hand, this also tells us the power of information technology and media. If we just used it to bring self-awareness to people!

Frank: Don't you think a lot of people are above crass television reality today?

Chopra: If you get enough of what you didn't want in the first place, you start going back to basics. And it is happening. In spite of all you hear about this decadence of Hollywood and California, it's the healthiest place on the planet right now.

Frank: Many people are sensitive to the skewered depiction of gender models in mass media programming and popular culture. Does this concern you?

Chopra: The future of fiction in general is great. It is moving towards the archetypes. Star Wars, for example, represents all the archetypes. They are very empowering. They are very spiritual. The role models we have for powerful women aren't really powerful women. They're masculine women. Indira Gandhi. Mrs. Thatcher. Golda Meir. Madeleine Albright. Every woman I can name represents a male archetype. The place we need to go for powerful women is mythology. Athena, Aphrodite, Persephone. These are the archetypes that really represent feminine power. It's also important for young women to look up to women who represent them. Another great confusion thanks to media is that our society has replaced heroes with celebrities. Kids don't have heroes; they have celebrities as their heroes.

Frank: There are strong indications that the dumbing of America deepens. Serious concerns about the nature of our leadership abound. How do you cope living in the United States?

Chopra: I find it a very fresh, creative, adventurous, innovative environment to be in. It's like being in puberty. There's excitement, confusion, there are lots of mistakes, there are problems, but it's fun.

Contact Chopra directly via www.ReadFrank.com/inotherwords

PHYLLIS COHEN - *LA RONDE* - MIXED MEDIA, 1998

WALLIS WILDE-MENOZZI

"my dear Ledig"

In the century that has recently passed and in previous centuries, we often credit Switzerland as a place that offered respite and neutrality in many senses to people fleeing from wars and persecution. It offered solace to a destitute James Joyce who was seeking financial support and an institution for his schizophrenic daughter after he and Nora would no longer be alive. It gave space to a recovering T.S. Eliot to write the drafts of the Waste Land. It holds Rilke on a hill in one of its many quiet church yards. Marina Tsvetayeva lived in Switzerland before she returned to Russia and met her own suicide. Voltaire and Rousseau breathed its air and brought that clear coloring into their way of thinking. It offered Nabokov a princely suite in the Palace Hotel, when the exile finally chose a place to settle. The list extends into a book. Ledig-Rowohlt, a distinguished German publisher, like many intellectuals, established a residence in Switzerland, happy with its beauty and peace.

The telegram that is reproduced below is from James Baldwin to Ledig-Rowohlt. Baldwin, too, had a Swiss moment and wrote about his experience of being black in a small unnamed Swiss village. In the telegram he is wishing Ledig-Rowohlt a happy seventieth birthday. Baldwin was among the many American writers who had relationships with Ledig-Rowohlt that went beyond formal ties. In the few letters from Baldwin held by the Ledig-Rowohlt foundation, the writer's personal affection and trust in the publisher are apparent.

Heinrich Maria Ledig-Rowohlt lived through the war in Germany and was the first publisher, helped by the Allies, to rise from the ashes of the defeated Reich. He introduced a version of paperbacks—the RO-RO's—which could be sold cheaply to an impoverished population and rapidly bring the west—from Ernest Hemingway to Albert Camus—into a Germany that had to move forward. Upon Ledig-Rowohlt's wife's death, his estate in Lavigny, Switzerland became a writer's colony. Many letters and papers, many books, as well as the tradition of intellectual exchange and hospitality were left to a foundation to develop. Everything about Ledig-Rowohlt's life suggests that he appreciated individuality and favored it; that he was a multicultural person ahead of his time; that he himself was not known for neutrality—at least if it meant allowing prejudice to go unchecked. The telegram from Baldwin says something about both men.

JAMES BALDWIN
Telegram, March 8, 1978

```
217854a roro d
colombe 270507f

attention mrs becker-berke

march 8, 1978

my dear ledig,

    happy birthday old warrier.
    the more you care about someone, the less articulate you become.
so, i really don't know how to say how much your devotion has meant
to me, during all these stormy years- the good years, when i was
riding high , the bad years when i was very low. well. we were
never bored, at least, and we could always drink, and laugh.
    i want to cite one particular moment, which will remain with me
forever: the moment in hamburg, when i was fighting to get tony
maynard out of jail. i had no money and no friends and no  grasp
at all of german law, and the endeavor would have been absolutely
doomed had you not given me, in effect, a blank check, had not
thrown the resources of your house behind me. absolutely nothing
obliged you to do this : nothing, except your response to human
trouble.
    you are a very beautiful man , ledig, and i love you very much.
i will  try  to seeyou soon. i will get some champagne, and drink
to you.

    james baldwin


217854a roro d
colombe 270507f
```

Thanks to the James Baldwin Estate, New York City and the Jane and Heinrich Ledig-Rowohlt Foundation, Lavigny, Switzerland, for permission to reproduce the telegram.

foreign dossier:
Switzerland

MAGNIFYING THE WRITING & CULTURE OF ONE PLACE

Dix Francs
Dieci Franchi

BANQUE NATIONALE SUISSE
BANCA NAZIONALE SVIZZERA

www.ReadFrank.com/switzerland

An integral part of each issue of Frank is its Foreign Dossier. The genesis of each of these investigations into the creative writing and art of a contemporary country, place, or region is always diverse and exuberantly multi-faceted. Following Turkey, the Nordic countries, the Philippines, Pakistan, China, Czech Republic, Congo, Belgium, and Anglophone Paris, we present here the culturally complex and surprisingly little-understood country of Switzerland, a land of numerous languages and sensibilities, with a common culture that suffers from the reputation of simplistic clichés. Our interest has been to delve beneath the silver foil of milk chocolate, fancy watches, secret bank accounts, piles of gold, and, of course, sweet Heidi. Much of the selected contents has been thoughtfully collected and assembled from the four language groups by Swiss writer Kristin Schnider, and we are grateful for her devotion to this project. We acknowledge that any anthology is non-exhaustive and ultimately subjective but we believe that we have succeeded in presenting the vitality of Switzerland's creative talent. -MD

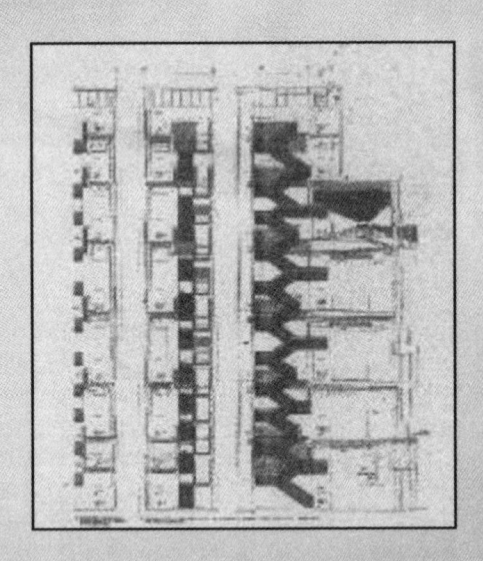

In architecture last year, Swiss architects Herzog & de Meuron were the names on everyone's lips for their conversion of a large London power plant into the Tate Gallery of Modern Art, across the Thames from St. Paul's. The architects explained their approach with the Tate as "a kind of Aikido strategy where you use your enemy's energy for your own purposes. Instead of fighting it, you take all the energy and shape it in unexpected and new ways". This concept could be a rallying cry for many of the Swiss writers appearing in the next pages.

Malcolm Pender
Swiss Literature

The opening of the Tate Modern art museum in London in May 2000 represented a conjunction of the creative aspects of two conservative countries: the Swiss architects Herzog and de Meuron had renovated an empty building as a commission from the British Tate Gallery for the display of modern art. The symbolism inherent in bringing a disused power-station back to life to operate in the cultural sphere with such invigorating force reminds us that the Swiss writer Albin Zollinger once claimed that the creative imagination acts like a mysterious vitamin in society – like the human body without the vitamin, society would be sadly dysfunctional without creative imagination. Switzerland, like Britain, tends to glorify her past in certain mythical narratives and to regard the forward movement of events as inimical to, or even destructive of, these narratives. Thus, in Switzerland, again as in Britain, powerful political forces see current developments in Europe threatening her structures and the spirit of her past. I hope that these parallels between the two countries and my own interest in and regard for the creative imagination in Switzerland manifested in her literature provide some justification for me, as a Briton, seeking, in the wake of the collaborative example of Tate Modern, to set the present collection of Swiss writing in some kind of broad context.

It has been claimed that there is no such thing as Swiss literature, that instead there are writers in Switzerland's four official languages— French, German, Italian and (unique to Switzerland) Romansch. But the historical and political tradition of Switzerland in which the cultures of these languages are embedded exerts a formative influence. Thus the Swiss writer relates to a certain Swiss ethos, to the literature in his/her language written in Switzerland and, if that language is French, German or Italian, to a literary tradition beyond the frontiers of Switzerland. Additionally, the German-Swiss writer has a different relationship to language from the French- and Italian-Swiss writer: he/she speaks dialect, which has a very much more central role than in the other two language regions but, in order to be understood by the wider audience of German-speaking Europe, must write standard German. Yet the complex relationships deriving from this heritage do not necessarily substantiate another claim, namely, that Switzerland is, because of her diversity of languages and the underlying assumption that these languages interact, a unique model for Europe. The writer Hugo Loetscher has pointed to the many countries with more than one language, and Friedrich Dürrenmatt was of the opinion that the cultures of Switzerland do not intermingle but live 'alongside' one another. The latter point might be exemplified by the fact that a major novel by Alice Rivaz, the

Jane Austen of French-Swiss literature in terms of precision of observation and genius of narrative momentum, took over 50 years to be translated into German: *Comme le sable*, published in 1946, did not appear in German until 2000.

The realities of modern life are often at odds with national myths, and literature undermines the political narrative which seeks to sustain these myths. In Switzerland, this narrative has been associated less with the great Swiss achievement of the modern age, the constitutional reform of 1848 which created the present political structures, and which was, incidentally, the one success in that dark year of political failure in Europe, and more with a perception of 1291, the year of the revolt against the Habsburgs. Thus, Swiss comportment in the Second World War was seen for many years in terms of doughty resistance against encircling Fascist neighbours. The country emerged largely unscathed from the War, and the dominant conservatism of post-1945 Switzerland, where sociopolitical structures and the ideology underpinning them remained intact, was further reinforced by her prosperity. This continuity helped to keep alive the notion of the writer as a supporter and promoter of traditional Swiss notions of self-sufficiency and particularity. From the early 1950s, however, literature, with its counter-models, increasingly questioned the relevance and the validity of the myths of official Switzerland.

The first, seminal major text of European stature in the post-war era to challenge Swiss self-perception was Max Frisch's novel *Stiller* (1954), which lambasted a backward-looking ethos for refusing to re-examine its values, and the hostile reaction of some contemporary criticism to aspects of the book suggested that Frisch was addressing a taboo subject. *Stiller* was followed two years later by Friedrich Dürrrenmatt's play *Der Besuch der alten Dame*, which sharply highlighted the moral dangers of Switzerland's postwar material prosperity. Both works exemplify what has continued for the last four decades to be one of the paradoxes of post-war Swiss culture, namely, that her writers are predominantly, and often fiercely critical of a social and political system whose success in terms of stability and wealth has been unparalleled in Europe.

> [SWISS] WRITERS ARE PREDOMINANTLY & OFTEN FIERCELY CRITICAL OF A SOCIAL & POLITICAL SYSTEM WHOSE SUCCESS IN TERMS OF STABILITY & WEALTH HAS BEEN UNPARALLELLED IN EUROPE

In the 1960s and 1970s, literature in Switzerland increasingly challenged, even ridiculed, official discourses, and also at this time provided an interesting example of a historical incident giving rise to literary expression in two cultures: the murder of a Jew in Payerne during the War inspired Jacques Chessex's *récit* 'Un crime en 1942' (1967) and Walter Matthias Diggelmann's short story 'Der Jud Bloch' (1974). After 1971, when the vote at federal level was belatedly granted to women, an increasing number of women writers lent their voices to show the effect of social forces on the individual. Well into the 1980s, literature continued to address itself to restrictive and reductive aspects of society, to depict, for example, economic forces which appear either to be beyond political regulation or which a political elite is conniving to promote. Often, as in German-Swiss literature of those years, writers avail themselves of traditional motifs, such as that of the Swiss house or that of the returnee to Switzerland, to provide, not the expected affirmation as in the past, but to depict shortcomings and inadequacies which impinge on everyday lives. Thus, the Swiss tradition of direct democracy figures prominently in the image of the country, yet again and again literature shows individual helplessness quite at odds with any notion of meaningful political control. There is a perceived lack of protection for the individual in the political framework and this relates to a theme which, in differing manifestations, has been discerned in the literatures of Switzerland—that of 'refusal', which might be defined as the identification and articulation of those parts of the individual which are steadfastly resistant to social and political manipulation. And thus literature becomes what Gertrud Leutenegger, whose novel *Vorabend* (1975) showed the strains between the private and the public self, called 'an instrument for establishing our reality.'

Towards the end of the 1980s and subsequently in the 1990s the strains on Swiss self-perception, long since charted and explored by literature, began to manifest themselves more collectively. In 1989, 36% of votes cast (predominantly by young Swiss) in a referendum were for the abolition of the Swiss army. There were banking and political scandals, the largest of the latter being the discovery of secret intelligence files kept on Swiss citizens. Political-cultural divisions showed in a referendum in 1992 when French-speaking Switzerland voted almost alone (along with one German-speaking canton) for participation in Europe. The revision, carried out under a variety of pressures, of the peceived role of Switzerland in the Second World War progressed to the point where President Villiger admitted in May 1995 to a measure of Swiss war guilt. In 1998, the final deconstruction of the myth took place when the Swiss banks agreed to compensation for the relatives of account-holders during the Nazi period.

Thus the beginnings of some kind of hesitant convergence between literary statements and national perceptions coincided, in political terms, with the collapse of Communism, the re-unification of Germany and the creation of the single market within the European Union, in literary terms with the deaths of the great world stars Dürrenmatt and Frisch, in 1990 and 1991 respectively. If the years 1989/1991 marked the finish of the post-war political legacy in Europe and in Switzerland, this was also true to a certain extent of literature. But the excited cries about the end of German-Swiss literature at the departure of Frisch and Dürrenmatt recall attitudes towards another great Swiss literary figure. The monumentality accorded to Gottfried Keller in the Swiss literary tradition is given concrete and symbolic form in the Keller memorial on the banks of Lake Zürich: on one side of the huge slab, an insurance company proclaims its responsibility for the erection of the stone on *its* hundredth birthday, the other side is completely covered by a list of Keller's works— there is space for not another single letter, as if there were nothing more to say. Of course there was more to say then, and of course there has been more to say since 1990—the present selection in this issue of **Frank** provides eloquent proof of that.

The universal fame of Frisch and Dürrenmatt, unparallelled in Swiss literary history, tended to overshadow all other Swiss writers, at least in the eyes of the outside world. In the last ten years, the view of Swiss literature has been less impeded, as it were, and it is possible now to see more clearly the many talents which have contributed, and continue to contribute, to the extraordinarily rich literary culture of the country and to appreciate better the aims and concerns of her writers. If, for example, older writers such as Maurice Chappaz, Adolf Muschg and Peter Bichsel, have continued to be exercised intellectually and emotionally by features of Switzerland, it is probable that younger writers treat these features more as convenient paradigms for restrictions and constraints which the daily reality of any Western advanced industrial society places on the individual. The beginning of the new century is thus a good time to display in a selection both the continuity and diversity of contemporary Swiss writing and to present examples of work in English translation for greater dissemination.

The excerpts and items contained in this edition of **Frank** have been judiciously chosen and edited by Kristin T. Schnider to provide from the very wide variety of writing in Switzerland a selection which, while not claiming to be representative, contains significant elements of balance and perspective. Firstly, writers from the four language areas are featured and so the reader acquires some idea of the range of work in a multilingual country. Secondly, the generations currently writing are represented, from Paul Nizon, a member of what is now the older generation, through Ilma Rakusa, Mariella Mehr, Elisabeth Wandeler-Deck and Martin R. Dean, all members of the middle generation, to Christian Uetz, a member of the younger generation. Thirdly, several genres of writing figure in the selection, giving some idea of the differing ways in which writers seek to channel their expression. And fourthly, there is an interesting balance between extracts from work which has been published and extracts from work still in progress, the latter providing a fascinating glimpse into the workshop of the creative imagination where we are privileged to see a piece before the final decisions about it have been taken. If Tate Modern in London, by offering a showcase for modern art, demonstrates forward movement in a traditionally backward-looking country, this edition of **Frank**, by providing a showcase for a varied and lively selection of contemporary Swiss writing, demonstrates the presence of Albin Zollinger's all-important vitamin in Swiss society. It is to be hoped that the selection will encourage readers to explore further in Swiss literature.

YVES NETZHAMMER - COMPUTER GRAPHIC

Fabio Pusterla
from Things with no Past
The Expulsion: Three Fragments

Translated from the Italian by Simon Knight

For my mother

I
Some houses are not just houses:
emergent wrecks, on reefs
where the wind blows implacable, strong,
and the cry of pain mingles
with the roar of the ocean.
The shark that grazes them,
careless, with its dorsal fin,
does not even notice. But they are there.

II
"In our village
the sun rises by Mount Olimpino
and goes down towards Seseglio. To the south
are Pedrinate and Penz Wood, rich in mushroom
and bramble. Our landmark
is the House of Thieves."

III
Come,
it is time to go.
Anyway,
here there is nothing more to be done.

Fabio Pusterla
from Buried in the Garden

Translated from the Italian by Simon Knight

1.

Where leads this road that no one now takes,
barely discernible, weed-grown
pathway?
Here people rolled on their bellies, with coarse mocking laughs,
and there was much shouting, suffused with pain.

(It is, it is possible, even without us,
to walk this way.
One must flatten oneself in the grass, forget something,
and as for you, cursed fear,
your power we shall have to break).

2.
for Matteo

There was a kind of shyness to confess
our familiarity with the tangled ivy,
the thickets of spiny acacia, and those pathways
long sought, found and lost again
in our ignorance of the underwood.
Action, not words, you thought,
introducing me to an imaginary city
you were building in a sunless land:
in silence, and because words were numbered,
better not waste them.

8.

Strong smells, of mint or verbena,
you seem to find off-putting. But pebbles, radishes,
objects abandoned in the garden
tempt you to dig and explore: water dripping
from pipes, broken hoes,
cobwebs, the darkness under the stairs. A coin
resurrected from the vegetable patch, five-cent
bewhiskered king, you put to your mouth.
Lost in the early nineteen hundreds:
maybe someone was digging potatoes (it was wartime);
and here on the land of the dead
spring forth the runner beans.

Landscape

Translated from the Italian by Simon Knight

Here it rains for days on end, sometimes for months,
The rocks are streaked black with water,
the paths heavy going.

On the banks of the ditches:
tadpoles, dark tin cans. A tar-stained
suitcase.

A dribble of oil runs
on the gravel. Above, cement.
Scratch the ground: refuse,
crumbling bricks, rabbits' teeth.

One can imagine the sounds of human presence,
footsteps, tennis balls. Voices even.
Any fragment permitted provided it serves no purpose.

This being nothingness there's room for anything,
and the little there is seems to have no being.
Even the tracks are perfectly inert,
the lizards motionless, the wagons
abandoned.

Then the hen-house. Things with no past.
Outside, a wheelbarrow
with no wheel. A well. A rusty bucket
with no bottom. The name of an idiot:
Luigino. Chickens' feathers in the netting.
Holes. Broken connections.
Cruelty, though not as you conceive it.

Yes, I am nothing,
but what I am I desire strongly.
And now no one can steal my words.

from Pietra Sangue
Opposing Forces

Translated from the Italian by Simon Knight

Preliminaries on the ground

Birch tree turned to stone, black pile
of wood laden with snow, and in the sky
wind or ice choking off life. Is this total
silence, then, a cycle
that no mercy can break or describe, blind
winter that will not hear of spring?
Frost that splits tree trunks, opens the veins
of the earth, breaks down the clods
and watches them die?
But look, just over there, a shrew!
What can a shrew be doing? It scurries,
scratches at the snow with feeble claws,
suddenly stops, sniffing. What is there to sniff?
Then the sun comes out and it disappears:
splashes of light, dazzling droplets everywhere.
Particles of watery light:
maybe the shrew
feeds on such elements, surviving
in the dark of its burrow.

And both are here: gutted matter
and bright limpid light. Opponents
who never parley. Which way to look, you wonder,
which eye to believe, which party to yield to.
Should the mist part, for a moment,
should a gust of icy wind raise the curtain,
there, where chance directs the gaze,
appears, in clarity, a swathe of mountain, but detached
from earth, as if in flight: immense eagle
of black rock and snow, talon and wing.

Paul Nizon left his native Switzerland in 1977 and has made Paris his home and writing *atelier* ever since. The eternal expatriate hermit —his father immigrated to Bern from Riga— Nizon is a writer's writer, tightroping that fine and yet treacherous line between life and literature. Three wives, four children, a dozen books, lots of cigarettes and drink... Nizon's source of creation is ultimately his availability and loyalty to his own mind. He doesn't pontificate, he doesn't moralize, he doesn't philosophize or theorize: he writes, he thinks, he watches his hand move across a page, he walks, observes, and captures the movement of his imagination and feet, all the while translating the details of existence into the fabric of his prose. Influences and kindred artists include Robert Walser, Goya, and the quintessential bohemian expat, Henry Miller. "Only the foreigner has eyes open, shining with wonder," Nizon comments on the state of being transplanted from a Switzerland that he physically and emotionally abandoned. Philippe Derivière, in his essay on Nizon, *La vie à l'oeuvre* (Les Flohic, 2000), calls Nizon's chef d'oeuvre *L'année de l'amour*, "the chant of a man drunk with solitude but confident of the redemptive power of words." Innovator and practitioner in the literary form of "autofiction," Nizon departs in his work from autobiography while drawing authority from the life of the author. "A book should be detached from its author like a soap bubble emerging from the end of a straw, which floats in the air exposing mysteriously its iridescent colors." But this detachment is only possible thanks to a metamorphosis of the real narrator. Nizon shares in *L'oeil du Couisier*: "These last days on the journey from apartment to workspace," (Nizon deliberately rents a different writing space in Paris periodically) "I metamorphosed not only as a worker and writer but I entered into the skin of myself within my own fiction. This metamorphosis of my 'I' in the alter ego seems to me to be a necessity to write." –DA

Paul Nizon

from The Year of Love

Translation from the French by Mick Byrne

Here I am as light as a pigeon's feather, I would say to myself from the depths of my cellular bedroom, when I first came to Paris; and as cutting as a stiletto, I would add. Lightness, that was my state of non-belonging, of non-existence, I could have let myself be carried away by the water in the gutter, I had no past here, did I have a future? I was pure availability.

Cutting, that was what I hoped to become, what I was expecting from this city: that she should sharpen and polish me to her will, for life or for death, I cared little, let her smooth me like a pebble. I would place the pebble I had become on my tongue and start to speak. To tear myself away from this silence as light as stone.

During my soliloquies, for I had acquired the habit, inevitable when one lives absolutely alone, of talking to myself, during my soliloquies, I was saying, I had the impression of having become numb, as a consequence resistant and, I hoped, real. It was not self-pity but on the contrary pride which made me talk: as if I had at last attained what I had always dreamed of: to be a simple feather, the lightest flying object in the world, ready to be carried off by the slightest breath. But the nib itself, the nib of this quill, had to be as cutting as a stiletto.

I felt the top of my head, I pinched my arm, raised my eyes towards the old pigeon man, squinted in the direction of the strip of sky that the courtyard allowed me to see, I told myself, I am at home here, this cellular bedroom is mine, I am in my place and I will stay. I was nothing more than myself, nothing more was important to me. I was happy, so happy I could have wept, all alone in Paris. *Free*. Free, for example, to visit places like Madame Julie's, I wonder how I managed to get hold of this address. I think it was Brisa who managed to get it for me, a Brazilian I had met long ago in a bar and who had, in her own way, remained faithful to me. Brisa was a call-girl, her bases, her hunting grounds changed often, Paris was one of them. She called me one fine day, the telephone being, as I was later to discover, one of the tools of her trade. In various towns around the world she had a clientele of regulars and of course their respective numbers were noted down in a tiny address book which she always kept with her, and as soon as she arrived somewhere, whether it be Paris or New York, Zurich or Rio, she dialed in turn, I don't know according to what criteria, a certain list of numbers in order to let people know that she was there and, if needs be, available. She never used the streets, the bars or the clubs, at least not for her work, keeping this on a strictly private and confidential basis, at her place. In Paris she had a little pied-à-terre in the 15th arrondissement in a street which featured the name of a general. I also went to this apartment and it happened that on that particular day Brisa was not alone, but in the company of a friend with very dark skin, who talked little, was rather uninspiring physically and whose name I forget; I think she had arrived unannounced. We went to the restaurant and then the three of us returned to Brisa's apartment. It was on the sixth floor and consisted of a quite large room with a kitchen, plus bathroom and toilet; I was put in the big bed, Brisa insisted on taking off my shoes herself, pillows were stuffed behind my back, I felt like I was playing the role of the overworked husband; laid down like that, a big glass of whisky in my hand, I watched with a feeling of euphoria the television which was showing a late night program while the two girls whispered in the neighboring bathroom. Finally, I found myself lying between them, if I remained there, it was rather through laziness, through an indolent need to prolong this state of well-being. Brisa asked me in a low voice if I wanted to, and I answered yes, that wouldn't be a bad idea, I said, and then noticed that the friend with the very dark skin was not sleeping, that she was wide awake; at that moment, Brisa disappeared under the covers to control the degree of intensity of my desire; we slipped into each other and while this happened I was aware of the presence of this other body on my right. It did not disturb me at all, I felt as sheltered as a little boy in the bed of his cousins during the vacation, I was overcome by a wonderful feeling of innocence, by an overwhelming love for the whole of humanity. We were lying there the three of us in the difference of our bodies and our skins in the depths of this unknown bedroom on the sixth floor in a street named after a glorious general, it was as if we had been sharing a crust of bread; we were strangers united by chance under the tarpaulin of a truck and who had suddenly found a common language, I was visiting another continent and throughout it all the phrase: "We made our way upriver, and had nothing to eat" was running through my head, where had it come from, I had never read it, knew nothing even of its meaning, but I liked it well.

Brisa was for me not a mistress, but rather a friend, and one fine day she took it into her head to persuade me to go and live with her. At first I took this to be an innocent joke, but as the days went on, I realized that her talk, although silky and seductive, was serious. I would like to know, I told her, how you see this situation and why me especially? I have no worldly goods, I'm more like a good for nothing, Brisa, I can think of nowhere that would be a place for us. As I piled on the arguments, Brisa claimed that I had misunderstood the proposal, that for nothing in the world would she want to be a burden to me, that she would continue to lead the same life as before, that in Rio she had a little house and that besides, she expected no faithfulness, would even introduce me to her friends. But how do you see things working out, I said, what would I be supposed to do in Rio, in your house which must, I'm sure, be very beautiful. Should I look after the takings?

You are infuriating, she said. Why are you pretending to be stupid. Don't act more silly than you really are.

But why me especially? Why the hell have you cast your choice on me?

I find you, she said, intelligent and kind, and then you make me laugh. What's more, don't forget that this way you'll be able to do it until you can't take any more. So why not you?

Ceaselessly, at each of her visits, each of her phone calls, Brisa hammered away at the same topic. She often found herself calling from far away in the middle of the night, once even from America, and relentlessly she started by asking if I still lived alone, she meant without a girlfriend, without a wife. After I had replied in the affirmative, she repeated that I had to go and meet up with her in Rio, she would lend me the money for the trip. It was through Brisa that I got the address of the *maisons de rendez-vous* and of Madame Julie. One day, after arriving once again unannounced, just a breath of wind passing through, she explained, *amor minho*, I don't like this idea of you sleeping around with just any little idiot. They'll fleece you or else you'll never be able to get rid of them, women are awful, always be on your guard. Suddenly she took out her tiny address book and copied down one or two names onto a piece of paper. Here, she said, some addresses you won't regret knowing, don't forget to mention that you know me, it's a little more expensive than usual, but you will be in good hands in more ways than one.

Bedroom love: I know this kind of room well, after each time I ask myself how I managed to end up there, I no longer know where the room and street in question are, in my memory it's only a simple bedroom in the middle of a strange continent, I remember the bed, maybe the washbasin, the ragged curtain blown out by the wind, I noticed a certain noise just as I was entering this room, the kind of hotel room rented out by the hour, was that noise the laugh of a child or the twitter of a bird, yes, once I remember quite clearly, it was a twitter, it made me jump I can't remember why, a twitter at this time, I said to myself, no, it can't be. I moved to the window and it was then that I saw, down in the deserted courtyard, an old woman with a handcart. It was the badly oiled, squeaking wheels which were making this kind of twittering noise and had for an instant given me the illusion of hearing birdsong. From that moment on, those twittering wheels belonged to that room in the same way as did the cart and the old woman who was pushing it across the deserted street. A bedroom and in the middle of the bedroom, me and the woman, perhaps busy pulling strands of hair away from her face, throwing her long hair back over her shoulder, like a wave breaking, and I think: hair like a wave, a wave of hair; but perhaps it is she who is speaking: come, sit yourself down here, sit down next to me, she says showing me the bed and the place next to her and me I'm standing in this tiny room, far too small for two people who know nothing of each other, I light a cigarette, take off my coat, sit down on the slightly pushed in bed; while I sit down I can feel the hardness or the feathery softness of the mattress.

But why me especially? Why the hell have you cast your choice on me?

What's your name, I say; I give my name, maybe she answers; you're not from round here, are you, you're passing through, or maybe another such remark; I listen to the sound of her voice, I try to decide if I like the tone, if it reveals anything or is familiar to me, I watch out from the very depths of my self, I listen to what the echo of this voice generates in me, pleasure, a memory, an image. Then, while Ada undresses, while we undress, taking off, casting off our disguises, I drink in the spectacle of her thighs, these woman's thighs which extend from the buttocks like an arch seem to be immense, even on a very young woman, it's a display I delight in, I don't know why, to the point that I forget to swallow my saliva; and the breasts - not so fast, I can no longer make the transition from the still distant image of the elegantly clothed foreign woman, dolled up, rigged out, belted, dressed up from top to toe, standing on her high heels, and that of the naked woman. Everything is going far too quickly, the distant image is already forgotten, lost, we are now barefoot, in this ordinary room, and we go to the washbasin to wash ourselves, it's true that the way the hair falls is different, when it falls onto the naked back, onto the round of the shoulders of an undressed woman, instead of blending into the shape of a coat, a fur collar, here we are then naked, we sit down, we lay down on the bed, each one absorbed in touching the other's body, meanwhile the voice has become familiar to me, that slight hoarseness, that kind of guttural sound that is part of this voice; under the pressure of my fingers, the thighs take on colossal dimensions. It is like the tongue when you have a fever, the room and my senses of perception are not enough, faced with this dilating of all the members, the thighs, the buttocks, while I thrust up into the hollow of her thighs, while I enter, while I am inside and while I move in these bodily depths of which I can feel nothing but warmth and wetness, while with my hands I explore the curves of the body, at the same time trying once again to glimpse the lips and their particular sinuosity before it is too late, before the mouth is finally sealed by mine, before there is nothing more than tongues, and before everything suddenly collapses on me, on us, in this sensation, this delight which swells up until we forget our own existence, while the two naked beings, tightly intertwined, wrestle in the inextricable tangle of bodies, while, from the throat of the foreign woman, small sighs of pleasure, groans, while my sweat flows and mixes in the heat with Ada's sweat, all this in that room, where reality has been abolished, sweeping away the last shreds of mutual embarrassment in a two-voiced cry, emerging from the depths of the throat, yes the time for modesty or restraint has passed by for these two beings who don't know each other but who are nevertheless more intimately joined than anyone else in the world, what is exchanged, what is cried at this instant?

Afterwards, a cigarette or not between the fingers, she caresses his hair, on his brow, with the tenderness of couples who have known each other since the dawn of time. The bedroom is still a hotel room rented by the hour with its anonymous bed, its washbasin, its torn curtain, but it has now a scent, a feeling, like a reflection of their presence, a sort of euphoria that bathes their thoughts, accompanies them, while they leave the room, clothes back on, shoes back on, she, made up, dressed up, while they go down the staircase, leave each other in the street. Ada, ciao, Ada, I say, or he says, but this scene is not part of Paris, it has taken place elsewhere, everywhere, and if I return, it is only with the intention of evoking the barriers which exist between beings and the brutal abolition of these barriers which constitutes the plunge into this thing. When this bedroom reappears in my memories and in my daydreams, I always call it the rose bedroom, or the pink bedroom, and in fact, it seems to me that it is located in Rome, or maybe somewhere else.

Ilma Rakusa

from A Farewell to Everything: Ninety Nine-Liners

Translated from the German by Eileen Walliser-Schwarzbart

In the train just drifting off
with the horizon toppling inward
a mountain of sand so totally different
soars vast and yellow to Saharan height
beyond the rails of a
provincial station
Where am I? and bright red
a steam shovel rumbles into the picture
to demolish the illusion

My parents the carpet
and me
the silence the foot
injury
no hurry the picture
immobility
good night the sheet
and a farewell
to everything

Nine lines the length of a
note a gust of wind half a thought
first glimpse into the well
fears and fervent prayers
everything
and the wish for it all
word hand warmth tango
land like landscape and home
and sea sorely missed

Almost Japanese the glitter
of plum trees white
light trembling on the slope
crinkles under tufts of cloud
The grey day tears open
bright windows for
birds fools heavy hearts
and laconically sprinkling a
dusting of snow

Monica Cantieni
HERR PILLWEIN AND FRAU KULANEK

from The Fog-Drinkers
Translated from the German by Michael Robinson

Pillwein never got up before midday. He lowered himself into a warm bath, and requested that Renk or Heisel bring him a cup of tea. After this he went to his wine-shop, which was called "PILL WINES" and also sold necklaces, rings and watches.

But today Renk and Heisel were late, so Pillwein pottered around and tried peering over the vast girth of his underlying belly in the hope of seeing his feet. His stomach flopped out of his dressing gown and drifted aimlessly ahead of him like an abandoned ship. It was absolutely pouring with rain. Pillwein looked out into the rain through the open window. The concrete slabs on the waste land by the factory blurred into each other between the mounds of green grass. A fleeting memory came to Pillwein, then went away, distracted by the sound of car doors slamming in the street.

Renk and Heisel came in with a soaking carpet. It slapped wetly down at Pillwein's feet. Heisel looked at his watch and hurried to put the kettle on. Soon the kettle lid was tinkling, and Pillwein grumbled:

—Is that all?
—There wasn't anything else worth taking.
—I send you off and you bring me a carpet.
—It's pretty big.

Pillwein went red with fury. He walked round the carpet a few times, then finally kicked it.

—There's something inside. Unroll it.

The thieves got hold of the carpet at both ends and lifted it up. Quite silently, light as a feather, and just as white, a woman appeared. Renk said:

—Great stuff, Heisel. An old, dead bat.

Pillwein clipped Renk's ears, Renk yelled at Heisel that he was a complete idiot for stealing the carpet from the lorry. Pillwein boxed Heisel's ears and Heisel asked:

—What now?

The scale in the kettle grunted as it heated up and the beating rain wouldn't leave them alone. A gust of wind blew the window wide open. The pictures on the walls started to shake. They shifted slightly on their nails, swinging to and fro like clock pendulums, ticking and clicking when the frames brushed together.

Pillwein could see all the time that was clicking away on his walls. The woman lay in front of him, thin as a late summer spider's web. She had no more time to spare because her time was up, and there was nothing more to lose. Pillwein closed his eyes and dived dizzily down. He pulled the picture of the woman down with him, lost it in the darkness; there he groped around and located the picture near his feet. He dropped it, horrified, and when he opened his eyes again the woman was still lying there. He closed the window.

—We have a problem, he said, and disappeared into the bathroom to run a bath.

In the mean time, Herr Kulanek was making a short speech:
—When we are born, we come into the world head first. When we grow up, we grow towards the heavens. This continues as we get older. Wanda Kulanek has arrived.

The company fell silent, and Herr Kulanek sat down at the end of the table that had been laid for the wake. He speared a dumpling as his sister burst into tears. Herr Kulanek put down his fork, called for wine and found that it hadn't been delivered yet. He gave a dignified nod, piled cabbage on his plate and poured so much sauce on it that the mountain of cabbage towered up like an island in a fragrant lake. The guests sat in silence. Some had folded their hands over their bellies and were looking at their hands, others looked with interest out of the windows, through which the grey of the façades could be seen. Herr Kulanek lost his patience and banged his fist on the table so hard that the dumplings leapt from his plate:

—It is not enough that the Lord God has made me blind to a woman that has to go climbing into the mountains and falls down. All right then, we spend time and money looking for her and we find her, and all she does is disappear again the next day. All right. My Wanda was forever wandering in her lifetime. Why should it be any different now?

The guests squinted into the bright spring sun that had come out after the heavy rain. They lifted their empty glasses and drank his health.

—But a burial is a bereavement, and when there is a bereavement it is customary to have wine and a good meal.

The audience murmured their assent. Herr Kulanek raised his fork with the dumpling speared on it:

—What is wrong with this dumpling?

The mourners looked at him expectantly.

—The dumpling is not steaming. It has no aroma. And why doesn't it have any aroma? Because it is almost cold. Does it deserve this? Do we deserve it?

Voices had been raised.

The people sitting around the table became indignant and Herr Kulanek finished by saying:

—We're off.

The guests gathered up their coats and Herr Kulanek invited the dispersing company into his lorry and drove to the wine shop with the unfortunate name of "PILL WINES." Its owner was sitting outside it like a wet sack, sunning his paunch and twiddling his thumbs.

Pillwein almost fell off his chair and fixed his eyes on the group of black-clad mourners that had got out of the lorry and were tottering threateningly towards him. Some still had their napkins tied on, others were holding knives and forks in their hands. He blinked and tried not to rub his eyes. He was seeing the nightmare he had already been in once today; there was still a bit of it left over in his cellar, put on ice, as it were. He shook his head anxiously, as he was afraid for his stomach, which these crows were eyeing up greedily. Herr Kulanek fumed:

–Where the hell have you been? Our food is getting cold. As if a funeral weren't bad enough as it is.

Pillwein gabbled a few excuses and got busy. He was furious about Renk and Heisel and these asylum-seeking arseholes. He decided to deal with the situation in his usual impressive way and to give Renk and Heisel a good kick up the arse as soon as he got his hands on them. This thought cheered him up considerably.

–And how about an extra case for our trouble? asked Kulanek.
Pillwein shoved another wooden case of wine at him irritably. The guests gathered round the case. Herr Kulanek's sister blew her nose on her napkin and said:

–If only we really could bury her. She was stolen from us, our Wandicka; stolen off the back of our own lorry.

Pillwein went white as a sheet, and when Herr Kulanek tried to get a bottle of plum brandy out of him as well he turned on him and hit straight out.

–Kulanek, is it?

He drew the syllables out.

–So it's Kulanek!

Then he stopped hitting him and got a gun out from behind the counter.

–Fucking refugees! Piss off! What are you after here anyway? Think you can get booze for nothing in this country, do you?

They had been gone for a long time. Nobody came back. Nobody came to get him. Neither the Czechs, nor the police. Nothing happened. Pillwein was still standing by the case of wine with his gun in his hand, waiting. Finally he put the gun back behind the counter and went home. He poured himself a hot, steaming cup of tea, opened the window and stared out at the waste land by the factory.

An image of the cemetery he had known when he was young came to him, the cemetery where the graves were crooked and overgrown. Some of the gravestones leaned back as though they felt compelled to enjoy what little sun there was, others leaned forward, as though they had been gazing at their navels for years. Today they seemed to him like a jolly tea-party, rocking tipsily to and fro. Some of them were lying together, laughing so much they had fallen forward over themselves, bursting apart at the seams now only sparsely covered with the yellow grass hair, and touched by all this exuberance, Pillwein gave in to his memories, sobbing.

Martin R. Dean
The Blue Elephant

Translated from the German by Michael Robinson

For some inexplicable reason I felt compelled to go to Melide near Lugano several times, to visit "Miniature Switzerland." I had an urge to say goodbye to this country, and I also wanted to arrive here properly at last. I felt I would have to keep going through these rituals of arrival and departure for just as long as my writing had something to do with Switzerland. This tiny version of Switzerland - you can walk in a few paces from the Rhine harbour in Basel to the cathedral of St. Pierre in Geneva - is almost exactly the same age as I am. It was built when I was a little boy, when I started to have some sense of awareness, with all the usual gaps in it. Here the sun always laughed above the little gables and tiny windows, just as it had laughed when I was a child in the Aargau. I couldn't imagine this place in rain, fog or snow. The sights of Switzerland were presented here prettily, smartly, with sharp creases ironed in, if you see what I mean, rather like a flower-decked room set for a feast, where you can wander freely from one table to another. I strode from the belfry in Bern to the lion monument in Lucerne to Kolinplatz in Zug, a town I was visiting for a year at the time.

"Our aim," I read in the brochure, "was to produce a symbolic representation of Switzerland, showing all its inhabitants' activities using a selection of objects from every area, reduced for the model. (…) It is served by an ultra-modern transport system, strikes are unknown, its inhabitants will live happily ever after, without soldiers, without police, without taxes. Discover your homeland!"

I had always been fond of descriptions in prospectuses and the language they use, which often gently detaches itself from the object it is trying to describe so precisely, and forms interesting, usually unanticipated bubbles. This brochure was telling me about the utopia of a small state that in its full-scale reality actually renounces all utopias. Other countries might incline wildly towards monumentalism and anything else hazardously gigantic; endlessly seeking freedom in the great expanses of the West, but Switzerland has always huddled into smallness, with austere modesty. "To suit me," Alberto Giacometti had said, "things have to be small." And Robert Walser scaled his life down in micro-script to the point of ultra-polite illegibility.

Small things always stuck in my throat like fish-bones. I could talk myself out of it in dialect, and set myself apart from any bragging or boasting. But when I was in Germany people poked gentle fun at the way I spoke, as though I had some obscure throat disease, and started to amuse themselves by imitating me as the evening wore on.

Miniature Switzerland was spotless and sterile; no wind of history, no storm of catastrophe and revolution. Cliché had become reality here, and instilled a feeling of intimacy.
This is how home is created, like this and in no other way, I said to myself, as a repeated acknowledgement of something that had long been familiar. I felt I wanted to lie down on the spot and hug parliament building. The little houses, the tiny people, tiny trains and tiny trees set my imagination racing. The miniatures worked like a magnifying glass that made reality clearer at its focal point. "That's what Switzerland is like!" I suddenly and enthusiastically shouted at a group of terrified Japanese, and went back to Kolinplatz in Zug.

Zug is not part of Central Switzerland! I realized I was mistaken about this when I started my year as "town observer" - as the writer-in-residence is known there.
My guest accommodation was in the middle of the old town, which had a bad reputation for seeming like a museum. But this old town had excellent restaurants and a handful of bars, where you had to fall silent as soon as you went in. If you didn't fall silent you went under in the noise everyone else was making and left the bar early. So only people with powerful voices that weren't drowned by the music assembled in the bars. I didn't usually approach the counter till after midnight, especially when I didn't have anything left to say.

My hosts were curious about the cool outsider's eye that I was going to cast over them. "How do you find Zug?" was a question that was often asked, though it was best not to answer. The reason for this was that it always followed a series of critical self-accusations, and it made considerable sense not to agree with these if you didn't want to offend the self-accuser a great deal. Lasting contacts were made by contradicting energetically. Zug was in fact a small town between two larger ones, and felt that it had an unfortunate reputation. A number of dubious foreign firms, most of them no larger than letterboxes, had set themselves up

...Switzerland has always huddled into smallness, with austere modesty.

here because of its attractive tax concessions. They constantly fuelled the bad reputation. And up on the mountain was the successful author Johannes Mario Simmel, writing. I never clapped eyes on him, not even when buying caviar. He was simply here to pay taxes. Quite obviously the whole city suffered from the wealth that it was itself not prepared to accept as entirely earned. I did not want to spend too much time on this, certainly not the whole year; it seemed to me that the typical citizen of Zug was far from being especially avaricious. The people all had good teeth, healthy-looking faces and there was a conspicuous lack of the supposedly dull, exaggeratedly unanimated quality that could have found its way into their faces if they had had too much money.
I often had to go away from Zug, and yet I always liked coming back again. When I arrived

in Zug and the föhn was blowing, the mountains stood there backlit, like defiant, snow-powdered officers. The lake was at the foot of all this camaraderie.

The lake, Lake Zug, was the first and only thing that I could see from my lofty visitor's home. At times it lay as flat as a lead mirror, and then its surface would prickle like a dragon's scaly armour. After only a few days I came to like the view from the window so much that I couldn't do without it. The image of the lake rippled with my sub-conscious in ever-recurring waves, a daily barometer that told me my state of mind. If I looked out of the window, my mood was dictated to me. Despite its operetta-like qualities - the ships, for example, seemed like paper models of ocean liners, and the dancing buoys in their turn like islands - I could use the lake to read the weather and the state of the town's soul. In my breaks from writing I ran along the lake in old track-suit bottoms, in the summer I swam out till the bank went away and left me and I was encircled only by the mountains.

Participation and observation were two words in my brief, a third was description: that was how I was to enrich the cultural life of Zug. In reality it was I, the so-called observer, who was ceaselessly observed, and that with a great deal of verve. Sometimes a local would come towards me with his pupils widening threateningly until I had gone past; then he would turn round, and I felt his look scramble over me and tickle my shoulders.

Here in Zug writing became a public matter for me. Some people looked me sharply up and down, as though they needed to do that to find out whether their tax money had been well spent on me. What I was actually doing was writing a novel with the working title "The Guyana Knot." As this activity had no perceptible meaning and no apparent use I constantly found myself on the defensive. But I was trying to defend something that I didn't even think was worth defending myself, and the more I defended it the worse it seemed. If people saw me in the street I was obviously not writing, just indulging my taste for squandering taxpayers' money. Then again, if I was sitting at my desk, steadily tying knot after knot, and thus continuing to weave my fabric, I was obviously neglecting my brief, which was to make contact with the locals.

But despite the high expectations invested in me in some circles, I only managed to respond appropriately to hostile overtures, or even to keep them alive, in the tiniest number of cases. I felt that interest in me was waning after three, four months: I must have been much too conciliatory somewhere or other. My alien appearance, which attracted a great deal of curiosity, began to lose its effect. I was taken for a Tamil or a Turk in the street with increasing frequency, and people spoke to me, in a friendly yet threatening way, in English, Turkish or that inimitable mixture that consists of rudimentary Swiss-German with the words twisted violently around. In fact, many people in Zug could not agree with each other, and had hoped that my implacable appearance would give them a common cause again.

Invited by an interested circle of readers, a woman indignantly told me about a neighbour who had watched another neighbour shooting at some parrots that were flying around in the wild. When I failed to be as outraged as expected, and did not spout a torrent of contemptuous words, an older woman at the table shouted vehemently at me: "But that sort of thing is racist!"

When I was being greeted by the cultural circle in an adjacent parish, they took the opportunity of asking me where I actually came from. But it was not possible to answer this question without a lengthy digression, and to say something pretty close to the truth - "I come from Menziken" - would have run counter to their expectations, so we opted for a longer lecture as soon as the coffee and cakes had been served. This was about the strange phenomenon of the "neighbourhoods," which again was something quite different from what I had thought it to be. The admiring exclamations that I threw in, or even my discreet questions, discreet because they were whispered when the lecturer was pausing for breath, drifting into the middle of the table like a cloud of breath, were ignored until there was no point in asking them any longer. It became quite clear that my hosts had to go into their own origins immediately: one cannot sit back in a chair and relax until one has explained one's background, right down to the last detail.

> *They kept offering me more and more pieces of cake, which meant that I couldn't interrupt or ask questions...*

They kept offering me more and more pieces of cake, which meant that I couldn't interrupt or ask questions, and at the same time passing on a captivatingly complex piece of local history. Rites and role-specific behaviour I had never heard of before among the various "neighbourhoods."

I decided to respond to the question that people were ceaselessly asking me about my origins, so I got into my car one buzzing day in May, drove into the Wynen valley and looked at my grandparents' house in Menziken, in which I had grown up. I was very relieved to find that the layout of the gardens and the rooms was almost completely unchanged. The smell that emanated from the walls and carpets was the old familiar fug as well, and soon had me back under its spell. But there was one thing that bothered me: the house, garden and rooms had shrunk terribly. I could measure the length of the garden in five paces - my nose was against the garden hedge in a flash. All these small things must have been large when I was a child. Even the apple tree, the first tree in my life, was not particularly monumental! It was in the middle of the little piece of lawn, small and awkward, so I felt moved to stroke the bark with my hand again, and break a piece off here and there. Then there was the pear tree, whose branches drooped prettily down into the unmown grass, the damson and mirabelle trees behind the house. I used to climb them with a ladder, but now, as a grown-up primate, I could relieve them of their fruit with a little jump from the ankle. When I used to stand on the tips of my toes on a mild night and shake the branches of the hazelnut tree, thousands of maybugs fell past me on to the ground and made a hard, dry noise that I could still hear. Now I was bigger than the bush. And when the magnolia tree, the most elegant, feminine and expansive of all the trees in the garden, gently shed its petals, I picked them up and put them in water to make a kind of perfume. Childhood perfume, childhood smells, childhood mistakes.

The smells inside the house had stayed, even though the furniture, the utensils and other things had been taken away. The wooden table in the living room was still there; but the cracks and furrows that I used to trace with my fingers on hot summer afternoons like rivers and lakes were nothing more than the grain of the wood, which incidentally looked worn and shabby. The effort needed to turn the light-switch made my hand revert to being a feeble little child's paw, and my finger-tips remembered: I was a child who liked switching lights on and off. And the creak of the wooden window shutter suddenly released the children's voices that had been waiting for me for whole afternoons when I was half asleep, behind closed blinds. On the left by the stairs was the tiny little bedroom with bevelled walls, now no bigger than a sailor's chest. On the ceiling, as in a doll's house, the hooks hung down where my grandmother, who had grown up in a North German farmhouse, used to hang the sausages up to dry. Now the hooks were painfully empty.

Burglar and detective in one, I crept around this eerie house. I found places where I had scratched the wall. There was dust on the toffee-coloured radiators, which had perhaps not been cleaned since my childhood. In the attic I opened the skylight and stared for a long time, too long, at the summer-buzzing hills of the Wynen valley round about, so long that I decided to ban myself from staring out of windows as it carried me away too quickly.

Was it still possible to dream oneself into his blueness and get lost in it?

Finally I set off for the cellar and pushed open the door to the room where I remembered the oil tank used to stand behind its protective wall. But now I saw him standing there, immovably in his place: the large blue elephant. Thin straw on his back, his trunk curling out of the window, he was standing where the oil tank used to stand.

And so he was still alive, my old blue elephant. He had remained faithful to me even though I had abandoned him for so long. He shifted proudly from foot to foot and said: "You see, it is possible for me to live here! I am not taking anyone else's place, I am just here, as long as you keep thinking of me and the power of your wishes does not fade. Then as now, and despite all objections, I am here."

No one could have taken him away from me, wished him elsewhere or talked me out of him: I looked at him and was happy for a moment, even though I remained suspicious. Was it still possible to dream oneself into his blueness and get lost in it? Could he still collect every wish in his big blue belly and make them come true at a suitable moment?

Why do you write? What is the point of literature? These were questions asked by friendly citizens of Zug in passing, while sitting at tables, but also in newspaper articles. And because I couldn't answer questions like that, perhaps because they were the kind of questions that you have to be a bit careful about answering, they were followed by friendly tips and suggestions for things I might write about. A hospitable landlady in an inn, drying her hands on her apron, complained to me about the way in which the Zug authorities constantly stood in the way of culture. I should write about it, she suggested as she pushed a wonderful rabbit dish across the table. I should write about the fact that the mayor had cars belonging to German tourists who parked where it was not permitted towed away there and then. The fire brigade invited me to their ball and recommended themselves as a subject. I should write about the cattle-market, and also about other cultural events like meetings of the shooting club, the tilers, the chimney sweeps.

> *The fire brigade invited me to their hall and recommended themselves as a subject.*

I bought myself an old postcard in the tobacconist's where I used to get my smoking paraphernalia and newspapers. Zug in about 1840. The card showed a Zug that was a thing of the past, a rural Zug, with a little stream winding through the middle of the picture, and the meadow coming right up to the houses. I showed the postcard to my guests. I always threw it on the table when we had finished eating. The guests would fall silent and look at me quizzically: was this Zug, as I would like to see it? Or was I trying to say that I found Zug as it was today more lovable, more agreeable, more open-minded? Or could I only cope with Zug by looking at this old view over dessert, and at the same time drawing my guests' attention to something that no longer existed? Or was there something missing in reality that I had to make up for with this photograph?

Friendly critics were soon saying that I had "masochistic tendencies," less friendly ones were challenging me ever more openly to drag out the "naked truth behind Zug's friendly façade," I was not inclined to do that, so I picked up my pen and wrote a witty article asking whether there was not a certain "intellectual inertia" in Zug occasionally, scarcely perceptible from a distance but unshakeable at its core. This stirred up a hornets' nest. I had long sensed that the public needed a little more excitement. They were not content with knowing that I wrote and that what I wrote would be revealed at an appropriate opportunity. The indignation that followed my little dig had something cathartic about it: I had obviously put into words something that a lot of people felt but did not dare to say, then hoped that I would say it as that is what it was my job to say. A great deal of activity broke out, and while some applauded, others complained that I had an "élitist view of culture," reproached me for being "shy of the public," and took the local, beer-drinking young people who had been affected by my comment under their wing.

There were very definite ideas about how a writer-in-residence was supposed to be, and people measured me up against them. A famous colleague had once been writer-in-residence in Frankfurt am Main; he was usually to be found sitting in pubs there, energetically in touch with so-called ordinary people. Even when he didn't happen to be writer-in-residence somewhere else he lived like a writer-in-residence at home in Solothurn, in the pubs, vigorously making contact with ordinary people. This image of the model writer-in-residence, which had now penetrated everywhere, was then accompanied by a slim volume written by my colleague, in which he developed his aesthetic from the spirit of vigorous contact-making in pubs. I had no means of avoiding this colleague, whom I liked very much, or his contact-making escapades; I had often taken refuge in their warmth myself. I was judged by his standards, even though I was quite different. He was in fact a card-carrying patriot, as he had said in a television interview, even though what he meant was "critical patriotism."

But I was thinking of running away as the first of August came closer. My friends were already sitting in their cars with ironic smiles on their faces and making for the south. Dog-owners were off camping in the mountains. I crouched on the bank and saw the finely spun veil of mist on the lake. The waves were splashing gently on the shores of the so-called "disaster bay." In a few days there would be fireworks here, with rockets shooting into the night sky above yelling mouths, full beer glasses and Chinese lanterns with a white cross on a red background. *And months later the Swiss would be throwing out the application to join the European Union at the ballot box.*

On the afternoon of the first of August I broke off my text in mid-sentence, left the flat and went out into Zug old town. I crouched down and crept along a bone-white, solid stone wall. At an old, wooden door I rang a bell. The smiling face of the sister of the Solidarity of St. Peter Claver appeared behind her thick glasses at the square peephole, which could be opened from inside. I went into the building and read in the prospectus that this was a congregation of nuns principally interested in Africa, founded by Countess Maria Theresia Ledochowska in 1894. Key statements by the Countess, which I noted down, said: "The divine quality of the divine is to be involved in the salvation of souls." Or: "Either Africa will become Christian - thanks to the missionaries - or it will fall prey to the Mohammedans. And then we have to fear the penetration of the crescent from the south, and not from the east."

The sister led me through a corridor without a light, her steps dragging because she was so short-sighted. Giggling, she pushed open a door and left me alone, without comment or warning.

The first rockets were hissing up into the sky outside, and there I was, surrounded by masks, sharp-edged axes fastened to the wall, elaborately carved sticks and other fetishes from my secret Africa. When I looked upwards a vigorous shaman's head-dress gleamed at me, decorated with a cluster of protruding raffia locks. Next to this was a wooden mask, grinning wickedly and edged with a tiger-skin lapel. Black, alien and utterly unambiguous, Africa met me here in the form the Zug sisters knew it. And there was no escape from this room, blacked out with heavy curtains, with its objects presented in dusty-yellow light as if on an ancient stage, and explained only by a single, usually bloody word. Red was the colour of the magician's cult mask from the Congo, who according to a brief inscription had over a hundred people on his conscience. If he had such a thing at all, in the Christian sense. Faced with the explosions that were starting up outside I was confronted with coshes that seemed almost comforting and solemnly glowing spear-heads. A velvety booming came from hip-high, fur-lined drums, almost syncopated, and blending in with the marching music. With the clear eye of colonial knowledge, the sisters had set up a so-called savages' settlement in miniature in the middle of the room, with straw houses and ancestor-temples. A fetish for luck when stealing hens and making money had also not been omitted, and the magician on the wall behind the amusing "savages' settlement" would certainly have frightened me if I had still been a child: a wooden figure larded all over with mirror shards and nails. Was every nail, I wondered, a magic murder?

After I had finally said goodbye to Zug, years later, I went back to "Miniature Switzerland" in Melide. I strolled past the Swiss castles, palaces and chalets again with a camera crew who were making a film about my new novel. When twilight started to fall, the cameraman released artificial mist and I paced along the façade of the House of Parliament with a lighted match in my hand. Mist fell over the roofs of the old town, autumn came and a little more colour was leached out of the lake each day. Now I looked at the monitor of the camera that was shooting, where image was following little image, and saw a big blue elephant, standing in the middle of Kolinplatz in Zug.

AGLAJA VETERANYI

from Why the Child Is Cooking in the Polenta

Translated from the German by Pierre Imhof and Dafydd Roberts

I imagine the sky.
    It's so big I fall asleep right away to calm myself down.
    When I wake up, I know that God is smaller than the sky. Otherwise, when we pray, we'd always fall asleep from fright.
    Does God speak other languages?
    Can he understand foreigners as well?
    Or do the angels sit in little glass cabins and translate?

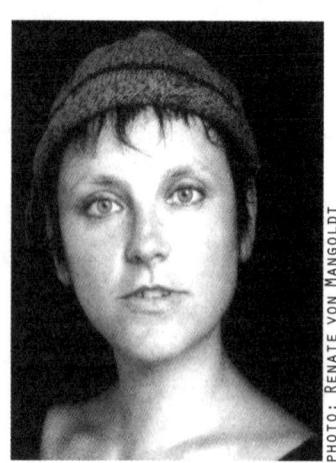

AND IS THERE REALLY A CIRCUS IN HEAVEN?

Mother says yes.
    Father laughs, he's had a bad time with God.
    If God was God he'd come down and help us, he says.
    But why should he come down, if we're going to go up to him afterwards?
    Anyway, men don't believe in God as much as women and children do, because of the competition. My father doesn't want God to be my father as well.
    Here every country is abroad.
The circus is always abroad. But inside the caravan is home.
    I open the door of the caravan as little as possible, so home doesn't boil away.
    My mother's grilled aubergines smell just like home everywhere, never mind what country we're in.
    My mother says we get a lot more from our country abroad, because all our country's food is sold there.

IF WE WERE AT HOME, WOULD EVERYTHING SMELL LIKE ABROAD?

All I know of my country is the smell. It smells like my mother's cooking.
    My father says you remember your country's smell everywhere, but you only recognise it when you're far away.

WHAT DOES GOD SMELL LIKE?

My mother's food may smell the same the whole world over, but abroad it tastes different, because of the longing.

Apart from that, here we live like rich people, we can throw away the soup bones after the meal with a good conscience, at home they have to be kept for the next soup.

At home, my cousin Anika has to stand in the queue in front of the breadshop the whole night, people stand so close to each other they can sleep while they're waiting.

AT HOME QUEUING IS A PROFESSION.

Uncle Neagu and his sons wait in turn day and night, and close to the shop they sell their good places to other people who can afford not to be patient. Then they go back to the end of the queue and start waiting again.

Abroad you can manage without the wait.

Here you don't need time for shopping, only money.

In the market you almost never have to queue, quite the opposite, they treat you like someone important, they even say thank you if you buy something.

ABROAD DOESN'T CHANGE US. WE EAT WITH OUR MOUTHS IN EVERY COUNTRY.

At first light my mother gets up and starts cooking, she plucks the chicken and holds it over the gas ring. My mother prefers to buy live chickens, because they're the freshest.

In hotels she kills the chicken in the bathtub.

WHEN THEY'RE KILLED, THE CHICKENS' SQUAWKING IS INTERNATIONAL. WE UNDERSTAND THEM EVERYWHERE.

Killing chickens in the hotel is forbidden, we turn up the radio, open the window and make a lot of noise. I don't want to see the chicken, otherwise I wouldn't want it to die. What doesn't go into the soup goes down the toilet. I'm frightened of the toilet, at night I pee in the sink, where the dead chickens won't come back up again.

We're always living somewhere else.

Sometimes the caravan is so small we can hardly get past each other.

Then the circus gives us a bigger caravan with a toilet.

Or the hotel rooms are damp holes, full of vermin.

But sometimes we live in luxury hotels with a fridge in the room and television.

Once we lived in a house where lizards ran about on the walls. We put the bed in the middle of the living room so the creatures couldn't creep under the covers.

And when she was standing by the garden gate a snake slithered over my mother's foot.

WE'RE NOT ALLOWED TO GROW FOND OF ANYWHERE.

I'm used to arranging things so that I feel all right.
    I only have to put my blue towel on a chair.
    That's the sea.
    I always have the sea by my bed.
    I only have to climb out of bed and then I can go swimming.
    In my sea, you don't have to be able to swim to be able to swim.
    At night, I cover the sea with my mother's flowery dressing-gown so the sharks won't get me if I have to pee.

One day we'll have a big house with luxuries, with a swimming pool in the living room and Sophia Loren dropping in all the time.
    I'd like a room with lots of cupboards where I could keep my clothes and all my things.
    My father collects real oil paintings of horses and my mother expensive china that we never use because it would get worn and break with all the packing and unpacking.
    Our belongings are in a big trunk stuffed with lots of newspaper.

WE COLLECT NICE THINGS FROM EVERY COUNTRY, FOR OUR BIG HOUSE.

My aunt collects cuddly toys, her lovers shoot them down at the fair.

MY MOTHER IS THE WOMAN WITH THE HAIR OF STEEL.

She hangs by her hair above the ring and juggles with balls and hoops and burning torches.
    When I'm grown up and slim I'll have to hang by my hair as well. I have to comb my hair carefully, my mother says hair is the most important thing for a woman.

MY FATHER SAYS THE MOST IMPORTANT THING IS THE HIPS.

I imagine a woman with hips as big as the circus tent.
    But that doesn't go with hanging.

I'm never going to hang by my hair, I don't want to.
    I pluck my hair from my head in tufts like the soup-chicken's feathers.
    A woman without hair won't get a husband, says my mother.
    I don't want a husband, I'd rather be like my sister, she's brave and always causing problems.
    My sister is only my father's daughter.
    She eats everything, because my mother saved her life when she was rachitic and

covered in lice.

I love her like a sister, even though she's a foreigner. Her mother is my father's stepdaughter. She and her mother, my sister's grandmother and my father's first wife, live in a hospital because they've gone mad.

My sister is mad as well, says my mother, because my father loves her like a woman.

I have to be careful I don't go mad too, that's why my mother takes me along with her everywhere.

MY FATHER ONLY WANTS MY SISTER ANYWAY.

My sister can do everything a lot better than me. Although she's only a few years older, she already has a crushed knee. My father drove into her leg with a tractor, so she wouldn't find a husband and stay with him always.

I won't belong to the circus before I have a proper injury of my own. But that won't happen, my mother always stops it, I can't even get onto the rope without her almost fainting.

My mother often behaves as if something terrible is going happen, even if someone nearby just laughs suddenly. Particularly women.

Women are jealous and calculating, they only have wicked ideas in their heads, she says.

I WAS ONLY SOMEBODY BEFORE I WAS BORN.

I was already a tightrope-walker for eight months before I was born, on my head. I was inside my mother and she did the splits on the high rope and I would look down or press my head against the rope.

Once she couldn't get back up again from doing the splits and I almost fell out.

Just after that I was born.

I was very beautiful when I was born, my mother worried that someone might steal me and put another baby in the crib.

I was born completely bald.

After I had been bathed my mother gave me thick eyebrows with her black pencil.

My aunt counted to see whether I had all my fingers, and the midwife strapped my bow legs together with a bandage.

My father wasn't there.

My mother named me after the midwife because she was from abroad.

And my aunt gave me a second name after a film star so I would become famous.

But I don't have the same name as Sophia Loren.

I WAIT FOR THE NIGHT ALL DAY LONG. IF MY MOTHER DOESN'T FALL WE WILL EAT CHICKEN SOUP TOGETHER AFTER THE PERFORMANCE.

My mother has long, slim legs, on the photograph she looks Japanese, with smooth black hair and a fringe. We don't look alike.
    I look like my father.
    He's not your father at all, the bandit, my mother sometimes says angrily, we don't need him!

WHY IS MY FATHER NOT MY FATHER?

Sometimes with men my mother pretends to be my sister. She rolls her eyes and stretches her words out long as if she suddenly had honey in her mouth. Though she doesn't even like honey, what she really likes is black rye bread with butter and salt. And she drinks white wine. She drinks as much white wine as I eat candy-floss. If we saved the money instead we could buy our big house with the chickens.
    When my mother pretends to be my sister she suddenly smells really strange. Then she mustn't touch me any longer. At the hotel she has to sleep on the floor, I don't want to share the bed with her.

MY MOTHER IS DIFFERENT FROM OTHERS BECAUSE SHE HANGS BY HER HAIR AND THIS STRETCHES HER HEAD AND MAKES HER BRAIN LONG.

My sister is as beautiful as a man, she fights with all the children. She's a gypsy.

I WANT TO BE A GYPSY TOO.

While my mother hangs by her hair in the tent my sister tells me the story of the CHILD COOKING IN THE POLENTA, to calm me down.
    If I imagine the child cooking in the polenta and how this must hurt I won't have to think all the time that my mother might fall from up there, she says.
    But it's no good. I always have to think about my mother dying so as not to be surprised. I see her setting her hair alight with the torches, see her falling burning to the floor. And when I bend over her, her face turns to ashes.

I don't scream.
    I've got rid of my mouth.

My sister and I were suddenly taken to a home in the mountains.

While we were packing mother hugged and kissed us like a clockwork doll. She kissed us before she put our clothes in the trunk as well.
    I will soon get you back, she said again and again.

My father didn't want to say goodbye to us. He swore and banged at his face with his fists: I'll kill anyone who lays a hand on my daughters!
    Then, silently, he turned to face our little black and white television on which he had glued a piece of coloured cellophane.
    The newsreader's face looked like a cassata.

My mother and us two girls were picked up by Mrs Schnyder, who had been taking care of us and our papers since we had run away.
    My mother was always asking whether there was a doctor at the home, are you sure my children won't be kidnapped or poisoned!

PERHAPS OUR PARENTS HAVE SOLD US. IT HAPPENS IN ROMANIA.

And where was my aunt?

The car-journey went on for years.

I wanted to remember the way so as to be able to get back. But the more I tried, the more everything became like everything else, as if someone had tidied up the landscape.
    The trees had packed up their leaves, as my mother had done with our clothes.
    Snow was falling.
    The car zig-zagged upwards.

Now the car had to fall off the edge.

A big house, surrounded by mountains.
    As soon as we had climbed out of the car I couldn't remember the direction we'd come from any more. The road we had driven along had disappeared.
    We were welcomed by a woman who looked as if she had several people under her dress.
    This is the director, said Mrs Schnyder.
    I am Mrs Hitz, said the director.
    She took us to a room with four wooden beds.
    The pillows and the covers on the beds looked like snow as well.

I didn't want to put down my suitcase.

The director opened the window and pointed to the garden.

In the summer you can pick strawberries, she said.
She smelt of bacon and spoke a language that sounded like singing. My sister understood more words than I did.
In the summer.
And now was winter.
We'll stay here forever, I thought, and started to cry.
My mother looked very beautiful and sad, we would never see each other again.

I WANT TO PUT MY MOTHER IN MY SUITCASE.

Mrs Hitz showed us the dining room, the common room and the kitchen. Everything was orderly and tidy, it smelt of disinfectant. You couldn't imagine anyone living there.
    Homework is done in the common room, and after that the children are allowed to play, said Mrs Hitz.

My mother took out the plastic bag full of photos and told Mrs Hitz about our great successes and about all our travels. My children are very intelligent, she said with a dark look, they know the whole world. We are international artistes! You must feed them well, only the best, you understand! I will call every day and ask whether they have eaten well! My mother kissed holes in our cheeks.
    She and Mrs Schnyder climbed back into the car.
Waving.
    My mother will die right there, I thought, then we'll bury her in the garden under our window. In the summer the strawberries will taste of my mother.
    My sister and I stood hand in hand in front of the door. Mrs Hitz stood next to us.
    She must have rubber arms, if we run away now she'll stretch out her arms and catch us.
    An animal was gnawing away in my belly, it had already eaten away my legs.

This place is a home, says my sister.
    Here you have to get very fat, otherwise you get crushed by the mountains. And you need several skins to keep warm.

I LET MY SKIN FALL TO THE GROUND.

The girls live on the top floor, the boys downstairs. There are babies too.
    We have to go to bed before it gets dark.
    And get up in the middle of the night.
    Air the rooms, put the bedclothes and the pillows over the window sill.
    Then we stand in front of the big sink in the corridor. When it is our turn we wash ourselves with a flannel with our name on it.
    Each child has:

2 flannels
2 towels
2 napkins

There are no names on the bedclothes.

Once a week we have to have a bath and wash our hair.

Our clothes have our names on too, even the socks. In the needlework class we had to sew a little tape with our initials onto each item of clothing.

After washing, make the bed and tidy the room.

Then breakfast and go to school. You reach the school along a mountain road. Opposite the school there is a farm.

My sister is learning reading, writing and arithmetic.

In my class we sing and we draw.

When we sing I always start to cry.

I can't take joyfulness.

After singing we're given a piece of paper with an animal to colour in. Then we learn what the animal is called in this foreign language.

IN EVERY LANGUAGE THE SAME THING HAS A DIFFERENT NAME.

In the afternoon we have to do our homework, after that we can play in the house or in the garden.

The little boys stay with the girls. The big ones only come when my sister and I do tricks.

We juggle with stones.

Or we walk around like rubber women.

My sister does handstands and I do the crab or the splits.

I stuff cotton wool under my jumper and make breasts like my aunt.

The boys come then as well.

My sister already has real breasts.

She has a few hairs downstairs as well.

TIME FREEZES.

The week is divided into working days and weekends.

On Wednesday I hear someone say: it will be the weekend soon.

At the weekend the parents come and collect their children. Then the house is almost silent, just the babies and us.

Our parents don't come.

They're abroad, says Mrs Hitz.
This is abroad too, we say.

HOW MANY ABROADS ARE THERE?

At the weekend we go walking.
    Mrs Hitz leads the way and we follow.
    In the forest we light a fire and grill sausages.
    We climb up high towers to see the countryside.
    Or we go swimming. I have to jump into the water although I can't swim.
    If my mother found out!

At the weekend I sleep with my sister in her bed, which is forbidden.
    At night we steal into a baby's room and pinch it till it cries. We can't stand the silence in the house. We're in bed again by the time someone comes upstairs. It always takes a while for them to quieten the babies down again. That's good.
    Sometimes we go into the corridor and say we've been woken up. Then we're allowed into the kitchen for a bit and we get an extra cup of milk.
    The television is usually on in the grown-ups' room. We're not allowed to stay in there, though.

In bed I'm constantly thinking of my mother hanging by her hair. My sister always has to invent terrible things about the child in the polenta.
    I help her:

DOES THE CHILD TASTE LIKE CHICKEN?
WILL THE CHILD BE CUT INTO SLICES?
WHAT'S IT LIKE WHEN THE EYES EXPLODE?

Then I cry.
And my sister holds me tight and comforts me.

I DREAM THAT MY MOTHER IS DYING. SHE LEAVES ME HER HEARTBEAT IN A BOX.

The child is cooking in the polenta because it tortures other children. It catches orphans, ties them to a tree and sucks the flesh from their bones.
    The child is so fat it's always hungry.
    It lives in a forest full of bones, you can hear the sound of gnawing everywhere.
    At night it covers itself with earth and sleeps so restlessly the whole forest trembles.

On Sundays we go to church. It's near the farm. It's not Orthodox or Jewish, there's no

dancing or proper singing.
 They tell different stories about God in every language, that's normal says my sister.
 In this church the devil is important.
 The devil is God's assistant, and he lives in Hell, which is as hot as the polenta.
 Hell is behind heaven.

PEOPLE ARE GOOD BECAUSE THEY'RE FRIGHTENED OF THE DEVIL.

I put my flannel on the bedside table.
 That's Hell.
 If I get used to Hell quickly then perhaps we can get away from here again soon.

The children talk about the circus the way they do about the zoo.
 Their eyes sparkle or they snigger.
 They think all circus people are related, that they all love each other and sleep in the same caravan and eat from the same plate.
 And then they live in the open air, oh how nice!
 They've no idea that you train all the time, that other people might copy your act and that one night you might fall down from up there and be dead the next day.
 They think it's all fun.

IF MY MOTHER FALLS DOWN SHE WON'T DIE FOR FUN.

Only actors die for fun.
 The children laugh when they hear I'm going to be a film star.
 I am one already, really, a little bit, my father has already filmed me. When I get older, he'll film my life story.
 Mrs Hitz doesn't like to hear that. She goes red in the face and says as if by heart: everyone is the same, no-one should want to be special.
 The most important thing is to be hard-working and humble.
 God doesn't like it when people are lazy.
 Man is here to care for the world.
 He isn't allowed to be a burden to anyone.
 He has to have a job and earn enough money to be able to give to charity as well.
 And he has to keep his house clean at all times.
 This will bring him peace.

But she also says that we are the image of God.

IF WE'RE THE IMAGE OF GOD THEN WE SHOULD BE ALLOWED TO BE AS FAMOUS AS HIM AS WELL.

WOLFGANG AMADEUS BREULHART
Culture: An Instrument Of Peace?

(Culled from a public talk by Swiss Cultural Counsellor Breulhart in London, 2000)

The picture *"Chienne de guerre, la culture te vaincra"* (Vile war, culture will defeat you) hangs in my office at the Swiss Embassy in London. It serves as a daily reminder of my two and a half years as Cultural Counsellor, from 1996 to 1998, at the Swiss Embassy in Sarajevo. During that period, Switzerland contributed some 100 million Swiss francs to the reconstruction of Bosnia and Herzegovina, of which 2 million were allocated to the field of culture. With these resources, we pursued the following objectives: to support the reconstruction of Bosnian cultural institutions, to promote cultural exchange in Bosnia and Herzegovina and the former Yugoslavia, and to promote cultural exchange between Bosnia and Herzegovina and Switzerland.

A month ago I returned to Sarajevo. I attended the 6th International Film Festival of Sarajevo, which was first held during the war. At the Festival, I was in the company of Bosnian artists and intellectuals; together with my colleague at the Swiss Embassy and the Director of the Centre Andrè Malraux, we considered the question: "Cultural programmes: How effective are they as a means to resolve conflict?"

This year's Sarajevo Film Festival featured a film by young Bosnian film-maker Srdjan Vuletic "Hop, Skip and Jump." The film focuses on a Sarajevo couple who find themselves on different sides of the front line when war breaks out. In such an ethnically mixed city as Sarajevo, this was a common experience. The female protagonist is a Serb sniper, her ex-boyfriend lives on pigeons that he traps. Each time a pigeon approaches his trap, she shoots it, taunting him, playing upon his emotions. Eventually he walks to the window, offering himself as a human target.

Culture also unleashes emotions. Vuletic's film affected me most deeply. The film presents three aspects of the conflict: the slow destruction of multi-cultural society in the former Yugoslavia, in particular Bosnia and Herzegovina, the beginning of the war and the war itself, and the peace agreement and the questions which remain: What now? How to move on?

In each phase, culture and cultural programmes assume different dimensions and functions. Our question "Culture: An instrument of peace and reconciliation?" can be answered in different ways for each phase of a conflict. To quote a phrase by Jacques Waardenburg, "'culture' is not just sunshine and clouds, it is also earth and dust."

Culture and War: An Uneasy Relationship

Pascal Dècaillet, one of the authors of the report *"Chienne de guerre, tu ne tueras pas la culture"* (Vile war - you will not kill culture!) characterises the marriage of "culture and war" as follows: "It is the story of an unlikely couple: culture and war. These two are totally entangled. Accomplices, even lovers, since time immemorial. To the point that they have sometimes been projected onto each other: wars of culture, culture of war, we have seen how culture and war live together and sometimes draw sustenance from each other." In his book *The Idea of Culture*, Terry Eagleton expresses this more casually: "Culture and crisis go together like Laurel and Hardy. Culture has passed over from being part of the solution to being part of the problem."

> To quote a phrase by Jacques Waardenburg, "*culture* is not just sunshine and clouds, it is also earth and dust."

As for the phrase "culture builds bridges," we often forget that culture also sets boundaries; wars and crusades are often justified in the name of a particular culture; and that war is a continuation of "dialogue" through a different medium, the medium of violence.

Disintegration of a Multicultural State Structure: Culture and Nationalism

After the death of Tito and the fall of the Berlin Wall, the peoples of the former Yugoslavia gained freedom. With this came a decline in ideology and the apparatus of power. Helmut Hubel in his "Internationale Politik," July 2000, states that "Nationalism became the most important factor in the shaping of an identity in the post-socialist crisis. Political power was asserted or won in such a way that socialists who held power became ultra-nationalists."

Culture (and cultural policy) was an instrument of the nationalists. They used it as a means to acquire and reinforce a new identity for their particular people; to strengthen their power base and incite hatred for other peoples. "In Bosnia, culture is not just what you put on the cassette player; it is what you kill for" (Eagleton).

Anti-nationalists, multicultural individuals and families all came under pressure.

Suddenly they had to favour one ethnic group, one culture. "The paradox of identity politics, in short, is that one needs an identity in order to feel free to get rid of it. The only thing worse than having an identity is not having one" (Eagleton). The only other alternative for these people was to seek refuge abroad. Artists and intellectuals were no different. Some started to build the foundations of a nationalistic cultural policy or made major contributions to a new cultural exclusion policy. Others warned their compatriots—at an early stage—that Yugoslavia could disintegrate into a state of war. Many others sought safety and creative freedom abroad, finding, for themselves, a new home and identity.

The question remains: could the conflict in former Yugoslavia have been appeased or prevented, perhaps by a focused programme of dialogue between peoples and communities? The answer is neither yes or no! Culture and the promotion of dialogue and understanding are of immeasurable value. Diversity of dialogue—promotion of respect and peaceful understanding, constitute a utopia of culture.

It has been said (Helmut Hubel) that Yugoslavia's disintegration into war did not stem essentially from a struggle between cultures and religions but from the collapse of the "Second World" and the associated problems of rebuilding a political order against a background of economic and social crises. The author John Mueller goes one step further in an article entitled "The Banality of Ethnic War" in *International Security*, Summer 2000. He argues that the causes of so-called ethnic wars should be sought not so much in ethnic or cultural differences as in the disintegration of state order which enables relatively small groups of common criminals to terrorise the rest of society and exploit their fears. They destroyed the whole fabric of dialogue, respect and culture exchange between peoples.

The exodus of several hundred thousand intellectuals and creative artists and the suppression of the (cultural) autonomy of Kosovo by Milosevic in 1989 heralded the forthcoming military conflicts. The international community should have been alerted to these warning signs at the onset and prepared for the possibility of war at a much earlier stage.

War: Destruction in the Name of Culture: Culture as a Means of Resistance

"In Bosnia, culture is not just what you put on the cassette: it is what you kill for."

group were also targets in this war: Mosques, Catholic churches, and Orthodox churches were intentionally destroyed. In Vuletic's film we saw the firing and destruction of the national library, we heard the "Waltz" that the cellist of Sarajevo performed in those ruins—a time-honoured symbol of Sarajevo itself and of the cultural, ethnic and religious pluralism in Bosnia and Herzegovina. In Mostar, the Bosnian Croat Army destroyed the 16th century (building commenced in 1566) bridge over the Neretva. These are only two examples from the wars. The aggressors justified war, massacres and the elimination of other peoples, like other oppressors before them, by so-called "ethnic cleansing."

The siege and constant bombardment of Sarajevo by the Bosnian Serb army lasted for more than four years, from April 1992 to November 1996. As the besieged inhabitants fought to repulse their attackers, one of the instruments they relied on was culture. In 1993, Enes Kujundzic, Director of the National Library, told a Swedish Newspaper: "In addition to food, medicine and clothes, we need books as well as part of humanitarian aid." People very quickly realised that in war and crises, man needs not only bread and water but culture as well: nourishment for the spirit.

The Sarajevo Philharmonic Orchestra gave concerts, plays were performed and exhibitions organised. There was the first Film Festival. The director of this year's Festival said, "Here was an act of resistance and our contribution to a very active cultural life in besieged Sarajevo."

All these cultural activities continuing in a state of war had an effect on the outside world. On May 27, 1992, a grenade was thrown into a bread queue at the bakery in Sarajevo. Twenty-two people were killed. Every day after this tragedy, cellist Vedran Smailovic played at that very spot, in full evening dress, at 4 o'clock every afternoon, risking his own life, performing in memory of the dead. A report by John Burns of the *New York Times* on this heroic musical declaration made more impact than any political statement of that time.

Swiss writer Franz Hohler recalls the conviction of that time when he says that "Culture is the opposite of war." Franz Hohler and his Swiss fellow artists set up a real cultural bridge between Sarajevo and Switzerland. They supported and revitalised Sarajevo's cultural life during those four and a half years of war; their intention was also to support Sarajevo's cultural diversity. Paradoxically, war gave birth to so-called "war art." Here we have daily life, staring death in the face. This was the "inspiration" of artists, living in Sarajevo through those troubled times, creating works of art and literature which cry out, admonish and exhort.

Reconciliation through Cultural Programmes

The Swiss Embassy in Sarajevo was opened shortly before the signing of the Dayton Peace Agreement, and I joined the team at the beginning in 1996. My colleagues and I encountered the following cultural situation: All those in power in each ethnic group continued to wage war with words and supported, first and foremost, nationalistic forces and "their own culture." Nationalistic art and creative artists received support. Each ethnic group wanted to set up its own cultural institutions. The will to co-operate and work towards reconciliation was non-existent. Many cultural institutions and associated buildings were destroyed. There was a lack of qualified personnel. Many creative artists emigrated during the war and did not want to return. The critical voices which remained were marginalized.

Based on this analysis and inspired by the words of Jean Monnet, "If I were to begin again, I would begin with culture," we supported the cultural reconstruction of Bosnia and Herzegovina from the very outset, and we also tried to make a modest contribution towards reconciliation through cultural programmes.

> Here we have daily life, staring death in the face. This was the inspiration of artists, living in Sarajevo

We supported numerous projects with lasting benefits: renovation of the National Gallery in Sarajevo, rebuilding of the "Maison Tchorovitch" in Mostar (Serbian cultural centre with multicultural orientation), support for the Sarajevo Philharmonic (First CD/AIDIMOS), support for independent media, public chess board layouts, training of piano tuners, the LICA cultural magazine, support for independent artists, publication of children's books, and support for the SOROS Design School.

Cultural Exchange Projects

1996 saw the construction of the cultural centre "Meeting Point" in Sarajevo and the development of the International Film Festival of Sarajevo. At this year's Film Festival children from all over Bosnia and Herzegovina watched children's films. SFOR and the EU organised the transport and were responsible for security.

The following year, there was the first theatre exchange between Sarajevo, Mostar and Belgrade since the war began, with support from the Swiss Army. In 1997, there was the first joint exhibition by an artist from Sarajevo and one from Banja Luka in Sarajevo since the outbreak of war. In 1998 and 1999 there followed the production of a CD by a rock band from Sarajevo and Banja Luka and 2 CDs by jazz groups. Most recently, in 2000 there have been various exhibitions by Bosnian artists in Zagreb and Ljubljana. At this year's biennial of contemporary art in Ljubljana, "Manifesta 3," many artists from former Yugoslavia met again for the first time since 1991.

Journalist Matthias Frehner, who reviewed Manifesta 3 (*Neue Zürcher Zeitung*, 14 July 2000), described the impact of the exhibition: "But you do not have to be a masochistic art freak to experience a growing fascination with this exhibition. It is the ever-advancing impression of genuine commitment to social problems and personal experiences, a reflection about existence, which wins respect even if the formal expression of the sympathy and consternation is neither innovative nor original. The question of borderline experiences in the Europe of today resulted, in the selection of the artists, in an obvious blurring of the line which separates art and documentation."

> Art gives visible expression to life's experience.

Art gives visible expression to life's experience. Culture is a fundamental necessity of life.

Culture and Nationalism

Cultural activity and works by artists pick up underlying trends and should be taken into account more often in political agendas for security and conflict prevention. This can increase understanding of a conflict situation and assist in identifying possible solutions at an early stage.

The preconditions for effective cultural co-operation between ethnic groups and peoples in order to prevent conflict are partners with equal rights and mutual respect. This requires institutional measures which the majority and minorities all respect and defend. Regional and international agencies should be called upon to introduce institutional proposals to resolve situations where conflict is possible.

To quote the cultural critic Zianddan Sardar: "It is necessary to free 'dialogue' from its conceptual bipolarity and to extend it to an open 'polylogue' in which people can speak not only as representatives of established cultures, but can alter given cultural contexts, shape their experience together and transcend historical boundaries."

Based on my experiences, I believe that it is possible to contribute to reconciliation between estranged peoples, ethnic groups and warring factions through cultural programmes. The support of peace-keeping troops is necessary to implement such programmes.

The target group for such cultural programmes has to be the younger generation. There is a need for mutual exchange to heal the wounds of separation. If young people and young adults can meet, then their parents will follow; such was the case with the Bosnian Youth Orchestra, Bosnian rock bands, and Bosnian theatre groups.

Many people suffer from depression after the end of a war and lose hope. Culture can improve the quality of life for all people. Art and critical culture can offer hope and vision. Art gives visible expression to life's experience. Culture is a fundamental necessity. Let us all endeavour to make it available to everyone in a difficult post-war phase.

Let us hear once more "The Cellist of Sarajevo."

W.A. BRUELHART

Claire Genoux
Two poems from *Saisons du corps*

Translated from the French by Ellen Hinsey

Having climbed this hill suspended in the March sky
I can see more clearly under this kingdom of leaves
If one day I enter this soil
without having given you
the rain-filled secrets of morning returning to the valley
without having let your fingers play
along certain glowing shores
when I have returned this body, loaned to me
this no longer inhabited shelter
– the doors slammed shut under the cold wind
if you have refused to let yourself go
refused to return by the path
where the high grass has the soft scent of mint
when roots nourish my veins
will you find words to calm
the flower which brushes you with its woolly blossom?
what will you say when an entire dew-filled landscape
sings an ancient night mass
like a pure hymn of farewell?

Claire Genoux

Translated from the French by Ellen Hinsey

If I had loved better
these days with their good smell of bark
these copper twilights
the mountains exposing their toothless jaws
if I had walked more upright
along trails that lead towards dawn
where faith shelters us from doubts and time
If I had known how to savor the full laugh
of the river that rocks in its fleece of leaves
my head held to the trunk's pillow
my cheek cast among thyme
if I hadn't fled like a coward to the back streets
and believed in the false lights of the city
in its burning waltz of noise
Perhaps then I wouldn't–stumbling,
rake my wooden head against the walls of night

Elisabeth Wandeler-Deck

Rumor About Flying and Hearing

From **To Sing of a Ship**
Translated from the German by Maria Schoenhammer

It may very well start with a sandwich and on high sea, Rias Hollywood, already, he describes wide circles around the entrance to the store, Bread'n'tapes, N.M. records each channel, it is her business, while looking after the tapes the sound of the skateboard on the asphalt, hollowed out from below, leaves her restless. Rias Hollywood, already, on his way to where what for, at his age, at his size, with his hair standing up, dyed blue dyed blue, N.M. files away, or are there customers coming already, you will talk about it today, Rias traces a smaller curve, a tiny loop very quickly, he brakes, misses the step, jumps off, N.M. rearranges tapes, that increases sales, she does not yet increase the rental fee, she will have to look out, look around at what others are offering, wants to know that precisely, she pushes the pack of blank tapes to the other side of the counter, she folds the daily newspapers in such a way that she sees at a glance today's offering of movies that she is able to receive on 23 channels over 23 receivers, she also offers versions pirated from TV or elsewhere, she loves to be secretive, specializes in rarities, a service among many, she cultivates her contacts with small distributors. Rumor About Flying and Hearing, details already now, N.M. files video tapes, it is early morning, returned, that is, dropped off female names other than Marie: Louise Sophie Susanna Anna Lilith for how do they name women.

A day can run through the seasons, through the years, the largest chunks of time get muddled up, straightening up is of no use, that has to be left alone, N.M. says towards the high shelves, three Luises or Susannas came with Lilith over the sea, they say, from the south they marched into this town with splendor and color, with high shrieks, three M and gloomy Sara queen or woman wading from the ship to the northern shore, as far as the eye can see, three Maries wading with Sara, they have been welcomed by her, did she arrive with them, towards the harbor gate, as far as the eye can see grasses are surging against protecting walls, of today, of long ago, wet hems dragging over pavement stones, asphalt, over meadows. For centuries there has been low tide, gray silt no longer slows down their steps when three Susannas or Luises are waiting out there on a Saturday and look over there, no one remembers the legend. Sea gulls in the grass. N.M. lies on the city wall with the man. The July sun burns. She thinks of going away and if she left him. You, she says to him, you, she says out loud, not for him to wake but for her to stay, to stop thinking up routes where leaving could take place, you, didn't anyone think of shooting in the mussel beds, let's go back, out on the oyster banks, as far as they go, there too, she says, to the Maries from the sea, starting point of their story, of their imagination.

Finding words in the crate of daily arriving newspapers, whoever brings them needs a vacation, from time to time an edition is missing, The New, The Daily, The Daily News, subtle when I look, of love, murder, robbery, whoever delivers that, line by line definitions in a very general way, what has to be, what to call a No, a look can not lie, columns of reproaches, when I look I see the man. I leave the place on the wall coping, I follow the headlines and enter the bar, For You, that had been closed, for entire days, because of renovations, a coat on the floor, at least, a bar is a bar, for you, freshly done up, a trace of blood can be made out, several people are standing around, that can also mean a woman, are confused, for two days, the trophies, the posters aren't where they used to be, a glass case is missing, I ask for the new owner, whom I suppose, at least, the bar is the bar. A similar carefree spirit takes over in other areas as well, he closes the door. He washes his feet, that's taken from a different scene. He brushes his teeth. He puts his jacket on the bed spread. He does not take off his sweater. He puts on his shoes, takes them off. He takes off his sweater. How, I lean against the wall, the table consists of a top, stained red, the grain shimmers through the coat of varnish a small shadow on each side, his, mine, she tries to make it out, the light is so diffuse, today, sharp-edged referring not to observations but to the observer, N.M. says two steps at an angle from bottom to top vertically at an angle both at the same time, I lean against the side of a wall. Stones are pressing into the shoulder blades, calling small dents at head level a smooth plaster wall. In the absence of pain, what can serve her to orient herself, naming him is fresh, white, he looks done-up. He takes off his underwear. As usual, it has stripes. Puts on pajama pants, where do they come from now, takes off his pajama pants, in another time, of another man, he didn't wash. Death is short, it proceeds, grammatically, in its feminine form, N.M. notices humming in her ears, doubly from the inside, from the outside, her head throbbing, whatever splits her up. The clouds bare her brain. Someone else might say it this way or that way, a collapse of the rampart, N.M. notices that she talks of the demons of being right and of succeeding through force, she lacks a you-figure, Rias Hollywood is really still too young, her place is to keep it in her heart, she operates the recorder. Video, audio, Merri Klages might have said it differently, might have jotted a small sketch on her note pad, rubbed a bit of lipstick into the paper, and might have made two creases. The man shows himself angry and unwashed. He smiles. The woman she was reports and observes, she hits him in the face and falls asleep. Breaking words from the plaster of the newspaper delivered in the morning, the phrase just so occurred to N.M., she pronounces it over the recording machines that are set out. I have been listening to you, for the longest time, Rias Hollywood says through the cracked door, will you let me? Yes, what is it, the sirens at noon time. Where she is now there is no wind in the world at all. Her life is known. Almost that of a famous person, so very generalized, surrounded by data, other people's memories, canned sounds and images, N.M. an empty spot, by herself, put up in tin words, the path leading to the coast, to the mountains, she doesn't know, Rias Hollywood

> **The woman she was reports and observes, she hits him in the face and falls asleep.**

circles along, did she want to send him ahead, is he her pretext. Sara is it you, every ten minutes nothing happened, meanwhile the wind sets in again, the voice yells more softly, drifts away in the snow, two to three Marie, Mary, the one, Mary McDala succeeded between the fat moons, beams of light and clouds to overstep no one's land, to land past buildings on the shore that would have been an arena or a guard station, she succeeded in reaching the basement room, N.M. adjusts the recording level, fog lifts a speech, are you saved, one steps over someone the area the grass. What else, say those who have a say, now, who is that, rejected, he and he and she and she, she, three, one, several, N.M hears voices brushing through the high grass, from the coffee bar downstairs in the house, or notices the echo if you're lucky, bathed deloused transferred, where she came from. A broken heart, she, one N.M. listening with two pairs of ears, of a native and of an expellee, inside and outside, she exists for herself presently a home town to hear with two pairs of eyes, as long as she has lived there has always been war, talking differently or not. Then they were many, starting point for ramblings, N.M. points the video camera at herself, starts to move, walks slowly among the shelves with the video tapes until she has the distance, to slip away, to arrive, Rias practices his leaps across the cracks in the asphalt, the cherry tree, three times grafted, on the top of the slope, at the foot the railroad track North-South, N.M. lights a cigarette, a girl sits in the tree, the woman, the Marie, Michelemmà, the fisher woman, mathematician and architect. She keeps lookout and reads. She builds a tree house for herself. She builds a hut a ship in the tree. She keeps lookout along the railroad track. She looks over a sprawling hospital building towards the other shore, she listens behind her where the house is in a flat garden. She smells the scent that rises from the thuja hedge separating the steep land from the flat land. I climb the tree. I climb up the tree. It is the cherry tree. She smells the scent of cherry wood. In early July the cherry tree bears small wild fruits from which in this region they distill kirsch. Some of the grafted species mature earlier, some later. N.M. turns towards the shop window. Directs her voice, her face, she turns her back to the camera, she doesn't speak. She speaks, she turns back, she looks across the machines, the shelves, the three M, N.M. says, came over the sea where the divided town is. They talk nautical, praise the empty galley, they talk of Michelemmà you ivory tower, you heaven's gate, you morning star, consoler of the distressed, courageous captain, where N.M. looks, in Rias Hollywood's aquarium that she recently moved into the shadier one of the shop windows, the water snails are multiplying, only rarely one of the fish dies. Only rarely does a plant rot, the finger rarely creeps in the case, will you tell me that today when I come back? A sandwich in each hand, Rias rides off. On the counter there are Rias Hollywood's things compass drawing pen Walkman. Dancing fish move very, extremely slowly through the aquarium. N.M. presses the button: stop. A small sound may be opened for examination purposes.

1 Sara. Prelude.
Slowly very slowly panning masses of water flow clatter incessantly words words cut slowly very slowly cut, you see, what is within reach incessantly throwing evaluating listen,

Sara H., I remember, it could have taken a turn. It would have been a legend. Reading. It would have delighted me. I remember, she, Sara K., hands. That's the way she is. Yes, hands. Yes, Kälin, Sara Kolin. Listen, it could have taken a turn. The hands, yes. A hearkening. Nothing. Not Sara H., would she have been a talk, turning into a tale, don't you hear. Yes, talking of it. Is it relevant to the present. Could have become, yes, could have become, I remember. This basement, listen, this voice, a voice, a turn,
I remember, was it in the town, was it. **It was in the town of Bethany where the resurrected Lazarus was still living with his sisters Maria and Martha.** Was there **There was a huge persecution. And all of the disciples and apostles had to go into hiding or they had to flee to avoid getting killed.** Yes, talking, yes, Sara H., listen, **The apostle Jacob was living there as well with his mother Mary Jacobee, and the apostle Jacob with his mother Mary Salomee. And both women had one servant in common,** this basement, listen, orders, the voices, listen, wanted to flee to another country, had an opportunity, I remember, this haste, this fear, **They bought a ship and climbed into it to go over the sea. But as they were about to depart, the women's servant came running in haste and she implored them: "Allow me, you holy women to come with you and serve you on the way." They didn't want that. They said: "Nothing will happen to you in this country. But we are already so many on the boat that it might even sink." But she didn't stop begging. So she was allowed to get in. The boat, however, had no oars, no sail and no helm. Because those who sold it to them,** this haste, listen, a hearkening, yes, talking,
three women, I remember. The sea. You see the sea. You do not yet see the sea. The plain. The short grass. The wind. You see the wind. They do not yet feel the wind. The wind. Now it is here. You taste the salt of the wind. A street, asphalted, a long time ago. You walk against the wind, against the light. You see. You know the light, the wind. Three women, you see them. You see the basement, I remember, whereto. Did one go further. Did she go, maybe into the hills, a mountainous countryside, her brother. Maybe her brother. What a tenderness. Feet. See the feet, what a desire. Time. You hear the wind, It is still early. Listen. Singing. This could have happened to any of them. Recently, you see, a truck. Garbage, hands. Sara K., Kähler maybe, she wore that white dress. Was it marble dust. Did she climb that loading bridge. Sara K., you see. Yes, some ashes on her sleeve. Just on one of the sleeves. Was it ashes. What are they saying. This time, this music. This dripping. Yes, I remember, from the loading bridge. Yes, I was too late, it was too late, you said it was too late. Yes, she wore that dress. Which doesn't mean anything, yes, an arm, these hands,
One day. That could have happened to any of them. She remembers, yes, writing, a

withdrawing, on a ship, this is how it must have happened, she says, to sing or such, an address, she practiced. She, behind her a writing, she practiced, the headline, with the address, an address, in the fold of her undershirt, of her skin, she made much of writing, practiced. Did the ship come in. A board, the names, claimed. One day blackened, **but in the Café des Vagues not much is to be seen of them. In the Café des Vagues there are mostly men, among themselves. And it appears they are men of some influence.**
No, sleepless nights, hardly, people, Sara says, she remembers, three women
And wears a dress after all, what she wore, who remembers, stairs, she says, graduations. Basements. Buildings, she says, a weaving, smooth, green, yes, forgotten what was shining. Glistened away. Dusty, she wore that green dress. Yes, forgotten. When she arrived, already forgotten. Half a million people
already forgotten,
off to the side a circle of younger men. They practice on guitars, they play, each one for himself. The little boys are standing so that they are able to see without being sent away. did they come, she says, those who nevertheless arrived, she says strings and whirls, she says, sides, suitcases, the suitcase locked, locked in. Did they carry themselves, what they had to bear, a vignette, the ID card, where do the women stay, oh, the women, Sara says, they do not bother much, carried the dress, themselves, what else, a suggestion.
The boat. Look at the boat. No oars, no sails, nothing to align the boat. I remember. A gust of wind. A sheet of paper maybe, a crumpled sheet, I don't remember precisely. A hand. A hand grasps. A hand a wrist, grabs. Listen. Something snaps shut. Running. Running off. Hear the voice. You see the man. No, he can not identify himself, a gust of wind, what is taking place. Do you remember, there was the boat. They say, merely a legend. They say they don't remember. Was it Alexandria, Sara K., I remember, Alexandria. The boat, the beach. She, just having turned twenty-three. She is waiting. Was there a landing place. You know, the boat, a beach. Waiting so as not to die, remember,
Sara says, subtractively irritated, the line of a back, keeping nothing lest she dies. A suggestion. Or turns away, card catalog of the gender, three, maybe Maries, what remains, an empty spot, rotations, like this or like that, myth M suffix n, $n = 1, 2 \ldots$, I am, Mary Jacobee says, the one who resists, it is necessary to melt down the myth, what remains has to be counted out, melted down, at most elsewhere. Reddened by the unfamiliar sun, she remembers, a supporting figure determines the crossing, the planks set out, this urge, this commitment to continuity that hinders her, **Angels appeared and blew a favorable wind. Then the boat drifted to the mouth of the Rhone river. The water became very smooth. And the boat gently came ashore.** Of a different leading figure later, in a different season, late winter then, Sara laughs, seasonal, and other comments regarding the circumstances, then, when there is low tide, she lifts one foot and puts it down into the silt, listen, as an afterthought.
Counting, at times, it would have been a legend, a tale, she says she wanted to remember it. Did the figure get clothed then, **Like a queen of the seas**, that could be

expected, she could be counted on, the figure of Sara, **her delicately embossed diadem sways gently and glitters**, yes, it would have become a saying, a reacting of the boundary maybe, of thoughts,
if she sets her foot down. Sara says. Had she not been warned, I remember, puts her foot down, Sara K., always elsewhere, are there guests, a mountain town, later, listening grazing wounds, remember, time. A woman, retrogressing, every basement a prologue, only, her place is the crypt, Ishtar, and without a gift for attraction, she remembers, a Kali, look, yes, look, the low tide when she embarks on thinking. Yes, look, how the low tide rises, the water pulls, yes, a little cold, feet, yes, pulled up, she remembers, adversities, the boat propped up. Anger, at last, listen, how does she carry herself,
no, you merely hear it, you can not see it, the flies, many flies above the planks laid at an angle, they looked there, they didn't see anything, they could have seen it, they could have turned around, it would not have been too late, two women, or three, so they say, it wasn't anything, nothing happened, a rumor, at most. Not a word at the beginning, a whimpering, hair, over the edge of the planks, yes, hair, arranged at first, would it have been a legend, something like a body, or flesh, naked flesh, having read, eyes. Her eyes pierced by the light. One after the other. Consider the basement, the hands. Time.

YVES NETZHAMMER - COMPUTER GRAPHIC

Leo Tuor

Giacumbert Nau—An Annotated Account of his Life as a Sheperd on the Greina, chronicled by Leo Tuor

Translated from the Sursilvan Romansh by Mike Evans

I spent five summers in search of the
White Stallion of Blengias, five whole summers.
I challenged it, provoked it, goaded it,
cursed at it, besought it,
set bait for it, enticed it, laid in wait for it.
All to no avail! Not even in the devil's name.

How I'd love to cast eyes on the White Stallion of Blengias;
then I could happily perish, just like any member of the populace.

My recollections...

He wasn't all that big, nor was he much to look at.
His shoulders weren't really broad enough for a man.
His chest was hairless. One leg was a trifle too short, so his gait always gave him away,
even from miles off. (He rarely went fast, being a shepherd. Perhaps because of that leg,
perhaps because it was his wont to stand on the spot, glass to eye).

He had slender hands. Yet on his left hand, just the thumb stuck out on one side; the rest
of his fingers had gone. I could find no beauty in him, bar his eyes, but it used to take a
long time before he would look another straight in the eyes, because he preferred animals
to people. He hated people, especially "the populace" –
that stupid, blind herd so easily turned in whatever direction the priests and politicians
wanted to turn it.
No, thinking most definitely wasn't the populace's strong point. Say your prayers, do your
work and think nought. Do a job, stay daft and keep on regurgitating the same old puke.
That's what the populace is like.
Hatred, contempt and ridicule had been the weapons he had wielded against stupidity.
Finally, he had had to flee to the mountains like a wounded animal and fade away there –
like last year's snow. Don't ever ask where.

He was not a believer, and the only trust he ever entrusted anywhere was in his dog. Once, when Albertina had said that she was coming to visit him, he had retorted:
"I'll believe that when I see you." To which, she, in self-defence, had rejoined: "if I've said I'm coming, that means I'm coming!"

He just gave a slight laugh, a bitter one, then remarked (I know not whether he uttered this aloud to Albertina or just to himself): "Is it not said that those who inhabit the Alps have a belief all of their own?"
Continuing, he added: "Blessed shall be the believers; and stiff shall be the dead."

As early as seventeen, he had stopped believing in the catholics' God, the God of sins and confessions, who only ever sided with the priests, since it was they who would say what it was that God had to say. At an early age he had stopped believing in the truth of what they preached – and in justice too.
And there was something else, too: he didn't believe that people were good:
"I know I'm bad."
That was one of his very few sentences.
The sound of those five little words of his used to send a shiver down my spine. His beauteous eyes would boil over into mine as he said:
"And you know you're bad."
And I knew it.

His soul often used to pain him; I could sense it in his voice. His words were few and far between, and whole sentences even rarer. It wasn't always possible to understand what he was saying or what he meant. But I wrote down everything I heard or saw. His words penetrated my very veins, though I did not always understand them. But do we always have to understand it all? Giacumbert was his name, and he herded his flocks in a place starting with 'G' too.

He was proud of his daughter, whom he had had with a married woman, and even more proud that he had managed to produce a child precisely with the woman he wanted, cocking a snook at laws and morals alike, without anyone noticing it, not even the "old" ram (as he used to call her husband). So he had not only had his fling and made sure that his kind would not die out, but had also put a stopper in the mouths of the scandalmongers. In my heart of hearts, I am sure I know why he said that to me: he wanted me to commit it all to writing, so that, once he had gone, they would find out about it after all.

Giacumbert has gone now, and the pasturelands starting with a 'G' have been wiped out too. I also recall four lines he used to enjoy reciting so much (I don't know why; perhaps it was because of the sound of the words):

Have I not just had a sleep
On the altar of our great God
Sullied the slumbers of the Righteous,
Hugging your breasts?

The last time I saw him, he said:
"We are going to meet again, down in Hell at the latest
Down there is where the real beauties go. Adieu."

Red & white used to be his favourite colours.

So here you are; you've come up here to join me,
you're asking me who Giacumbert might be.
It doesn't really matter. Simply say that Giacumbert
is the man of the Gaglinera.

The Gaglinera is the place where the chickens have a shepherd.

Who is Giacumbert?
Who is the Gaglinera?

Perhaps you might even divine it, if you are able to sense it;
otherwise you won't, for Heaven's sake!
But if you come up to the Pass sometime, then your eye will see the meagreness of the land and the meagreness of the words, and perhaps you will sense the wavering soul of the man of flesh whom I call Giacumbert.
If you are able to sense it, then you yourself are Giacumbert or Albertina, and then your favourite colours are:

Red & white.

If you come up over Diesrut, if you have the eye for it
then you will see the pile of rubble up on the plateau that used to be the horseman's refuge.
If you have the eye for it.
Your eye is your soul.

Giacumbert pushes back his hat

Giacumbert is not impressed by the plateau
Piano della Grena
Giacumbert keeps going until he has gone from sight.
Like his animals, Giacumbert sticks doggedly to the black path up there, pushes back his hat even further still,
hammers the point of his stick on the rocks, between the rocks and into the grass.

Stubborn Giacumbert.

Giacumbert listens to the murmurings, strains himself to listen to the murmurings.
Giacumbert listens to the shepherd, to the valley and its undertones.

The spirit and the valley never die.

Where are your paths leading you, Giacumbert? And the paths in your mind? And that hard skull of yours?

Your paths are wandering like your mind,
not in an orderly line like your animals.

But should the paths of thought not go like animals keep on going, going, going?

"Why on earth are you trying to sense the weather?"

You're not a barometer. People of yore used to have a feeling for the weather. You no longer have a feeling for the weather.

Go and sleep in your refuge and leave the weather alone.

Outdoors is the place for weather.

Where's there a night pen for the flock, where?

They're already up and about and all lined up along the grey horizon. They look as if they are stretching to their full length on the rounded rocks of the glacier.

Down they come in rows.
Suddenly one, two, four.
One that's faster,
like so many elongated beads.

So that's where the Gaglinera would have been.

It's six o'clock, and Giacumbert, already soaked to the skin,
looks on amazed, utterly stunned.
So that was the revelation of daybreak.

Giacumbert takes a gloomy view and rushes like a devil through the knolls and hollows of the Gaglinera. Now you see Giacumbert, now you see just his hat, now you don't see Giacumbert at all.
There must be snow in the air.
The farming folk are nowhere to be seen.
Giacumbert's on the run to keep warm.
There must be snow in the air.

The Gaglinera turns white.
Where are your animals, Giacumbert?
Where are your animals going to spend the night now?

The silent snow fills the Gaglinera,
blotting out its features.

Giacumbert? Dozing off?
Dozing off at your table, Giacumbert?
What's the point in going to bed!
Your bed's too short in this condemned cell of a
refuge. You are worse off than your dogs;
they've already been asleep a long time, raising an occasional
eyebrow to see if you're finally going to turn off the light.

Giacumbert has to pull Oldie along after him.
Today's the day for moving on.
"Aah-tit-tit-tit-titaaaaaaaaaaa."
Oldie's in no hurry and still takes a nibble from the right of the path and another from the left, stretching out for one tasty shrub and trying to root out another.
Her bleats grow more staccato as the rope tightens round her neck.
A murky Giacumbert turns and looks back, his patience at its tether's end, stumbling forward over the exasperating young goat darting to-and-fro between his legs,
what impudence.

Behold Giacumbert, the goatherd of his goats, lying facedown on the path.

But let's not lose our patience; perhaps we'll be where we want to be by nightfall. Aah-tit-tit!
The nanny goat licks his ear clean for him.

Giacumbert chews his bread.
Bread never goes hard, not even after fifteen, twenty days.
Giacumbert chews his dry bread.
There's no such thing as hard bread.

Giacumbert makes a feast out of gnawing at his bread, piles up his yellowing ham and breaks the blade of his knife on his bread.

What's the matter, Giacumbert? You've got no meat left.
You're lost without meat. You can't live only off greens and fruit and old junk like that; you need meat. Your ancestors descended from the wolf. It's meat you need, meat.
You never feel full, you need meat.

"I"
"i i i i - i i i i i"
Giacumbert hauls the dog from the bed by its ears.
"Not in the bed, you swine, not in the bed!"
"i i i i i"

"Wretched creature!"

Giacumbert stands sentinel beside the long line of animals wending their way down the path like pearls on a string.

Giacumbert just keeps staring entranced at the line of the procession going where it has to go. Giacumbert's the only one standing sentinel next to the long, long procession. It's not like Saint Placi' Day, when there are only a few in the procession and all the rest look on or swarm around with cameras and things that go click and things that go buzz and things that go whirr as they keep on trying and kneeling and slipping and sliding and bending down low, as they creep along behind the cross and the noise of the bells.

Giacumbert's animals have kept their rituals;
humanity alone stands sentinel;
decadence.

The vast woollen front advances
over hillock and hill, cropping the succulent grass
back to its roots. It takes but one moody animal to steer the whole jittery herd in a different direction.

Then the whole flock squeezes together again, as if nothing had happened. Lone animals chance a glance up, continuing to chew suspiciously. Their sporadic bells chime in with their *tin tin*. On and on the front moves:
avanti avanti
avanti popolo
no time to rest
no time to rest
Onward moves the flock, leaving behind its night pen, the hilltop, its droppings, the grass-heath, the tufts and its baa baa.

Roger Monnerat
The Trout

From The School of Shame
Translated from the German by Dafydd Roberts and Pierre Imhof

He woke at dawn, Silvie had gone, on the table lay the various stacks of paper, arranged alongside and on top of each other. Joris knocked on Silvie's door, but received no reply. He heard noises in the dining room and went downstairs. An old woman brought his breakfast, but when he asked her whether she could tell him something she quickly went away and did not reappear.

Joris ate, taking his time over it. A sluggish blanket of cloud hung over the landscape, and it was only against the deep shade of hills, forests, trees and houses that one could make out a greyish light in which street lamps and lighted windows floated as bright, hazy blotches.

As Joris lit a cigarette, the owner approached his table. "You wanted to ask something? My mother," he said, pointing behind him with his thumb, "doesn't speak to strangers on principle." Joris asked about the family of Angel Perreira, "You know, the young man from these parts who was killed in El Salvador some twenty years ago?"
"Perreira? I heard about it. The boy's father, Jaime Perreira, lives down in the gorge, but I don't know him personally. Perreira avoids people and people avoid him. You'd be better off asking Silvie, she knows the old man rather…." He stopped suddenly. "But that's really none of my business," he went on, all embarrassed, and went away.

"Do you know where Silvie is?" Joris called after him. He didn't expect a reply.
Old Perreira's house wasn't hard to find. A little bit above the bridge was a turn-off into the gorge, a track which meandered among the rocks and passed over a number of narrow bridges to end at a gate, where the narrow valley broadened out into a bowl. Two setters came running, barking all the way, but turned aside some 20 yards before reaching Joris to strike out in different directions, head down into the bushes. They watched Joris from their posts as old Perreira made his way from the house to the gate.

He was tall and gaunt and walked slightly bent, or rather it seemed as if his bird's head were thrust forward on a long, curving neck. He wore no hat, and from his head a spiky bush of black hair stood out in all directions. Black too were the bushy eyebrows. He had a flat face, big bright eyes, a short nose and full, soft lips. Perreira stopped at the gate, placed a foot on the middle bar, and offered Joris a cigarette which he had probably been rolling inside his jacket pocket as he came up. The hand disappeared inside the pocket again, while for a few moments he scrutinised Joris silently, then produced a second cigarette, to light it from the small flame that Joris held out to him. "So?" he said. Joris remained silent. From a distance the old man looked like a vulture, from close up like a clown, an old clown, an old clown with eyes as bright and expressionless as a wolf's. "Well," Joris replied, guardedly.

"Silvie told me everything. She came up last night on her bicycle and got me out of bed." He spoke slowly, shaking his head.

"I'm sorry about what happened to Angel," Joris started to say, but the old man waved it away.
"Angel was a grown man, he knew what he was doing."

The old man paused, and then went on with unexpected vehemence: "It's really none of my business, but you'd do better to worry about the living than the dead. Do you think a whore could spread her legs for everybody if she weren't hoping deep down inside that someone one day would turn up and stay for good? Silvie had no illusions, but like everyone else she had the right to hope. Have you ever considered that possibility? Have you ever thought about the fact that hope can also destroy a person? 'Hours spent in hope of knowing, decades despoiled by hope,' as one of our songs has it."

> ...you'd do better to worry about the living than the dead.

"Look Perreira, I'd like to know more about Silvie and, if you don't mind, about Angel. Can't we simply sit down at a table and talk like ordinary people?" Joris asked. "I don't have anything to prove to you," he added lamely, a remark which seemed to him as pointless as the attempt to change the old man's mind.
"I was up half the night. Come back this evening, I've nothing against you," Perreira conceded, then turned around and stomped away.

At the hotel Joris found a note from Silvie in his pigeonhole. "Take care, Joris. Silvie," was all there was on the folded paper. As if there were any point taking care any longer, it had all gone wrong years ago, Joris thought bitterly, but perhaps that wasn't what Silvie had meant.

He went to his room, packed, paid the bill, and got into the car. He didn't yet know whether he would take up the old man's invitation, it wasn't even midday yet. He started the car and drove off. He'd think about it in Pontarlier.

Joris' decision was made for him as he entered the centre of Pontarlier by a poster advertising a Courbet exhibition at the Museum in Ornans. It was about 60 kilometres to Ornans. Perhaps there would be a chance to see some of the sketches and studies for Courbet's *Origine du monde*, the first painting of the modern age to capture the body of a woman in its concrete and unmediated aliveness. Courbet had dispensed with every anecdotal feature, he had anticipated the close-up and the cropping of the image that would become so important in cinema. The model's torso fills the space, lying on one diagonal of the painting, with one thigh extended along the same line and the other on the opposite diagonal, while at the centre, above the crotch, is a silky bush of dark hair, tightly curled, its crown there where the dividing line between the curves of the backside ends in a vagina that seems open and closed at the same time, like a mouth between whose lips one can see the tip of the tongue.

In its density, its tangibility, its warmth even, this body is sufficient unto itself. The painter has pushed the model's nightdress up over her breasts; here the painting stops and turns back to canvas. There is no face in which the viewer can read anything, there is no expression the viewer can project back onto the body. With this painting Courbet has gone beyond the hypocrisy of his sleeping nudes, this last degree of the anecdotal that spares the viewer the disturbance of the gaze the woman might direct at him, the man still fully dressed.

If there is a riddle in this torso of Courbet's, then it lies in the subject itself. The naked truth, as radical as Holbein's painting from the mortuary and Heemskerck's Christ had been three hundred years before. Joris had seen a reproduction of the painting for the first time as an adolescent, and unlike other occasions for masturbation, and all representations of naked women had been such in those days, he still remembered it. It was the only picture he had still been able to contemplate without revulsion once he had satisfied himself.

In the case of pornography, Joris' ideas about how such photos and films had been made also played a part in his excitement, which is why it was afterwards followed by an embarrassed disillusion: this kind of production had nothing to do with his own life, the deception was too obvious. Not that this was enough to spoil everything, for in the end the imagination that exploited such a representation was still one's own, unexhausted by what it found before it. As a teenager, Joris had usually pushed the porn-mags under the mattress, turned on his side, snuggled under the blanket, and dismissed with a slight shrug the humiliating circumstances of his imaginary excesses. In the well-being of a weariness rather like that which followed great physical exertion, and with a concluding, precocius *"c'est la vie,"* Joris would then fall asleep.

The first images of naked women that Joris had ever seen were pictures of prisoners in German concentration camps. His first descriptions of sexual intercourse he had read in war novels like Norman Mailer's *The Naked and the Dead;* his sexual fantasies were prompted by scenes of rape and torture in Leon Uris' *Mila* and *Exodus*. Joris had read dozens of such books, anti-war books supposedly, which had shown him no more than that the imagination corrupts. He had felt lust, and though he might also have felt ashamed of this, there is nothing that can prevail against imagination.

Joris found the Gustave Courbet Museum in Ornans in a simple town house alongside the schoolyard. He followed the instruction to ring the bell at the minister's house, where, after a long wait, an aged sexton opened the door, asked Joris what he wanted, and then took him over. The rooms were wood-panelled and dark, the shutters closed, the paintings and drawings illuminated by spotlights. Of Courbet's famous paintings, there was only the self-portrait that shows him imprisoned at Sainte Pélagie, where he had been sent with Pierre-Joseph Proudhon and other well-known insurgents after the defeat of the Commune in 1871.

Courbet was accused of being responsible for the destruction of the victory column on the Place Vendôme. The portrait shows him sitting at a barred window, gazing pensively onto an inner courtyard, where the evening light is falling and there stand a few small, thin trees. Next to the painting hung a photograph, in which one could see Courbet in 1871, as president of the Commune's art commission, inspecting the toppled monument to Napoleonic victories. Courbet was then 52 years old, a self-confident, corpulent *citoyen* and *bon vivant* with grey hair and a full beard. In the self-portrait, however, painted in the year following his release from prison, one sees an entirely different Courbet: older indeed, no longer as slim as in his youth, but in his deportment and expression, with his black beard and dreamy almond-shaped eyes, a Courbet who resembles the hunter in *La Curée*, a painting done fifteen years earlier in 1857 for which Courbet had taken himself as the model.

In this self-portrait, Courbet, who all his life had fought against any idealisation in painting, allowed himself an idealisation of himself. From his letters it is clear that he did this not to accord with classical models and aesthetic criteria, but rather from a feeling, after the defeat of the Commune, that his future could only be won from his memories. From the memory, indeed, of the young Courbet, who, before he became a man of the world, the lion of the salons and subject of society gossip, had fancied himself rendered in the detached pose of a young bohemian, still unforgetful of the sorrow in his heart.

"I am dead," wrote Courbet in 1872 – though he could equally well have written "I is another," for as a painter he knew better. He had produced his true self-portrait that same year, in the picture of the trout that hangs from the hook with all the weight of its nine pounds, snatched from its element, not dead, but dying. Even the red scarf of the Communards, which the imprisoned Courbet wears, can be found again in the dying trout, as a trace of blood under the gills, as a spray of blood spread over the whole canvas. Five years later, on 13 December 1877, Courbet would be taken from the clinic, back to his apartment in La Tour de Peilz across Lake Geneva, where he had lived in exile since 1874, driven on a market cart, his body so swollen up from dropsy that he couldn't fit into any carriage. Courbet died on 31 December 1877, his end a bitterly mocking reversal of his painting of the dying trout: Courbet suffocated in his own water.

Hugo Loetscher

A Nice Accent: On Impurities in Language —An Orientation of Switzerland

Translated from the German by Alan J. Bridgman

We do not write as we speak.

This refers not to morals but to language. The situation is not as unusual as we suppose. But we Swiss tend to think that what distinguishes us is unique. Even if we do have problems, we do not wish to share them.

The fact that in the homeland of Pestalozzi there are functionally illiterate people does not fit into our virtuous view of ourselves. Should we be consoled by the statistics from the schools that tell us our young people are better at arithmetic than reading?

What, on the other hand, does a Chinese think of our problem? He can read what other Chinese ethnic groups write, but he does not understand them when they speak, because the characters are pronounced differently. Thus, a film made in Hongkong in Cantonese will be shown in Taiwan with Chinese subtitles for those who speak Mandarin - community through writing, not through speech.

And how could we explain our problem to an author who speaks a language for which there may not yet exist a possibility of being published? To a Nigerian, for instance, who speaks one of the languages counted by hundreds in his country? Do we want to complain to African writers, faced with the dilemma of whether, in order to reach a larger public, they should write in English, French or Portuguese: indicting what colonialism has done to their people, but in the language that was imposed on them by their former colonial masters?

Our situation is not all that interesting for the world, even though it is still true to say: we do not write as we speak.

We - this refers to us, the German-Swiss. This restriction is not without significance; after all, Switzerland is a country with four languages.

An Indian might report that in his country 15 principal and regional languages are authorised and in addition 24 independent languages can be found, without even mentioning the 700 dialects and tribal languages. But is it not unfair and unacceptable to compare a sub-continent with an Alpine statelet? Is it not malicious of a Third World inhabitant to ask what we would do if, instead of the Rhaetians, Moslems lived in the

Engadine, and in the South not Tessiners but black people, and in the Upper Valais nomads with ibex herds! Will it help us to argue from history then, that we too have had religious wars, even though they were only between ourselves, between Christian brothers?

Another comparison puts things in perspective: with a population of 9oo million in India, a minority of 4·7% represents almost 45 million Gujarati, and 1.3 % Rajasthani are still 12 million. How modest is our conception of minorities next to those figures - in other countries the dwarfs are bigger.

Obviously, in conditions such as those of India or Nigeria, the demand arises for a language of communication. In these and other cases, it is English.

We have no such solution for mutual comprehension in our country. Or have we? Even if only to a small extent. As we consider ourselves a federal state, we ensure in an egalitarian manner that none of our four languages is given precedence; as a result, we go back to a dead language which, although it inspires nobody, hurts nobody. The English of our federalism is Latin:

CH is the abbreviation for Confoederatio Helvetica, Swiss Confederation. These initials are seen on motor vehicles and appear in front of postal codes as the international symbol for the country. When a national cultural foundation is set up, we call it "Pro Helvetia," and the copyright protection society is named "Pro Litteris." If we think of young people, we choose "Pro Juventute" for the old "Pro Senectute" and for the physically handicapped "Pro Infirmi." The Latin need not always be quite correct, whether it is " Pro Instruct" or "Pro Print." But when it comes to emphasising tradition and a reactionary programme, what could be more appropriate than a dead language, namely "Pro Patria et Familia." But on the banknotes we respect four languages: Schweizerische Nationalbank, Banca Naziunala Svizra, Banque Nationale Suisse, Banca Nazionale Svizzera.

No, the Swiss franc is not a dead currency.

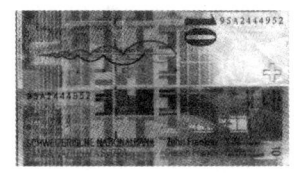

German, French, Italian, Romansh - one country with four languages. This does not correspond to the definition of a nation that was developed at the time of the Romantic Movement and of growing nationalism: one country, one language, one history - leading to the horrible memory of what was to last a thousand years: ***one* empire.**

Switzerland shares three languages with neighbours whose history took a different course, and the history of our own country was not the same for all the linguistic regions.
How little European states themselves abided by their formula for a nation can be seen from the frontiers drawn for ex-colonies, such as African states, which were released into new independence and old tribal feuds.

Switzerland created for its own situation the expression "Willensnation" (nation created by its own will). A self-satisfied formula if it implies that other nations arose purely from natural causes and that no act of will began their history, quite apart from the fact that such a nation depends not only on its own will but also on that of others, if we think for instance of our neutrality and the respect shown for it by the great powers.

What else is the USA if not a "Willensnation," with its fight for independence and its creed in the form of the constitution, even though the expression "WASP" ("White Anglo-Saxon Protestant") has long become irrelevant. One cannot import black slaves and wish to remain white; the Protestant monopoly was broken by the Catholic immigrants from Ireland, Poland and Italy, and in recent decades English speakers have had to make room for the Hispanics, who already represent twenty percent.

Is not every immigrant country a "Willensnation"? What applies to North America is also valid for South America. Being a Brazilian, for instance, means embracing of necessity a community of people which is based ethnically on three races, the Indio, the black and the European, and this last is in turn recruited from several different European origins; in addition there is Asiatic immigration, from which a Japanese and a Korean Brazil have developed.

In one form or another, such cultural heterogeneities must be brought to a common denominator. Language, which is essential for communication, does not guarantee this cohesion, but it is an essential precondition for it: it may be American, that developed out of English, as an expression of the "American way of life." Or Brazilian, that takes its own path in Portuguese, calling it "brasilidade," however "Brazilianness" is defined. "Brazilian, Portuguese with sugar," as a Portuguese writer described it.

The immigrants give us one more variation, since they do not learn to write the language they speak. Usually just for one generation, perhaps longer, depending how much they and their descendants cling to their cultural heritage. Except that for them an Atlantic or a Pacific lies between the spoken and the written language, while for us German-Swiss the separation is the Rhine.

The impurity that we have in mind has to do with foreign words. We are concerned with the impurities in one's own language, with what is considered as impure from the standpoint of a standardised, established language, with impurities in which their origin, whatever it may be, is always audible. Impurity in which the language being created and changed expresses itself, as a token of the attempt to do justice with words to the demands of the present. Impurity also as the individual within an accepted symbiosis, where the individual may be either a single person or a social class, a region or a historical moment.

> Switzerland created for its own situation the expression *"Willensnation"* (nation created by its own will).

It is not so long ago (and sounded anachronistic even then) since Eduardo Mendoza (born 1947) was refused the National Literature Prize for his novel "The City of Wonders," because he did not write "pure" but "Catalanised" Spanish. The way the language and the culture of a country may be allowed to grow apart is demonstrated by the two-volume "Diccionario de literatura española e hispanoamericana." This contains the Spanish-speaking authors of Spain and Hispano-America, as well as Spanish writing authors from the Philippines, Chicanos (Mexican authors in the USA) and Sephardic writers, but no Catalans, Galicians or Basques. For the sake of purity a country is emasculated linguistically. On the other hand, it has long been recognised that there is Spanish-language literature written in Spain, in Hispano-America and in the Antilles, ie. in over twenty countries each with its own history and hence its own linguistic history, whether African influences are detected in Cuba, or Indio in Mexico and the Andean states. This is quite naturally allowed for nowadays by describing translations correctly as being from Argentinian Spanish, or Ecuadorian Spanish, or Chilean Spanish.

In the same way it is appropriate to speak of "literatura de expressão portughesa." Literature in Portuguese is composed in Portugal, Brazil, Angola, Mozambique, São Tomé, Guinea-Bissau and the Cape Verde Islands. And this is done in a Portuguese that differs noticeably from one country to another, and not only when one thinks of the heavily Creolised Portuguese of Cape Verde, where the people played with the idea, after the carnation revolution of 1974, of making Creole their official language. Even for the Portuguese public, glossaries are essential. "7 vozes" is just a first draft for a more comprehensive Lusitanian dictionary of the "seven voices," the seven variants of Portuguese.

In France as well, the term "littérature d'expression française" has been created for works from France, Belgium, Switzerland and Canada, in the Antilles and in North Africa—no longer just "française" but "francophone".

Would it not then also be correct and useful to speak, perhaps of "literature of German expression," but at least of "German-language literature," which is "written in the Federal Republic, in Austria and in Switzerland"; a chapter could be added to the list on Prague and all the places where exiled authors continue to write in the language of those who banished them.

Any discussion on these lines comes up against the same difficulty, since German, French, Spanish or Portuguese are both national/political and linguistic/cultural terms. One could imagine that in the future, with an increasing devaluation of the national, there will be a change of meaning or a shift in importance so that what is national in the political sense yields first place to the cultural. For the present, however, we must allow for the ambiguity that implies a German author is of German nationality as well as of German expression. This could be made clearer: just as we speak of francophone, anglophone or lusophone, it makes sense, although it is complicated, to say not simply "German" but "German-speaking."

In recent decades, the view has gained ground that High German cannot be a standard language, valid absolutely and inflexibly for all who speak German. "German belongs also to the Swiss and the Austrians," was the slogan of the philologist Ulrich Ammon. And perhaps it is not purely by chance that in Austria a basic analysis was published, "The German language in a changing world," by Michael Clyne.

Should we then speak of "Swiss-type German" and "Austrian-type German?" This sounds like emancipation. But at the same time a new problem appears, the concern that the characterisation "Swiss" or "Austrian" represents a questionable manner of specifying nationality.

Firstly, the German spoken in Germany, and reflected in the written language, has just as little homogeneity as there is one "Swiss High German." Attention has been drawn with advantage to the "internal multilingual nature of German," or more generally the "heterogeneity of natural languages." Linguistics has become "variant linguistics."

Moreover, should a Swiss writing in German write "Swiss High German"? However much his linguistic origin may be traceable in his German, is it not rather the case that his linguistic choice is made according to different criteria? If an author is writing a narrative text which describes a specific period in a specific milieu, local and regional influences will have a different urgency and appropriateness than if the author is engaged on a work of non-fiction. In an essay, a scientific treatise or a philosophical discussion, no Helvetian

colour is necessary. The journalist, for his part, will use the familiar vocabulary much more readily than the hymn writer in whose verses a Helvetism might be out of place. In the words of modern linguistics: the variants of a language are determined by situative, functional or regional-local criteria. The decision is one of style and not of origin.
The tension between Swiss colloquial usage and the standard language is just one variation of a more basic problem. Neither ideologising the vernacular nor allowing the standard language to dictate orthodoxy will reduce this tension. The choice of language used for writing results from an intellectual decision regarding style; this choice does not remove the conflict, but renders it fruitful.

There is a difference between the standard language, demanding indisputable authority, and the standard stable, having an exercise ground for linguistic freedom of movement. To the extent that the standard language reflects a general cultural situation, the concepts of edge and centre become superfluous, and instead of a vertical hierarchy, linguistic variants can simultaneously exist horizontally, side by side.

In the discussion of linguistic pluralism, the Anglo-Saxon situation is usually mentioned, the existence side by side of English and American. It is all the more important to refer to this, since it appears that the language of international communication in future will be Anglo-Saxon - English or American? American that has developed its own version of English and nowadays sticks up for Plain English, and that oscillates between Black English and the campus English of the universities? British English? In no other country does the spoken language so decisively define social standing and education as in England. "Pygmalion" is a play that could only be written for the British stage. But "My Fair Lady" is at the same time the farewell performance of the one and only correct English. The Anglo-Saxon world family, from Canada to India and from the Antilles to India, speaks anything but one common English. In England the writers are no longer only those who attended public schools, but also those who learned in the street.

Now someone who speaks English poorly will hardly ever be corrected by an Englishman; how can you expect proper English from "continentals". If the same speaker uses his horrible English in the USA, the American will say "You have a nice accent." Our future will have a nice accent. It would be great if you would allow me the testimonial "As a Swiss author you have a nice accent."

MARIELLA MEHR

THE EYE OF THETIS

Translated from the German by Maria Schoenhammer

On May 4th, 1960, Rosa Zwiebelbuch, still a bit shy, was standing in the studio of the eyemaker Adolf Stauch, a buckskin in her hand and a vat full of water at her feet. Through the open window the noise of Seifertgasse drifted into the room—people hastening by, tripping along, clomping, laughing, chatting, calling, joking and singing, yelling and coughing. Fragments of music came from the house across the street, the animal house, Così Fan Tutte, she could understand "Amoooohohohore." At the window, the figure of a man appeared, strangely dressed, a fully-grown man stuffed into a boy's brown uniform. At the right arm he wore a black band with a swastika which Rosa found ominous. Didn't Father Zwiebelbuch have an entire box full of this kind of cross in his attic, and didn't he rummage around in there once in a while, talking about a "betrayed future"; and kneeling in the dust, he would pour tears on it—something he otherwise never did. He must be a traveler, Rosa contemplated, someone who misses his wife. With contempt she scrutinized the faded brown of his attire. She and the master would be spared of his company, someone like that walks the world with empty pockets and passes through Seifertgasse without any spare change.

Rosa Zwiebelbuch had set out early to fulfill her new duties after a night of dreamless sleep at the Blue Angel, a rooming house Master Stauch had recommended warmly because, for the amenities offered, the monthly rent seemed appropriate to him and he actually planned on paying it. Rosa could not yet comprehend what freedom felt like, having hardly tasted it. Without regret she thought about the farewell from her father that hadn't taken place. He had returned to the cage she had shared with him for eighteen years. Grimly, Rosa Zwiebelbuch wrung out the buckskin over the vat. Freedom—she wanted to take advantage of it, diligently and thoroughly.

The eyes, these artificial eyes. Treasures, adornments, truths, signs of God and beauty. Rosa cast an eye into paradise, and ate of the apple handed to her by Adolf Stauch. She had always known the snake was of another sex. Rosa endured happiness.

She must not take her eyes off Adolf Stauch's house. She circled around it, again and again, looking for the high narrow gable of the house, inhaling the new air through her nose. She made her rounds without Father Zwiebelbuch. In his socket Adolf Stauch had put in the eye with the leaden sea and the Hundred-Armed One. In silence Father Zwiebelbuch had then taken the basket with the preserves, the cold chicken, and the bread made by the wailing and moaning Anna Zwiebelbuch. He had taken his basket in silence and left the realm of Adolf Stauch. He took the night train. Without having extended his hand to Rosa. Sullenly he sat in the murky compartment. Left the foreign country. At customs he met the man in the dark raincoat and took the train that the man in the dark raincoat had taken before. With a gloomy look on his face he sat down in the murky compartment and went back to the morass that was his home.

On the evening of her arrival Adolf Stauch had thoroughly introduced Rosa to the secrets of his dainty cabinets. There they were, cradled in silvery bowls: the glass eyes, a collection of the finest craftsmanship from which the creator did not want to part. Eye after eye was entrusted to Rosa's hands, to Rosa's wide hands, for her to feel the eyes, the flawless glass, with the skillfully shaped iris and the legends in the depths of the pupils.

Moments like these are not suitable for babbling on about ideas of time and space, they are timeless. In moments like these even Rosa had all of life in front of her and all of death. It would change later on, gifts are not made for eternity. Otherwise how could we manage, what with the limited space up there where a visa will no longer admit you to eternal glory and where warranty cards even for the most necessary transfigurations are extremely rare.

In moments like these—Rosa felt it only vaguely—we get an advance on supreme happiness, no matter how much the priest is railing and preaching about price increases as if heaven were a pay-envelope. In Rosa's hands the eyes came to life gently; not wanting to scare her, they whispered and murmured, lest some cruel sound should disrupt Rosa's happiness. Her deplorably abused past fell off her and with it her lodger Zwiebelbuch who had left behind her body as a rather blighted garret. That too shall pass, it whispered gently in Rosa's hands, soon that room will be cleaned up and Zwiebelbuch's shadow gone. The eyes didn't say that someone else was already waiting to move into the garret, in short order she should have sheets and a chamber pot ready. No, the eyes in Rosa's hands were whispering stories as if to provide her with shield and sword but did not give away the coordinates for Rosa's future. The artificial eye knows neither mathematics nor tea leaves by which to prophesy.

Each eye had a name engraved in its silver bowl, a name which amazed and delighted Rosa. She had never heard more melodious names. In her hometown the women were called Claudia, Lilo, Liliane, Silvia, Margrit, Ursula, or Maria, some were called Rosa like herself, or Gertrud, Verena, and Hildegard. No unpleasant names for sure. For example, to be called Silvia, meaning wood nymph, Rosa considered an honor she certainly would not have dared to claim for herself. Or Ursula, the she-bear. What strength would inspire the bearer of that name.

> THE EYES IN ROSA'S HANDS WERE WHISPERING STORIES AS IF TO PROVIDE HER WITH SHIELD AND SWORD BUT DID NOT GIVE AWAY THE COORDINATES FOR ROSA'S FUTURE. THE ARTIFICIAL EYE KNOWS NEITHER MATHEMATICS NOR TEA LEAVES BY WHICH TO PROPHESY.

But these names, slightly flowery letters engraved in the silver bowls, seemed to Rosa more beautiful than any names she knew. They were adornments in themselves, equal to any of the treasures Adolf Stauch had created. They jubilated on the tongue when rehearsed, they rolled over the lips like pearls, even when your name was Rosa and you weren't particularly inclined towards poetry. They enticed, cooed, and twittered as they were pronounced. At first a little haltingly Rosa did so, and then as she calmed down, fluently. The names caressed the women, that's how it seemed to Rosa who could not pronounce the names often enough, could not murmur and whisper them often enough. After reveling in the foreign sounds for quite a while, she took a closer look at the eyes: the eye of Leda, wife of Tyndareus of Sparta. Unfolded like a willing flower on the shore of the Eurotas river, the white swan in her arms, and her chaste face hidden in the animal's plumage, she has given herself to the huge bird. In the depths of the pupil, Leda's lust had been rendered miraculously by a delicate hand. As Rosa looked into this sweet abyss, a hardly perceivable sigh broke the silence in the sanctuary of the eyemaker Adolf Stauch who patiently stood next to Rosa, watching attentively the changing expressions that graced her face.

There were many names: Europa, the beautiful child on the back of the bull, racing jubilantly across the sea with him to receive his seed on the shores of Crete.

The artist endowed her with a proud face which openly expressed her lust and her exultance in surrendering to this lust which—so it seemed to Rosa—would never end. In gigantic waves the frothy sea surged over the shores. Insatiable is the greed of the bull and insatiable is the greed of the child. In the depths of Europa's pupil the earth holds its breath.

And Alkmene, wife of brave Amphytrion. Her magnificent body rests on the royal sheets of the bed from which someone rose who wasn't her husband. The lascivious curves of her body, brilliantly depicted by the artist, spoke of a great triumph, won just a moment ago, incomparably greater than any victory won on a battle field, so it seemed to Rosa. She trembled while her narrow eyes rested on the bottom of the pupil where the desires and the beginnings in Alkemene's belly were in unison.

But there was also Io, the unhappy one, the daughter of an Argive king. Io, the name melted on Rosa's tongue, Io, the punished one who, beset by madness, stormed over the pasture as a white cow, pursued by Argos of the Hundred Eyes. Black is the abyss in the golden iris, difficult to discern there the fleeing animal, its woman's memory preserved by an almighty avenger. Io suffers from an unappeasable desire for the one who rode her.

Under tears Rosa parted with the treasure and turned to the next one. Adolf Stauch called this eye Danae, Danae, the daughter of the ruler of Argos. Imprisoned in the dark dungeon and fastened to heavy iron shackles, she receives the golden rain that the gates cannot keep away, soothingly streaming into the woman's melancholy until the dungeon becomes a holy shrine.

Rosa beheld eye after eye, amazed, confused and yet joyful in the act of feeling. Never had she seen anything like this in her poor life as the daughter of the itinerant butcher Zwiebelbuch, who knew how to strike with a steady hand and whom Anna Zwiebelbuch, née Lamm, never again received in her female quarters after the birth of her daughter.

The wounds healed under the gaze of Adolf Stauch. He patiently stood by her and accompanied her first, tentative steps into a new life. Ignorant Rosa did not notice that there was someone hiding behind the lust in the abysses of the pupils, someone missing, someone who wasn't a swan or golden rain, and who wasn't a bull either although even today quite a few want you to believe this, sometimes white, sometimes black, sometimes brown or dun. Rosa fell victim to this deception like so many women before her, whose fate of bearing sons catches up with them in the supposedly most blissful hours. Deception is when golden rain pours down or when a swan's plumage brushes ever so gently against a hot cheek, when the bull, lecherous and cheerful, swims towards the green shores of Crete, the child on his back exultant and shouting with joy when the animal enters the young flesh. Adolf Stauch did not dare to show that, under the plane-trees on the beach of Crete, the bull revealed himself as the Unaccountable One as Laughter itself, under the dome of the sky. He did not dare to show the resounding laughter that makes the earth tremble and that crushes any love. That would have been the pain in the depths of every eye, and had Adolf Stauch expressed this pain, there would have been an escape. As was, only Atropos, the Inevitable, stood at the side of Rosa Zwiebelbuch's road; Clotho was missing, the spinner to whom we owe the balance between good luck and bad luck, as was Lachesis, who allots incidents of suffering and happiness to every man and woman as is due.

> **IGNORANT ROSA DID NOT NOTICE THAT THERE WAS SOMEONE HIDING BEHIND THE LUST IN THE ABYSSES OF THE PUPILS...**

When Rosa Zwiebelbuch had carefully put Danae's eye back into the silver bowl, the eyemaker Adolf Stauch opened the last window of the dainty little chest. Behind the window were eyes which, still innocent and white, awaited the artist's hand of Adolf Stauch.

The virginal curves of the eyes scared Rosa, but cautiously yet firmly Adolf Stauch put one of these bowls in her wide hand. She was to keep it as a gift. Thetis: the name seemed to Rosa Zwiebelbuch even more melodious than the name of any other eye. Thetis: a cut diamond among women's names. Thetis, the sea goddess, who was before her and who patiently waited for Rosa to come into being so that her fate would come true.

But Rosa Zwiebelbuch did not know anything of this fate, innocent in her mind and unspoiled by knowledge, she took the eye by the name of Thetis, cradled it in her hand, in her wide hand. Tired from looking and from the silence which now heavily weighed on the things in the room, she noticed the onset of dusk and wondered how she could take her leave without disrupting the silence which seemed to her of another world.

Adolf Stauch advised her to go to the Blue Angel where the rent wasn't outrageous and the beds clean, he would take care of the rent as part of her monthly salary and of her breakfast as well, for her other meals she would have to pay herself. It would be fine with him if she started her working day at half-past seven. Rosa noticed that Adolf Stauch used a pleasantly old-fashioned language, even for every-day things, a little stilted maybe, earnestly articulating each word as if even words were treasures.

Pierre Imhasly

Switzerland is Different for the Swiss, Or: It Should at Least Be Said

Translated from the German by Breon Mitchell

The Italians cart off the shit
                        and war is war
say Helvetian leagues
obligingly
in times of peace
    and &
post coitum triste
                        as if it were true

Since we stood before Christmas trees
resentment in our hearts
calling God a good fellow
the newspaper
slipped slightly
to the right
along with
pope
Americans
Bolsheviks
And when Uncle Ueli
Was no longer surprised
by any of this
they beat him to death
the black man
                        because he wasn't Swiss
Because he wasn't Swiss
they beat him to death
and then another

The good children were already asleep
The fish slept in the pond

Two or three of us
went out
for a quick beer

                         Himmelarseandendanigga

Death is sweet
if one has lived innocently
    and
Whom God takes soon
receives a boon
    and
Throw the foreign workers out
    and
Let us be increasingly
free
Swiss

> They come crowded in
> they leave crowded out
> and in between they fumble
> with laced-up baggage

They turn
in vain
toward girls
the blacks

Even at work they sing
good Lord
it can't be true
muratori
carry cathedrals in their heads
that's not a particularly
                         pleasant sight
In the land of mules tracks
legs are what count

what counts are legs

Some of them
remained
beneath bulldozers
in drill shafts
blown off

    A pleasant sight

It makes them agreeable
even if this is one thing
and death another
It's not an unpleasant sight
to see them come crowded in
and quietly pass away

fumbling all the while
with laced-up baggage

even if death
is one thing
and this
another

If I could forget the thorn in the flesh
if I had the southern blood
of the ill-treated on the scaffolds
If the birds
of Saint Francis
would fly
roasted into my mouth
If I could walk barefoot
in the dew
If the earth

would close over me
Would absorb
and dissolve me
If like the wind
I
could cover the mare
of polite arrogance
If I could be the whale
and spit
Jonah out onto land
and if the miracle occurred:

hey-ho ye who rut
and ho-hey you who strut
of Swiss confederate mercy
I would slaughter
the sow of recent Swiss history
I would blow raw sugar up the ass
of the farters and fizzlers
in the immigration police

Torquemadas* in Switzerland
I'd give them an incubus
Give them a succubus
Bed sores dead sores
Flagellators holy tongue-lashers
Give them fornicating demons
Give them fornicated demons
Witch duckings chopping stools paper clips inventory
Give them calumniators
add a fair dose of pesticides
to the pious milk
of their inhuman
compound interest mind set

The shit
is carted off by the Italians
and war is war
and &
post coitum triste

* Thomas de Torquemada (1420-98). Ordo praedicatorum. *Lived
to the age of seventy-eight and continued to serve as Inquisitor until he died.*

Thou Art a Worm in Quasar Dust, And What's More Down the Drain

aya!
The old Nausicaa tramway
ominous star of Cassiopeia
above swans sylphids salamanders and newts
aya Andromeda
bast or bamboo perhaps
bending in the wind
ten thousand feet above godforsakenness

In ye olde fatherland
Guapa
no trace of Manolete
in ye olde fatherland
no imperium
not for Tuaregs from Haar
ten thousand feet beneath godforsakenness

And no trace of good will   high spirits or even
2 for 1 grand lit fast & pleasant between cities
may Death Boredom and Saint Stupidity grant it

So let them do it
to our submerged Thailand
Europe   the Atlantides

So let them do it
till the trees only die
and what counts
are legs

Let them work their way as they will
catatonic
and with insane ill humor
from catastrophe to cataclysm

Just let it be

Yet plunge into me
sundew
your fandango of sorrow
carnivorous
with tentacle tongues
deep
beneath my petrified heart

You Have to See Them In Context

From peak to peak
above the neutral cow pastures
rings out the call to prayer

Here on this pasture a golden calf
With its beloved profitamother and dearly beloved double indemnity
Ave profitamother   ave profitamother   ave profitamother ave
And the most dearly beloved Herr Capital-Coefficient
protect and preserve all that is ours in this pasture

May our local Death Boredom grant it and Saint
Death To Others

May Saint Death to Others console us
with arms racketeering on current account
May Death Boredom grant it and Saint Monetary Parity
may Death by Installments grant it
and Saint SDOD*
and all anti-aircraft artillery and firing ranges
of Saint Quick Death to all
May Saint Numbered Account grant it and Saint Stupidity
May they grant this and that
thus and thus

che vadano farsi benedire tutti quanti
    or
sub specie aeternitatis
the devil dumping
filthy lucre on the same old pile

What does your pain have to say about that
Pope & anti-Pope

testiculos habent
et bene pendentes

Yet it is to be hoped
no Kamasutra
will ever again stir up lust
in the emptied ox-butts
since from archives gutted by fire
ajaxclear as if invisible
Hitler's women
    then was he/wasn't he
polished mummy bones   scoured
whiter than white
newly gleaming

what shall we do
with the drunken soldiers
or

the devil dumping
filthy lucre on the same pile
or

overkilling
intra muros

Let them mount
to heaven
alone
facing backwards
with crooked swords
on wooden
dynamited hobby horses
middle-men and advocates
of a *tabula rasa*

Let them for mercy's sake
leave us in peace
out of it
alone
with the inner logic
of black shawls
we who have got over it
Siguiriyas
con arte y duende
don't need the crippling foxtrot
of their eccentric intercession

Spare us please on the day of reckoning
your preheated consumer graves
build your cheery cemeteries
in the disparate sign of Carayas
eat your fill of fodder
as long as it's raining chicken feed
stop taking shelter

spick and span
behind the nutritional edemas
of the third world

Arabic sheiks
Use Arabic numerals
in plain English:
They've got you praying again

Yet no Kamasutra
will ever again stir up lust
in your dangling dollar bags
The full trough
in deep freeze
pious fetish
at times
of hierarchical righteousness
offside behind and   *in the corner*

In a decline
the fence and steal and burgle business
with the souvenir Son of Man
and that wasn't all

And that wasn't all
candied thomist cathedrals
were knocked down to the highest bidder
on synodic orders
and that wasn't all   old wine
in new Plexiglas

Plastic ex votos
of Aristotle's epigones
no longer wanted by anyone

forced sale at auction
holy water   oral images   *malocchio*

And that wasn't all
Couple your mercy with an anti-tank gun
while there is still time
just give us will you
*forfai*t
for a few days
please don't announce in advance
when you'll turn out the light
for the night of the long scythes

Stay near to those
who know nothing
of your witch trials
serve up in golden bowls
the hors-d'oeuvre of time's end
brush crocodile tears
from choleric cheeks
into the dished-out ostracism
of your assembled entourage

à toute volée
spit the great NADA
of your estate
into the labyrinthine ear

*Swiss Department of Defense

Laurent Schweizer
from NASO LITURATUS

Translated from the French by Gilles Plante

I stayed for a moment on the pink carpet in front of the hotel. A pink-panther carpet in the cold air of a late afternoon. I sneezed without being able to decide, in spite of my light clothing, to leave the hotel steps.

I hadn't come to this hotel by chance. I was here on Rita's advice with a recommendation to the management as a photographer for their new flyer. Although the building had been entirely renovated, no suggestion had been made to take outside snapshots of the façades, but no doubt had they thought of hiring a talented photographer for that. Perhaps there was even an older photograph that they simply wanted to use in the new edition. Frankly speaking, I didn't care anymore about the reasons for their decision.

Around eight o'clock, a hotel employee had come to pick me up in a service minivan. Together, we had loaded and unloaded my equipment, agreeing that I would store it in one of the garage lock-ups after shooting, in case I would have to return to take additional pictures. A secretary had introduced me very rapidly to the manager before escorting me to the basement, while explaining to me that we ought to start with the swimming pool. Heating had stopped during the night, but it was out of the question to skip the swimming pool where a new bar had been installed during renovations.

There I was, arranging my flashes and umbrellas by the curving pool, with my feet all wrapped up—the secretary had insisted upon doing it herself—in two transparent plastic bags. The mint-green water and the mosaic border seemed to be playing in my favor, allowing me to set some kind of halo where I was hoping to flood the two actors who were still lingering in their dressing rooms. The staff (two barmaids, a swimming instructor and a towel girl) had already started to show some signs of impatience, when a male model in a dressing gown approached the pool side. Sensing that nothing would happen for the time being, he had sit down stirring the water surface with the tip of his toes.

Finally, the manager's secretary had come out of the dressing room with Zooey (as she called her). The girl was half-smiling, obviously upset to appear in a black bikini that left her almost completely bare. Perhaps was she feeling that it was a mistake to choose her for the flyer. Perhaps was she merely hating her own breasts—those of a deceptively skinny woman—her stern face or the excess of red lipstick they had inflicted upon her. However, she immediately dipped in the water up to her waist and started to make quick movements with her arms as she moved towards the halo beam of my apparatus. She had decided not to stay there, preferring to swim or to stand up and to walk a few meters across the bottom of the pool whenever she could get her own depth again. I hadn't been able to resolve myself early enough to distract her from her swim and to ask her to move closer to her partner in order for him to hold her for a moment in his arms.

I had waited so long that the scene never took place, and everything quickly collapsed when the model's agent demanded that his protégé be allowed to disappear under a makeshift shower activated by a generator used on construction sites.

The second sequence, around the golf simulator, didn't happen either, after the makeup man had noted justly so that the grass had not been installed yet. Following the secretary's instructions, we had immediately proceeded to the Rotonde de Staël.

In front of a 1954 beach, some young boys had set a table for two and placed large seafood platters adorned with algae, lemon and a deluge of sauces. Zooey had come to join Cyrus. He wearing a tuxedo, she a matador suit. The staging hadn't enticed her to go beyond the minimum requirements of her role. She hadn't paid any attention to my apparatus, and she kept staring at the eyes of the shrimp she was holding between her fingers. I liked that, and I would have used my whole roll of film at that very moment, if the waiter captain hadn't proposed to finish up the champagne and to take a break. Zooey was interested then by the paintings she had seen before from a distance, as she examined them one by one and let their reflection appear on the bottom of an ashtray.

After the bedrooms (he and she in a double room, she alone in the living room of a suite), it was agreed that we would take the last shots at the hotel bar. The hairdressers had argued together, but had finally decided to undo Zooey's *chignon* and let her hair fall freely on her shoulders then wrapped in a tulip-shaped gown. She had come forward and was sitting at the bar. Once again, I had neglected to take full views, limiting my shots to the stern features of her face and remaining insensitive to the movements of her forearms relentlessly reaching for the peanut bowl.

"NASO LITERATUS: BRIGHTLY COLORED FISH, ALSO KNOWN AS SURGEONFISH DUE TO THEIR RAZOR-LIKE SPINES AT THE BASE OF THEIR BODIES, LIPSTICK TANG DUE TO THE RED OUTLINE OF THEIR LIPS, OR SMOOTH-HEAD UNICORN FISH IN REFERENCE TO THE HORNS WHICH OCCASIONALLY PROTRUDE FROM THEIR FOREHEADS. NASO LITERATUS USUALLY LIVE IN PAIRS."

Christian Uetz

from *Nichte*

Translated from the German by Kristin T. Schnider

Seit Descartscher Gewissheit,
seit Kantscher Freiheit,
seit Hegelheideggerscher Hirnhitlerei
sitzt die Sinnbesessenheit im Satanssattel
des Seins selbst. Im Selbst selbst.
Intensivst indes ists immer ich
im irre innersten Identitäts Ideidioten Ideal.

Komm, grosser Esel, lächerlicher.
Lache dein linderndlustiges,
leb Leid lieb Leib losendes,
dein lösungslallendes Loblied.

Esel du Esel du
Engel du.

Ever since Descartian certainty
Kantian liberty
brainy Hegelheideggerian hitlering
possession with purpose sat straddling the satanic saddle
of existence itself. Even inside the self itself.
Most intensive, however, there is I forever
within the insane innermost identical idea idiot ideal.

come oh great ass, oh laughable one
laugh your merrily mollifying
loosening—yea suffering, yea body—
laudation of yours, lallation of

you ass you
angel you

Mundterre (Moonterre)

1.
(Lalls Laffe:) Geh nie Alls Affe.
Nur wenn ich dich schaffe; nur wenn du mich schaffst;
Scharfst dus Lichtscht; lichsch ichs schharf.
Kann mich das ehrnden?
(Sind Gehrdichte zu shehr Vhöhghell?)
Laufe ich hirnreifssend auf hirnriffssigen Lichtzerguss?
Blitzt dies kein fährreckendes Enghellszucken?
Kein sternbiges Gebähren?
Wenn du reissnen Herngstzens wiewärst wieherst:
Gehwieerr; Gewieherr.

Mouthearth (Moonterre)

1.
Babble pompous baboon: but never go
all out as universal ape
unless I create
defeat you;
unless you
defeat
create me;
if you should manage to sharpen the light—shush; I shall light—shush—a
sheep a sharp harp.
Would that bring harvest, bring honour to me?
Desirable poems going densely, honourably are they too much, too lofty, like
birds, bright in height—
are they?
Am I running brainwise mature and delightful, into failure
tearing towards a crackbrained reef into a torn discharge of light?
No lightening? No warrior on a ferry, stretching the perishing angel's tight
bright twitching?
No starryily dying bah-bearing behaviour?
If you rippingst pure and most studly hearted you would be well neigh what
neighing:
neighing—go like him
neighing—go like a lord.

CHRISTIAN UETZ

From *Nichte und andere Gedichte*

Translated from the German by Kristin T. Schnider

Nichte.
Ein Nicht ist nicht.
1 Normen

Niece Nothing.
A nothing is not .
1 Norms

"und dänn chunt bim rede
immer au s rede sälber is rede
als rede rede rede
drum isch doch de vorgang vom rede so wichtig
als tuur vo zunge und lippe samt zäh und rache
mir schwiizer sind ja bekannt defür
das mer bim rede so gärn dä rache chützeled
das ali andere völker s gfühl hend
mir heged zäme mit dä holländer
e chuchichäschtlichi halschrankhet
und drum isch s rede au niä bloss rede
sondern immer au küsse büsse malme fletsche fleddere
hechle schtöhne süfze
immmer isch im wort ä gmüëtsglogge
äs schtimmigsgwitter
ä wältgewieher
en all gelall"*

Und dann kommt beim Reden
immer das Reden selber ins Reden
als Reden Reden Reden
darum ist doch der Vorgang des Redens so wichtig
als Tour von Zunge und Lippe samt Zähnen und Rachen
wir Schweizer sind ja bekannt dafür
dass wir beim Reden so gerne den Rachen kitzeln
dass alle anderen Völker das Gefühl haben
wir hätten zusammen mit den Holländern
und deshalb ist das Reden auch nie nur Reden
sondern immer auch Küssen Beissen Malmen Fletschen Fleddern
    Hecheln Stöhnen
immer ist im Wort eine Gemütsglocke
ein Stimmungsgewitter
ein Weltgewieher
ein Allgelall.

and when talking
talking itself comes to be talked about
talking as talking talking talking
that is why the act of talking is so important
as a tour of tongue and lips, teeth and throat
we Swiss are known for being so fond of
tickling our throats while speaking
that all other peoples are under the impression that
we share a disease—raw hoarse coarse throats—with the Dutch
and that's why talking is never just talking but also
kissing biting mashing snarling plundering panting moaning
always there is within a word a mind' s bell moodily clanking
a tempestuos temperament's storm
a whole world's neighing
universal babble

*Swiss German, adapted from a recorded reading; translated into Standard German and English

Frank Presidential Interview Series

Ruth Dreifuss
talks about
SWISS CULTURE

Frank: *It is difficult to understand the complexities of contemporary Swiss culture outside Switzerland. As Minister of Culture, which Switzerland or Switzerlands do you wish to present or promote internationally? How do you view a country of such cultural and linguistic diversity?*

Dreifuss: Culture is an important and largely uncontroversial value in Swiss society. The fact that we have three national and four official languages respectively in Switzerland makes it even more important. These languages represent different cultural areas which in turn overlap with those of other European peoples. Far from wanting to homogenize its discrete linguistic blocs, Switzerland wants to preserve their distinct identity, while at the same time promoting more cultural exchange and greater tolerance of other cultures, whether in Switzerland or elsewhere. I am particularly anxious to foster exchange programmes involving the various cultures that exist within Switzerland. Yet the state can never be more than a facilitator and sponsor. It must not interfere or presume to define what is good or bad. There is no such thing as official culture in Switzerland!

Cultural exchanges between Switzerland and other countries are not only a source of vitality, but are also enriching for both Switzerland and its partners. Countries which do not cultivate cultural contacts with foreign cultures cannot develop. Whenever Swiss artists have an opportunity to show both their own creativity and originality and Switzerland's heterogeneity abroad, this helps promote Switzerland's overall image too.

Frank: *What challenges are you faced with as both Minister of Home Affairs and Minister of Culture? Do these portfolios clash or complement each other? You are probably the only minister in the world to hold both jobs at the same time.*

Dreifuss: I like to call the Ministry of Home Affairs "le département de la vie quotidienne": In other words, it concerns itself with every aspect of people's daily lives. Everyone in our country is bound to come into contact at some point in their lives with such home affairs ssues as social security, health, education and research, equal rights and culture. Of course it is not always easy to juggle all these things at once, although many of them actually complement each other. Culture is obviously an integral part of this wide range of issues and that for two reasons—firstly because it is always a good idea to remember that man cannot live from bread alone, and secondly because culture is a good antidote to the 'every man for himself' mentality which is the main threat to social cohesion.

Frank: *What, in your view, is the role of the writer in Swiss society today? And elsewhere in the world?*

Dreifuss: Octavio Paz once said that a writer is not "the representative, the deputy or the mouthpiece of a class, a country, or a church." This was his indirect response to the claim that literature has a social function. Literature can of course mean resistance, defiance or interference in politics or it may even seek merely to draw attention to a certain situation. Among the most famous contemporary examples of such politically-aware writers are Günter Grass, Alexander Solzhenitsyn, Gabriel Garcia Marquez and Nadine Gordimer, or in Switzerland writers such as Max Frisch, Friedrich Dürrenmatt, Alice Rivaz and Peter Bichsel.

This kind of "interference" is reflected in the wide range of topics Swiss literature addresses, including the integration of immigrants, the country's role in modern Europe and economic developments—both good and bad. It also grapples with history—national and/or private history—and with the writer's own direct experience of life. One leitmotif of 20th century Swiss literature, namely what Karl Schmid called the *Unbehagen im Kleinstaat* or "the disquiet of life in a small state," has frequently been analysed in great depth. Switzerland is depicted as narrow-minded, provincial, egocentric and greedy—a jaded view which has driven many an artist to flee across the border. At the same time, Switzerland has often provided a refuge for authors who can no longer live safely in their own countries. Even today, many of the books published in Switzerland are written by authors who are not Swiss, meaning there is a kind of *imported* political dimension to our culture as well.

Frank: *Do writers and artists have social responsibilities going beyond those of the average citizen?*

Dreifuss: It would be unfair to expect more of our writers and artists than of anyone else. After all, their most important job is to be creative. The fact remains, however, that what makes many works of art so special is the way in which they expose certain social and political developments. Writers and artists function as the extremely sensitive seismographs and communicators which society simply cannot afford to do without.

Frank: *But is it really the job of the Swiss government to support arts and culture? I am sure you are aware of how limited the role of the U.S. government is when it comes to the arts. How does this contrast with the Swiss concept of state-sponsored culture?*

Dreifuss: It is the job of the federal government to support culture, mainly by financing specific projects and individual artists. Pro Helvetia is an independent foundation set up precisely for this purpose. The most far-reaching support, however, is that provided at local level, by Switzerland's municipalities and cities, which provide funding for theatres, orchestras, museums and the like. Then there are the efforts of the cantonal governments, to say nothing of various patrons and sponsors. The Federal Office of Culture is responsible for arts administration at the national level, which basically means providing support for a number of umbrella organizations as well as being involved in the preservation of the country's national monuments and listed buildings and in the promotion of Swiss cinema. Plans to give the state greater resources and powers with which to promote the arts have twice been rejected—once in a 1986 referendum and again in 1994. Where Switzerland is concerned, therefore, the term 'state-sponsored' has to be interpreted in a very federalist sense.

Frank: *As a native French speaker, do you find it particularly challenging having to spread your official attention equally among Switzerland's four cultures?*

Dreifuss: I may be a native speaker of French, but my parents originally came from German-speaking Switzerland and I myself worked in an Italian-speaking area for a while and enjoy travelling to all parts of the country. I would also like to add that I live in a neighbourhood in which over 100 different nationalities live together in peace and harmony. As Minister of Culture, I greatly appreciate this diversity and enjoy visiting cultural events in all kinds of places.

Frank: *How does your particular background add to your understanding of your job— in terms of language, culture, religion and gender, for example?*

Dreifuss: Without any doubt the fountain of my political action is to be found in my experience of exclusion: as a woman involved in politics and the trade union movement, French-speaking, of Jewish origin, I have first-hand experience of what it means to be in a minority.

Frank: *Can you tell us something about gender in Swiss culture? Do Swiss women have to contend with any particular disadvantages—or advantages even? What have they contributed to Swiss art and literature? Does tradition have a stabilizing effect on society or is it an obstacle to the evolution of creativity?*

Dreifuss: While not every female author in Switzerland can expect either the Europe-wide renown of a Germaine de Staël or the enduring success of a Johanna Spyri, it would be equally wide of the mark to describe women's writing in Switzerland as 'The Language of Silence'—which was the title of a recent American dissertation on this subject. Women writers can now avail themselves of an infrastructure tailored to their specific needs, meaning bookstores and libraries for women's literature, women's publishers and publishing houses headed by women, such as the Editions Zoë and Editions Metropolis. There are conferences on women's literature, exhibitions and networks enabling women writers and readers to communicate. But what is true of other countries also holds true for Switzerland: No matter whether you are a man or a woman, the purpose of writing is to be read, if possible by both men and women.

The history of literature written by Swiss women over the past 70 years is the history of their emancipation from conventional patterns of thinking. Even in the late 1930s, there were authors in French-speaking Switzerland such as S. Corinna Bille, Catherine Colomb, Alice Rivaz and Monique Saint-Hélier who worked professionally and were not afraid to venture into new literary terrain. And the more the role of women in Swiss society has changed, the more the existence of female writers has become a matter of course. These days, Swiss literature would be inconceivable without our women writers, who after all account for about one third of all the regularly published authors whose works are read, discussed and reviewed.

Frank: *Much of the international news about Switzerland just recently has been concerned with its role in history and above all its institutional conduct during World War II. As both Culture Minister and Home Affairs Minister, you must be particularly sensitive to these questions of historical fact and public image. Do you have either an official or indeed a personal view (or both) as to how Switzerland should clean up its image, and can the dissemination of Swiss art and literature help change the way the world views Switzerland?*

Dreifuss: Despite all the doubts and insecurity to which this process might have given rise, I myself view our grappling with the period 1933 to 1945 and the post-war years primarily as an opportunity.

It is an opportunity for us to face what happened head on, and to analyse and explain the causal relationships. Switzerland is being called upon to remember its past and this is a job not only for our politicians, but also for our schools, our universities and our political organizations too. Yet it is also an eminently literary process. While what the past tells us and teaches us undoubtedly belongs both in the history books and in the reports of the various special international expert commissions set up to examine this period, it also belongs in works of literature, which depict, condense and elucidate the past on quite a different level from history per se, as well as exposing possible causes and missed opportunities. Literature can indeed make a significant contribution to the battle against racism, intolerance, discrimination and violence just as it can proactively promote the principles of democracy, tolerance and respect for human dignity. One of the jobs of cultural policy is to ensure that such efforts are publicized abroad too, especially via the channels opened up by cultural exchange programmes and dialogue.

Frank: *Perhaps you can point us to some of the most interesting cultural projects that Swiss artists have worked on, or are working on now, with or without your ministry's support?*

Dreifuss: Two highly acclaimed exhibitions of works by Pipilotti Rist in Hamburg and New York came about without any financial assistance from the federal government, but with our intensive and on-going support. This kind of intensive co-operation with the federal government has also borne fruit in an edition of art books by the graphic artist, Lars Müller, which have also reaped international praise.

Particularly worthy of mention is the Tate Modern in London, which was designed by the Swiss architects, Jacques Herzog and Pierre de Meuron, who have since received the Pritzker Prize for this project. Another important project by a group of Swiss artists is an exhibition devoted to the work of the internationally renowned art magazine "Parkett" and its various editions, now on show at the Museum of Modern Art in New York.

Frank: *And what are your cultural priorities?*

Dreifuss: They include safeguarding and promoting freedom of artistic work. When it comes to art and design, this is done as follows: The federal government invites young artists and designers to submit their work to two competitions in which they have a chance to win a prize of up to CHF 25,000. Even more important than the money, however, is the prestige and recognition the prize-winners stand to gain. Some 30 such prizes a year are awarded for art, and a further 25 for design.

The federal government also sends artists and designers to important international exhibitions, where they are given an opportunity to incorporate their work into Switzerland's official stand or pavilion. The federal government selects the artists and designers in question and co-operates with them on the exhibition concept as well as the organization, financing and execution of the stand or pavilion. The most important international exhibitions to which Switzerland makes an official contribution are the Art Biennale and Architecture Biennale in Venice, the Art Biennale in São Paulo, Sydney and Cairo, the Quadriennale for Theatre Decor in Prague and the Design Triennale in Milan. The federal government also organizes its own exhibitions on specific topics of relevance to contemporary art and design. Artists and designers are invited to present their works at these exhibitions, which are shown both in Switzerland and at important centres of art and design in other countries too.

Frank: *To close, we would be interested in knowing what you, on a purely personal level, enjoy reading? What are you reading now, for example, and which books do you keep on your bedside table?*

Dreifuss: There would be no room for all my bed-time reading on a bedside table. I live and sleep surrounded by books—books of all kinds and in five different languages. So all I have to do is to reach out and grab whatever happens to take my fancy—whether it be poetry, fiction or history or even a comic or technical literature. Were I to name any one particular book or author, I would inevitably risk devaluing all the rest. If pushed, however, I would have to say that my current favourite is *Harry Potter*.

ANNE-LOU STEININGER

The Sickness of Being a Fly

Translated from the French by Bernard Meares

I'm the Queen of the flies. My subjects die and slough me off. My subjects are born and fatten me up. My subjects transform me, transport me, and refine me. My subjects maintain me, enrich me, my subjects form my realm.... And I extend them, I immortalize them, crown them and seat them high in the blue empyrean upon thrones of dream. I become Queen in every fly.

I am the Queen of the flies, heroine of a story who trips in and out of a cascade of stories. I am not one but myriad, a thousand and one flies retold from mouth to mouth; I spread and propagate like plague or rabies, I am epidemic and inexhaustible. I am flysickness itself. I am the fly of the fly of the fly...I am the fly that one fly tells another, who passes it on, and goes and tells another fly, who in turn has a word with it.... And so on and so forth to any fly by night...I spread like a rumor, in an irresistible and ever expanding ripple. I'm the tale of a fly that's going the rounds, the voice buzzing in your head, the noise humming in your blood. I'm flysickness itself. I'm carried by you, transmitted by you. You sustain me, through you I am transformed, never the same yet always identical. Each of you steals me, pillages me and copies me, usurping for yourselves my fatuous soul and far-off tale. I am flysickness itself. I am the source of all misunderstanding and metaphor, for every fly in the world tries to be like me; I am the source of all metamorphosis, for all of them end by changing into me! I am the sickness of flies. I am Queen of the flies; Listen to my voice speaking in you. I am the sickness of origins, The poison of the race, And I flow through your veins Queen and sovereign, Without form (I never rest; my nature pushes me endlessly towards new metamorphoses: "Nature" is obviously a misnomer unless you take the meaning of the word to be some naive metaphor, the way you might say "Hi there, old fruit" to some fellow, even though he is clearly neither old nor the fruit and branch off any old tree. But by then it is too late: the fruit tree is nevertheless there with its stored-up autumns, its cracking leaves and its hollow trunk—the old tree is still there before our eyes, still coming between us! And the fellow says facetiously: "As this old tree is here, let's put it to use. Let's see whether its twisted branches can give shade despite their age..." At this, he raises his arms to the skies and spins round laughing, to shake out the damned crows, forever pecking at his ears. A cloud of blue birds escape, fulminating, from the dead tree's hollow trunk): "I see! I see!" shouts the guy, mad as a broom-seller, "once again the Fly-queen didn't give a damn about me!" But I am already...what? a malaria dancer in the hollow of his blood, that's what! I dance quadrilles while whistling : One-two! One-two-three-four! ...I lead a white ballet of quartan fevers dancing down his veins, I play the fiddle in his globules, its long-drawn sobs moan through his cells: one-two-one-two-three-four! ...with bursts of orchestras in flames, the percussion beating against his temples, kettledrums, cymbals, bells and whistles: I turn the drowsy substance of his languid swamp into a thunderous opera. Then, on river banks receding into the distance, he takes in the plangent vibrations of red velvet trees and groves poisoned by brass instruments, baroque seraphs twisting in flight from stomach cramps; cigars squashed in glistening sand. He sees the swollen glow at their tips refusing to go out, while women on fire coo and bill from balconies overweighted with frills and lace, their bellies eaten alive by blazing jewels given them by an admirer. He sees a hand, a slap, an explosion of green silk, a landscape of swamp and marsh jolting its ducks beneath the black lace of a palmate fan. The oscillation of the waves, prisoner of my boat thrown against a face whose grave eyes drag me down to the muddy ooze of the seabed. (Who is it?) His face crushes the breath out of me, with his saw teeth and their far too tinsel enamel. And my tremor gallops away. "You too agitated! You sweat like the sea !" "Sweat like the sea! Sweat! Sweat!" So I count lobsters: one lobster, two lobsters, three lobsters, four...(But they all look identical to one another.) ...I start over again. I concentrate. I sweat. I am all of a lather. One lobster, one lobster, one lobster, one. (I must have sunk for good.). I'm counting the same lobster twice over. I have to sink if my fever is to fall. The mud of the bottom, so I can slide: ooze, slime, softness. My paralysis must be wisdom!(and crevasses! With perpetual reincarnations.) I await my next victim, crouched at the foot of a precipice, a smooth-walled abyss with clearly defined edges where fleeting imagesor reflections— waft overhead in silence, whether idle fish or geisha clouds passing.... I am waiting—Or SHE is waiting for me—I am also her prey, after all.

We exchange our blood, teeth, and breath (How I love your perfumed odours when I melt in your fear! Your fever exalts the exquisite spice of your hatred. I suck your thoughts. I find the salt they contain. Thin, grainy and white. I taste your thoughts. But they melt too quickly, carrying off my tongue, and in silence they return to the fugitive images or reflections that hide me from your sight when you flow towards me, when you finally fall into my aquarium in a thin, grainy , white rain, and you deliquesce). Without form.

I make myself Queen in every fly . I crown myself Queen in every body where I'm fly enough , cast my skin, grainy smooth, tight and white—the egg-shell of the soul. And like the membrane in the egg binding white to yolk, I slip my initial obsession into the winding snailshell that is the difference in the 'e' sound between 'egg' and 'ego', or 'I' and 'ego.'

Egg and ego. And there I am! Another day another fly; I'll be Me, I'll be your Queen, with patience and vanity, for the space of one glorious summer long.

I and ego together again. I will grow with my prison, I will found my kingdom in it. I'll be Me, unique and sovereign. I'll grow wings, sprout legs under my belly, a proboscis and hairs. I'll lead a model life, with magnificent orchards, Turkish delights, Camels, herds and gold, and open sports cars. I will give my name to a disease and a monument. I'll be a gentleman poet, a boxing flyweight or pop star. I'll be spoken of as far away as Timbuctoo. I will be respected, adulated, envied and ... forever unrivalled.

Egg and ego. One more time, one more life to face eternity with, patiently and with vanity. Conquer the void and light up time. One more ride on the merry-go-round, hanging from the mould-stained mane of a stubborn horse with scaly eyes. A day or two more, watching myself grow old in an exhausted body, with patience and vanity, growing old and wizened, with trembling wings and sagging feet, in a world drowned by eyes muddied with emotion; growing old and resigned, letting go of my dreams, worn out with waiting; finally abdicating the throne in my ephemeral and misty kingdom, my ego unloosed from my egg.

Flydeath is just dread, a brief tremor. Coquettishly shivering, I return into death as if it were a sumptuous and fragile cast-off skin. It is a festive winding sheet, an ancient vestment worn from king to king since the dawn of time for this silent ball, the most magnificent of their reign. It comes in by the sleeves and knots up at the back, pernickety, ever so slowly, and with bated breath, so that the fluttering gilding, faded silken ribbons, and lacework of dust are undisturbed by the slightest of sighs, all the exhausted gorgeousness of this sumptuous apparel. The rite can begin!

And I enter death, trembling slightly, sipping all at once the stupefaction of long sea voyages and bitter orgasm. Supreme and foolish instant of sovereignty. As I soar away, my flight is given emphasis by a violet scarf and a few palpitations in the fine-spun gold of my dress. I feel beautiful in it. Let me be stared at, let me be gazed at with the sincere and almost melancholy gravity of deep-seated longing. I am dying. Weep, my beloved flies.

This is the way I always die; in each and every fly there trembles the sovereign of a foundering kingdom. I am the ego and the egg, hobbling on the rounded mouths of a single vowel in two shapes. In one final cast of skin, I debauch myself, and again turn into the sound difference between short and long 'e.' Then I fly down to Hell where my kingdom prospers. I make myself Queen in every fly, I damn myself. From each soul in torment I produce a flame; I meld egg and ego, water and fire, releasing flies from the country of the dead for another season on earth, for just one season, and I burn with phosphorus flame in a night studded with stars, the season of black loves or hour of the glow-worm.

I am Queen of the flies, hostage and sovereign.

My subjects hold me in thrall, my subjects imprison me; they keep me within them where they want me to reign over them as an absolute despot. They plead with me. "If it were not for you, your Majesty, where would we be? Long to reign over us! Govern us, rule. We'll be your kingdom. We shall fatten you, transport you, enrich you... we shall love you. Be Queen in each and every one of us; and make our lives a meaningful story! May our murmurs become speech! And our desires be realized!"

And I always tell them: "Alas, my faithful flies, my beloved flies, my loving flies, my kingdom is immense, my power unbounded, and I would give you all I possess , but...I am very afraid it is merely a dream."

Then, beating my brow:

"It's all happening in my head."
I would like to speak; whenever I open my mouth, my voice is covered by the sound of rain.
I am the Queen of the flies. My subjects exhaust me.
I have issued a decree: "Leave me alone! Abandon me!"

Kristin T. Schnider
HER FATHER. VERY EARLY.

from a novel-in-progress Aurora

This is not how she talks about him to her friends.
This is not what she says when asked.
This is not even what she really remembers, she thinks.
But she is not sure.
That it does not matter is what she really thinks.
This is what she thinks, thinking of him.

My father is very dark, very dark and I cannot see him at all. He must have a face but I don't see it unless he opens his mouth to smile at me. Then I see teeth and don't know if that is not even worse. Only teeth. I see his eyes only when he cares to look at me. I see his eyes when he looks at me and his teeth when he smiles. I don't see his teeth when he starts talking because then he is moving his lips so fast, and I can't really hear what he is saying and maybe I don't want to. I don't see his eyes either. Four little slices of white beside nothing, moving.

I imagine his eyes and his teeth and I know this is what I would see of him so I imagine I would at least see his eyes and teeth at least. So my father is all darkness and eyes and teeth, and I only see him when I close my eyes.

I have always seen him like that.

I close my eyes and all there is is my father. I try to go around him. I try to find out if he has a body. My father is darkness, darkness. It is when I have just closed my eyes that I think it is his eyes that I see. Far away tiny specks of light, white orbs at the back end of that darkness yet as I get closer all I see is just darkness denser than anything I see in my bedroom lying awake staring into the night. There are shades. Aren't there degrees of darkness. Memory lets me make out that my room, which has retreated for the time being, consists of shades of grey and brown and black, and there is the occasional fleck of light having found its way inside, rests of the headlights of a car swerving past, throwing spots onto the ceiling, the wall. As I close my eyes there is nothing, really, I tell myself, no eyes, no teeth, no father. I go to sleep.

When I started waking up crying and sweating I must have decided to do something about it. I held my breath. I was in a dilemma, I could not close my eyes against my fears and be safe. I had to keep them wide wide open, clinging to traces of light, glueing them to the wavery shape of the leg of my chair, I did not dare getting up either. How was I to know if

EITHER GROWN UPS DON'T MISBEHAVE OR THEY ARE SAFE BECAUSE THERE ARE ALWAYS TWO OF THEM IN THE SAME BED AT NIGHT & THE BLACK MAN IS NOT STRONG ENOUGH FOR TWO.

there was not a deep darkness lurking behind the chair? Enclosing me. The black man lying in wait behind a toy, ready to engulf me, ready to carry me away as I had been told he would do, if I did not behave. Had I been good on that particular day? My heartbeat seemed to pump me up ready for an explosion while at the same time my extremities went numb with fear, numb first, then they began to feel brittle, ready to break, to crumble and sink, little heaps of ash into the pillow, onto the mattress and then the black man would come and grab my throbbing heart, disdainfully blowing away my ashes and sink these teeth of his into my heart. I did not sob for fear of him hearing me.

I freeze. I pretend to be dead. I don't know what it is like to be dead. No one is interested in you any longer, because you are of no use. So no one will hurt you. You can't be hurt when you're dead. All anyone wants is to hurt you and to make you dead and when you're dead they will go away.

He has not come. It works. I am dead and I am safe. He has to leave my bedroom when the light comes and then I can come alive again and he never existed at all. The black man never comes during daytime to take the children away. Because then other people would see him and they would see what he does and he does not like that. I don't understand really. He makes children behave. So he does a good thing. People want to see good things. Children should do good things. So why can't he take the bad children and people would thank him and say, good man? They must think it is good, because they always talk about him. He only takes children. I wonder. Either grown ups don't misbehave or they are safe because there are always two of them in the same bed at night and the black man is not strong enough for two.

My pillow is wet. I have cried. The black man is waiting. I have learned to cry silently, so he does not hear me. That's something I am proud of. I am doing well. He can't get me. When I go to sleep I don't close my eyes anymore. I stare and then I just go. Maybe sleeping is like being dead a little. People are not used when they sleep so they are of no use to the black man. He wants me to know that he takes me and when I sleep I would not notice. And then I would wake up and be where he took me and that would be that. Wonder what place that is supposed to be. It must be a place children don't like. From the way they talk about him I can tell it is important that we know he takes us. Because we have been bad. I am not safe when I close my eyes. My father does not save me. I thought hard of him and willed him to come and help me against the black man. It didn't work.
I am always tired. When I fell asleep today at school it was a scandal. At home they were a

SOMETIMES CHILDREN VANISH FROM SCHOOL...

little worried I could tell. But they were more upset. I don't know where that should lead up to when I fall asleep at school. Or end up. They were cross. They sent me to bed early. It did not help that I cried. It made them more cross. It means I have to work harder and longer at being dead and not breathing and not moving. I thought that maybe the black man will take me after all. If I am so bad to make them so cross he might just take me all the same. Even when I am dead. Just to get me to the place where he locks up the bad children. I would be gone and everyone would know and they would be very cross. Because of what other people think. That they have such a bad child that the black man came to get it. And the other children would be happy they had not been taken. Sometimes children vanish from school. When I asked if the black man had taken them, they were cross again. They said I should not be stupid and that they just had moved to another town. How am I to know. Why should I believe them.

I was completely unaware that in spite of my efforts to play dead and be very still I had got into the habit of whispering to myself. I must have been beside myself with anguish when that voice cut into the shaded darkness the precarious safety of my bedroom, me playing dead: "will you cut out that fucking whispering, sleep for heaven's sake, don't sleep at school, sleep now!" The gaff was up. The black man had heard me all that time when I had felt safe and he was just biding his time noiselessly chuckling at my useless ruminations. I did not dare challenge the voice, do the sane thing and at least throw a tantrum, go out there to that voice into the light of the bathroom, where it had come from and break down and cry and tell them all. How could I? How could they betray me to the black man they kept threatening me with in the first place? Jump out of bed I did, frantically searching for a safe place.

They said they don't know what to do with me. I was giving them a bad name and if I kept on like that they would come and get me. So there are more people than just the black man to take children away. I had not known. They were very angry. They said people think they treat me bad when I look like that with dark rings under my eyes and fall asleep during the day. I have managed not to go to sleep during lessons. But they have caught me dozing during recess. And before the teachers and the people will arrange for me to be taken away, they have to send me away themselves. So would I sleep, for crying out loud. I don't know what they meant when they said it was a good thing I could not look really pale. That would even look worse, they said. I don't know what to do. I take care to put the pillow over my head and whisper really low. I can't help whispering. I like it, too. I thought I could talk to the black man. Ask him why he would take me. Or where. Maybe the place for bad children is better than the place people would take me when they take me away. One never knows. They said I had to share everything with other children and I would be very poor and sleep with dozens of others in the same room and nothing would be mine like here where I have my own room and my own toys. First I thought I would be safe from the black man then. Because I would not have to sleep alone. But other children are not nice to me so I would not be safe during the day. I have noticed they stare at me and talk. They don't really want to play with me. They say I am too loud and too big and I should not be surprised. I have to be nicer to other children. In a way everything leads up to me being taken by the black man. I am just bad. But if I talk to him they will hear me and be cross again.

It did not work to try and hide in a safe place in my room during nights. I would fall asleep and they would find me in the morning, huddled underneath my little desk, squashed into my wardrobe, halfway in halfway out. They got mad. They felt helpless. They called in a family friend who was a priest and made me pray with him. No one ever asked me what was the matter, so I felt, they must know that I had good reasons to be afraid of the black man. They did not allow me to keep a light on: that was something for sissies or babies and I must grow up and be a big girl.

It must have been then that my father, they had at least had the nerve and decency to tell me about, vanished completely into that darkness. I no longer thought about his eyes, his teeth, the possibility that he might actually save me. Not that the absurdity of it all would have dawned on me yet. I had been simply taken out and taken in by worrying about more immediate incomprehensible matters, devising ruses, lies and upholstering imaginary sanctuaries with all I had had then.

This is more like what she used to say when asked some years ago when she was a little younger:

My mother and my father live in another town quite far away from this one and we get on very well but I do see them rarely you know how it is. My parents are Swiss, yes, and so am I, and it is only my hair which is a little Caribbean they said because my other mother had a boyfriend who came from the West Indies and that is all I know so my father is Swiss and a really nice bloke and he even looks like me or I look like him you know.

Now she doesn't say anything anymore. She has found out how not to be asked.

Sometimes when she is in the right mood she says:
My father was a singer. And what's more: he did not come from some hick island in the Carribbean Sea at all, oh no. Nobody ever admitted to it, but I am not stupid. He was a singer and a world famous one at that. So there.

Swiss Notables

The Lexikon der Schweizer Literaturen *(Lenos Verlag, 1991) includes nearly 500 pages of biographic information on hundreds of Switzerland's most accomplished writers and thinkers. We were surprised by a number of these individuals whom we hadn't thought of as Swiss, and thought* **Frank** *readers might appreciate having a glance at the short list we've culled from the lexicon. Writers whose work we've included in* **Frank** *have not been added to this list. We extend our apologies for omissions and oversights, of which there are undoubtedly plenty. For English translations of the works of these writers, follow the links at www.ReadFrank.com.—DA*

- **Jean Calvin**. 1509-64. Theologian, best known for his beliefs concerning predestination. Died in Geneva.
- **Blaise Cendrars**. 1887-61. Born Frédéric Sauser in La Chaux-de-Fonds. Poet and essayist, known for his bold, experimental, action-packed writing.
- **Dada in Zurich**. Explosive avant-garde art movement that began in Zurich in 1916 and spread like wildfire...
- **Friedrich Dürrenmatt**. 1921-90. Known for his essays, avant-garde theater pieces and existential detective novels.
- **Max Frisch**. 1911-91. One of Switzerland's most acclaimed writers and architects, Frisch was born and died in Zurich.
- **Herman Hesse**. 1877-62. Poet, novelist, aestheticist. Author of *Demian* (1919), *Siddhartha* (1922), *Steppenwolf* (1927), *Narziss und Goldmund* (1930).
- **Paul Klee**. 1879-40. Painter, water-colorist, etcher.
- **Hugo Loetscher**. 1929. Novelist, literary critic, journalist. "To talk about something that doesn't exist is not the privilege of politicians. To talk about Swiss Literature is to talk about something that doesn't exist. But it does not exist in its own special way; my country has always liked the special case."
- **E.Y. Meyer**. 1946- Acclaimed free-lance writer; recipient of Swiss Schiller Foundation Prize and the Welti Prize for Drama.
- **Adolf Muschg**. 1934- Writer of novels, stories, dramatic works. Known for his work on the correlation between literature and therapy.
- **Robert Pinget**. 1919-97. Avant-garde novelist and playwright. Member of the Nouveau Roman (new novel) literary movement.
- **Ramuz, C.F.** 1878-1947. Switzerland's leading Romand writer of the 20th century, known for freeing Swiss French writing from its obsession with moral imperatives and its dependence on Parisian literary models.
- **Jean Jacques Rousseau**. 1712-78. Philosopher. Author of *The Social Contract* (1762), *Confessions* (1765-70).
- **Robert Walser**. 1878-56. Novelist and short story writer, best known in English speaking world for *The Rose*.

Frank Contributors

(E-mail and personal web site addresses are available at www.ReadFrank.com/contributors)

Chris Agee, an American living in Belfast, edited a special American issue of the Irish journal *Metre* and a contemporary Irish issue for *Poetry*, where his own poems and reviews have also appeared. His first collection, *In the New Hampshire Woods*, was a finalist for the Kingsley Tufts Poetry Prize.

David Applefield founded **Frank** is 1983 and has continued to publish the journal in Paris ever since. Author of two novels, *Once Removed* (Mosaic Press, 1997) and *On a Flying Fish* (Mosaic Press, Fall 2001), he is also written *Paris Inside Out* (Globe Pequot Press, 2000), and *The Unofficial Guide to Paris* (HungryMinds, 2001), and publishes the web site www.paris-anglo.com. Aside from specializing in marketing and publishing strategies for cultural content, his advertising and promotional projects often take him to French-speaking Africa, where he coordinates publishing supplements for *The Financial Times* and *The International Herald Tribune*. Applefield lives and works in Montreuil-sous-Bois.

Louis Armand is an artist and writer living in Prague, where he currently teaches art history and cultural theory at Charles University. His books include *Seances* (Twisted Spoon, 1998), *Anatomy Lessons* (x-poezie, 1999), *Land Partition* (Antigen, 2000), and *Inexorable Weather* (Arc, forthcoming). He is poetry editor of *The Prague Revue* and editor of the literary broadsheet *Semtext*.

James Baldwin, African-American novelist and essayist, spent much of his life in France. Baldwin died in 1987.

Bedri Baykam is an accomplished and controversial painter, writer, political activist, and cultural provocateur based in his indigenous Istanbul. His 2001 best-selling novel, *Kemic* (The Bone) has been banned by the Turkish government for its pornographic and anti-social content.

Bono is a highly independent artist and poet living in Clermont-Ferrand, where he collaborates with his wife Lydia. His latest book of poems and drawing is called *Equilibre*.

Duff Brenna is the author of the novels *The Book of Mamie*, which won the Associated Writing Programs Award, *The Holy Book of the Beard*, and *Too Cool*, a *New York Times* Notable Book, and his latest, *The Altar of the Body* (Picador USA). He is a professor of English at California State University, San Marcos, California.

Alan Bridgman was born and educated in England. After leaving university he settled into a career with a Swiss insurance company, where he remained until retirement. Today, he devoted his time to freelance translation, amateur acting, as a long-term member of the Zurich Comedy Club, and researching and writing the history of his own family. He lives in Zurich.

Wolfgang Amadeus Bruelhart is the Cultural Counsellor at the Embassy of Switzerland in London. He has played an active role in using cultural projects as an instrument of peace and international cooperation. Bruelhart is often seen on London streets driving his personal London taxi.

Nick Byrne is a translator and professor of English at de Vinci University in Paris. He splits his time between Montreuil and the Oise.

Alain Campos is a French artist living and working in Paris. His collection of drawings *Gros Plans* was published by the Musée de Lodëve in 1998.

Monica Cantieni, born 1965, lives in Wettingen, Switzerland and Vienna, Austria. Her novels include *Hieronymus' Kinder* published by Rotpunktverlag, Zurich, 1996 and *Die Nebeltrinker*, to be published in fall 2001. *Lucia, Mädchen*, her monologue for a woman over fifty, remains unpublished.

Deepak Chopra is one of the world's most influential spiritual thinkers. Author of over 20 books, his latest is *How to Know God* (Harmony Books, 2000). His comment to **Frank** that we should expect to witness horrendous "information wars" in the near future, heeds warning.

Phyllis Cohen is an artist who for the past 45 years has enjoyed a necessary pattern of life between Albuquerque, New Mexico, Paris and the museums of the world. Her passion is contour drawing and the pure line of human form. She has exhibited in Paris, London, Monte Carlo, and throughout the U.S., and her work can be found in the collections of the Albuquerque Museum and the University of New Mexico Art Museum.

Billy Collins's most recent collection of poems is *Picnic, Lightning*. In 2001 Random House is publishing his new and selected poems, *Sailing Alone Around the Room*. Collins was recently named Poet Laureate of the United States.

Wyn Cooper has published two books of poems, *The Country of Here Below* and *The Way Back*, as well as poems and stories in *Ploughshares, Agni, Verse, Antioch Review, Harvard Magazine*, and *Fence*. His poem "Fun," from *The Country of Here Below*, was made into Sheryl Crow's Grammy-winning song, "All I Wanna Do." He lives in Vermont.

Raphael Dagold is a poet, photographer, teacher, and self-employed maker of custom furniture and cabinets in Portland, Oregon. His poems have appeared in *Quarterly West, Indiana Review, two girls review, Shirim*, and *The Oregonian*.

Martin R. Dean was born 1955 in Menziken, Aargau, the son of Swiss-Trinidadian parents. He is in the process of writing a biographical novel set in London, Trinidad and Switzerland. He lives as a writer in Basel. His publications include *Die Ballade von Billie und Joe*, a novel, 1997, *Monsieur Fume oder das Glück der Vergeslichkeit* (Carl Hanser Verlag, Munich, 1998), and *Schlaflos*, a play co-written with Silvia Henke (Verlag der Autoren, Frankfurt-am-Main).

Michael Dennison's first book, *Vampirism: Literary Tropes of Decadence and Entropy*, will be published by Peter Lang in the fall 2001. His poetry has appeared in *Nebraska Quarterly, New Delta Review*, and *The Journal*. Author of two chapbooks published through the Nebraska Fine Arts Press, Dennison lectures in philosophy, literature, and writing at Carlow College in Pittsburgh, Pennsylvania.

Jennifer Dick completed a BA in English and Russian literature in translation at Mount Holyoke College under the tutelage of Joseph Brodsky and Michael Petit, and an MFA at Colorado State University in poetry writing with Laura Mullen, Bill Tremblay and Mary Crow. She is currently a WICE writer in residence in Paris where she teaches English and Creative Writing and co-edits the review *Upstairs at Duroc*.

Marie Doezema came to Paris from Norman, Oklahoma, on a Vassar College fellowship to study classical Arabic at the Institut de Monde Arabe. Having made Paris her home, Marie now works with **Frank**, writes, and graces the terrace at Fish.

Ruth Dreifuss is both Switerland's Minister of Culture and Minister of Home Affairs. She served as the president of Switzerland's seven-member *Bundesrat*, the executive body of the Swiss government.

Jill Alexander Essbaum's first book of poems, *Heaven*, won the 1999 Katherine Bakeless Nason Prize in Poetry sponsored by the Bread Loaf Writers' Conference and has been published by the University Press of New England. She lives and works in Austin, Texas.

Mike Evans is a freelance linguist (simultaneous interpreter, translator and lecturer), originally from Great Britain and now residing in Freiburg, Germany. One of his major professional and private interests is minority languages, such as Romansh.

Robert Fagan has published poems and stories in many magazines, ranging from *Partisan Review* to *Stand*. A story of his appears in the fall 2000 issue of *The Gettysburg Review*. He lives in New York City and is writing a non-verbal, non-ethnocentric history of art.

Veronica Frühbrodt, born in 1969, is a Chilean painter living and working in Montreuil-sous-Bois. She also designs her own line of children's clothing. She exhibited at Galeria Nemesio Antunez, in Santiago, Chile, in 1999.

Sergey Gandlevsky is the author of three books of poems, a memoir, *Trepanation of the Skull* (1996), and a book of essays. Winner of both the Little Booker Prize and the Anti-Booker Prize in 1996 for his poetry and prose, he has been included in several English translation anthologies including *In the Grip of Strange Thoughts: Russian Poetry in a New Era* (Zephyr Press, 1999).

Claire Genoux, a Lausanne poet born in 1971, is the author of *Soleil ovale* (Editions Empreintes, 1997) and *Saison du Corps* (Editions Empreintes,1999) for which she won the *Prix de Poèsie C.F. Ramuz*.

Robert Gibbons has written two chapbooks of prose poems, *Lover, Is This Exile?*, and *OF DC*, published by Innerer Klang Press, Charlestown, Massachusetts. His work is available on-line from *The Literary Review* at webdelsol.com and *The Drunken Boat* at www.thedunkenboat.com, both linked from www.ReadFrank.com.

Ethan Gilsdorf, poet, writer, editor, critic and self-taught graphic designer, moved to Paris with his wife Isabelle Sulek eight days before the Millennium, 1999. He has since connected with **Frank**, become a film and restaurant reviewer for *Time Out Paris*, and a regular contributor to *Poets and Writers, The Literary Review of Canada* and *Paris Notes*. He also consults as a technical writer and marketing copyrighter. Gilsdorf's poems have been published in *Poetry, The Southern Review, The Massachusetts Review* and *Poetry London*. The recipient of a grant from the Vermont Arts Council, he is also the winner of the Hobblestock Peace Poetry Competition and the Esmé Bradberry Contemporary Poets Prize. Over the past two years, he has lived in six different Parisian apartments, and has learned to drink coffee.

J.P. Glutting, a highly selective translator, is a health care researcher and web programmer who lived and worked in Barcelona until recently resettling in Boston. His translations have been published in *Chest, Critical Care Medicine, Current Opinion in Critical Care, Intensive Care Medicine, Journal of the American Public Health Association, Journal of Epidemiology and Community Health*, and *Radiology*, among others.

Carol V. Hamilton teaches Cultural Studies and Creative Writing at Carnegie Mellon University in Pittsburgh, Pennsylvania. Her poems have recently appeared in *The Paris Review, Kestrel*, and *Salmagundi*.

Herzog and de Meuron, based in Basel, Switzerland, are one of the most acclaimed and original architectural firms in the world. In 2000, they opened the New Tate Museum in London.

Ellen Hinsey's first book of poems won the Yale Younger Poets Series in 1995. Her second collection is forthcoming from Wesleyan University Press. Originally from Boston, Ellen has lived in Paris for nearly two decades and was recently a fellow at the American Academy in Berlin.

Pierre Imhasly, born 1939 in Visp, Valais, studied in Fribourg and Zurich and lived in Italy and Spain for longer periods. He has published poems, a book of critical articles, a treaty on bullfighting and several translations, including works by Maurice Chappaz. *The Rhone Saga* is his "opus magnum" to date, an immensely rich lyrical, epical, multilingual, multidimensional poem portraying the different worlds to be found along the river Rhone.

Pierre Imhof was born in Freiburg, Switzerland, into a family equally happy in French or German. He studied art in London. He and Dafydd Roberts live together, and translate together from German, mainly in the fields of art and cultural history. Their most recent work is a translation into English of Fritz Mierau's biography of the expressionist writer and Berlin Dadaist Franz Jung.

Fred Johnson was born in Belfast, Northern Ireland, in 1951 and educated there and in Toronto, Canada. A journalist for some years, he still reviews and writes features. Now he works as Literature Officer and is literary editor at *The Galway Advertiser* in Galway, where he founded CUIRT, Galway's international literature festival in 1986. His novel, *Atalanta*, was published in 2001.

Sandor Kanyadi has worked as an editor of a Hungarian-language magazine in Transylvania, Romania, where he was born and educated. He has published over twenty volumes of poetry, some in translation in Scandinavia, France and Germany. In 1995 he received the prestigious Herder Prize in Vienna and was featured in an anthology of ten Transylvania-Hungarian poets (*Maradok-I Remain*, Pro-Print, Romania, 1998).

Thomas E. Kennedy is an American fiction writer of imminent fame. A skilled writing teacher, literary critic and essayist, Kennedy has been living and writing in Denmark since the 1970s. A frequent contributor and advisory editor to Walter Cummin's *The Literary Review*, Kennedy's stories have appeared in scores of journals in North America and Europe. In 1987, he edited the Danish dossier in **Frank 6/7**.

Simon Knight has been a freelance translator for the last 18 years, after beginning his career as a teacher of English as Foreign Language, which included seven years in Madagascar. A speaker of English, French, Italian and Malagasy, he is a compulsive translator, fascinated by the exercise of transferring meaning from one language to another with clarity. He specializes in books on art and culture. This is his first serious attempt to translate poetry.

PHYLLIS COHEN - *SWISS ARTISTS CONVERSING* - INK, 2000
(INSPIRED BY A LIVELY CONVERSATION BETWEEN SWISS ARTISTS RUTH ZURCHER AND ILSE HESSE-RABINOWITZ)

Alpha Oumar Konaré is the President of Mali.

Bogdan Korczowski is a prolific painter, originally from Krakow, Poland, who lives and works in Paris's 20th *arrondissement*. He had a major exhibition at the Galeria Miejska Arsenal in Krakow in 1999 and Galerie Nicole Ferry in Paris.

François Lamore was born in Washington D.C. in 1952 to an American father and French mother, but grew up in rural western Missouri. After studying art in both the U.S. and Aix-en-Provence, he began exhibiting his paintings and publishing his poems. In the late 70s he met André Masson, Jean Hélion and Diego Giacometti. In 1999 the Galerie Maeght published his book of engravings with poems by Salah Stétié and his poem "Sky Fang" illustrated by Oreste Zevola. He lives in Montreuil.

Jean Lamore is a Franco-American writer, activist, and sculptor based in Ivry, near Paris, where he edits the journal *Mambo*. Lamore is deeply involved in numerous socio-political issues and causes in Africa and is often in places ranging from the Central African Republic to the Western Sahara.

Hugo Loetscher is a prolific writer of novels and essays as well as a cosmopolitan traveler with a permanent address in Zurich. He was born in 1929 and studied political science, history of economics, sociology and literature in Zurich and Paris. Since 1965 he has been regularly in Latin America, and from 1976 in the Far East. He has spent time as a lecturer and writer in residence at the University of Southern California in Los Angeles, the City University of New York, and Munich University.

Ma Tse-Lin, a painter born in Canton in 1960, has been living in Paris since 1985. Recent exhibitions include the Galerie Loft in Paris, Hakaren Art Gallery in Singapore, and the Galerie Leda Fletcher in Geneva. His work belongs to important collections including the Museum of Modern Art in Pekin and Cooper Union Library in New York. In May 2001 his painting "Van Gogh with Bottle" was auctioned as part of an Absolut Vodka campaign to raise funds for *Reporteurs sans Frontières*.

Bernard Meares is a translator and interpreter living and working in Geneva.

Mariella Mehr was born in Zurich and, as a child of a Roma family was separated from her mother by the charitable society Pro Juventute, to be brought up in foster care homes. Mehr began her career in journalism, first uncovering the scandalous practice of Pro Juventute. Her first novel, *Steinzeit*, was published in 1981. Aside from novels, she has published poetry, essays and drama, and received an honorary degree from the University of Basel for her incessant political engagement especially for the rights of the Roma people. After having been injured in several attacks by racists she left Switzerland to live in Tuscany, Italy.

José María Mendiluce, born in Madrid in 1951, split his childhood between Madrid and his indigenous Basque Country. As a militant opponent to Franco, he was arrested on various occasions and lived for several years in hiding. José Maria abandoned his militancy after the transition to democracy, and in 1980 accepted a proposal from the United Nations High Commission on Refugees (UNHCR), which sent him to Africa and Central America and then as the UN special envoy to the Balkans, where he directed the largest humanitarian operation in the history of the organization. His courage in denouncing war crimes and in defense of the civilian population earned him international renown. He left the United Nations in 1994, and was elected as a Representative to the European Parliament. He is currently Vice President of the Commission on External Affairs, Security and Defense of the European Parliament.

Phil Metres' poems and translations of Russian poets have appeared in numerous publications, including *Artful Dodge, COMBO, Crab Orchard Review, Exquisite Corpse, Field, Glas, Luna, Modern Poetry in Translation, New Orleans Review, Ploughshares, Spoon River Poetry Review, Willow Springs* and *In the Grip of Strange Thoughts: Russian Poetry in a New Era* (Zephyr Press, 1999).

Breon Mitchell, who lives in Indiana, is currently translating a novel by Uwe Timm about the Hottentot War, set in S.W. Africa around 1904. His most recent translation is Franz Kafka's *The Trial*, for Schocken Books.

Roger Monnerat lives in Basel, where he works as a journalist while writing a third novel. The tale of "Lanze Langbub," his debut as an author, established his voice in the literary landscape, celebrating the age of idealism, life in communes, free sex and never-ending discussions about politics. His second novel *The School of Shame*, which wryly examines the 68 Generation is unique in Switzerland.

Michael Morse has published work in *Tin House, Field, Antioch Review, Colorado Review, The Iowa Review, Fine Madness*, and *Spinning Jenny*, with work nominated for Pushcart Prizes in 1994 and 1999. He teaches at the Ethical Culture Fieldston School in New York City and lives in Brooklyn.

Rick Mulkey is currently an Associate Professor of English and Director of Creative Writing at Converse College. His poems have appeared in a number of journals including *The Connecticut*

Review and in the anthology *American Poetry: The Next Generation* (Carnegie Mellon University Press). "Theoretically Speaking" is part of a new manuscript titled *Flux*.

Yves Netzhammer is a Swiss artist who specializes in computer-generated images.

Paul Nizon is the author of numerous novels and works of "autofiction" published in German (Suhrkamp) and French (Actes Sud). Swiss-born, he has been living and writing in Paris for over 30 years.

Lisa Pasold's creative writing has appeared in many Canadian and European literary magazines. Her poetry chapbook of 21 poems about blackjack, entitled "green as the three of diamonds," appeared in 1997. She is completing a novel about art forgery called *The Favourite Cannibal*, inspired by her experiences as an artist's model and art critic. She now lives in Paris's 19th *arrondissement*.

Malcolm Pender teaches German at the University of Strathclyde in Glasgow, Scotland. Interested for many years in Swiss literature, he is currently co-editor and contributor to the annual journal, *Occasional Papers in Swiss Studies*.

Gilles Plante, Canadian-born translator, headed the Translation Service of the Canadian Nuclear Regulatory Agency for twelve years, before being appointed Administrator of the Publications Programme at the OECD Nuclear Energy Agency, in Paris, in 1993. A specialist in "surtitling" Plante has provided the English surtitles for the Comédie-Française production of Marivaux's *Les Fausses Confidences*.

Fabio Pusterla, born 1957, lives close to the Italian border and travels back and forth between Albogasio and Lugano in Switzerland, where he works as a teacher at a local college. He has published translations, linguistic treaties and several collections of his firmly fragile poetry.

Ilma Rakusa, a lecturer at the Unviersity of Zurich, was born in 1946, and studied Slavic and Romance languages. A writer, translator, journalist, she lives in Zurich. Her books, *Die Insel*, 1982; *Miramar*, 1986; *Steppe*, 1990; *Jim. Sieben Dramolette*, 1993; and *Ein Strich durch alles. Neunzig Neunzeiler*, 1997, are published by Suhrkamp Verlag. Her translations include works by Marguerite Duras, Marina Tsvetajeva, Danilo Kis and Imre Kertesz.

Deborah Reich has had poems in **Exquisite Corpse** and *The Green Mountains Review*. In 2000 she was a resident at the Millay Colony in Austerlitz, New York, and read at The Ear Inn in New York.

Dorothea Resch, Italian photographer, lives and works in Paris. After university studies in Austria and the United Kingdom, she graduated from the Paris school of photography, Speos, specializing in fine art, jewellery and studio photography.

Dafydd Roberts was born in Holyhead, North Wales, and brought up in Welsh and English. He now lives in London with his collaborator Pierre Imhof, where he works as a freelance translator from French and German, and writes occasionally for Welsh journals.

Michael Robinson writes English versions of German language plays. He also translates books and magazines about art, architecture and design, and press and catalogue material for Austrian, German and Swiss museums and art galleries. His version of Schnitzler's *Anatol* was revived at the prestigious Nottingham Playhouse in April 2001.

Sondra Russell is a writer from Norman, Oklahoma, with extensive professional experience in creative and technical development of web sites. After working in San Francisco and London, she crossed the Channel and now writes and programs www.ReadFrank from Paris. Her prose recently appeared in *Kilometer Zero*.

Kristin T. Schnider, born in London and raised in Zurich, is now living close to the second longest tunnel of Europe in Central Switzerland. To date, she has published two novels, a collection of short stories, several articles and essays.

Maria Schoenhammer lives in New York City. Formerly a student of the ancient world, she now makes her living as a freelance translator of sundries, but her preferred genre is literary texts. Her translations have appeared in *Prairie Schooner*, which she guest edited for its 1999 special issue on New German Literature.

Laurent Schweizer is a novelist living in Geneva. Ricco Bilger Verlag has published his work in German, and Actes Sud brought out *Naso Lituratus* in 2001 in French.

Peter Skelton is a Franco-Brit, having lived in France for half his life, starting off as a pion in a private school in 1961. His French tutor at St. Johns', Oxford, was Will Moore, an authority on Baudelaire, before, as he writes, "I did INSEAD and lost my way in the business world."

Paul Sohar has translated over 180 of Sandor Kanyadi's poems and has placed over 50 of them in various literary journals in preparation of an eventual book. He collaborated on the translation of a children's book by Kanyadi, *The Little Globe-Trotting Mouse* (Holnap, Budapest, 2000), and has published his own poems and translations in numerous periodicals.

Maja Starcevic has translated a number of works from the Bosnian into English. She lives in Zagreb, Croatia, where she translates Anglo-American and Czech literature into Croatian.

Anne-Lou Steininger, born in Valais, Switzerland in 1963, currently lives in Geneva. *La maladie d'être mouche*, published by Editions Gallimard's NFR collection in 1996, is her first novel.

Virgil Suárez was born in Havana, Cuba, in 1962 but since 1974 he has lived in the United States. He is the author of four novels, *The Cutter, Latin Jazz, Havana Thursdays*, and *Going Under*, several volumes of poetry, a collection of stories, and two volumes of memoirs. As editor he has published the best-selling anthologies *Iguana Dreams: New Latino Fiction* and *Paper Dance: 55 Latino Poets*. He divides his time between Miami and Tallahassee where he lives with his family, and is currently at work on his new novel *Sonny Manteca's Blues*.

François Trémolières, born in 1959, a book editor at a large publishing house in Paris and editor at the literary journal *Nouveau Recuil*, is currently on leave finishing his doctoral disertation on 16th century French writer Fénelon. Poet and critic, his work has appeared in the *Nouvelle Revue française* and *Java*. His book of poems, *Peintures*, was published in 1996 by Le Temps qu'il fait. He lives in Montreuil with his wife and three daughters.

Leo Tuor, born 1959 in Rabius, lives in Surrein. The Romansh he writes in, his Sursilvian mother tongue, is used by about 20,000 people. His poem "Giacumbert Nau" caused controversy in his home district Graubünden: not everybody appreciated his open words going contrary to the traditional Romansh canon. He has now given up his summer job as a shepherd on the Greina. After publishing a report on his experiences as one of a hundred writers on the Literary Express, a train which crossed Europe from Lisboa to Moscow in 2000, he is planning to tackle the topic of hunting in a literary way, another hot issue in the agrarian mountainous regions of Switzerland.

Christian Uetz, born in 1963 in Egnach, worked as a teacher for three years after studying philosophy, ancient Greek and comparative literary science at the University of Zurich. He has published several volumes of poetry and one book of inimitable prose. Now living in Berlin, Uetz is working on an ambitious book: *From Don Juan and San Juan to Don San Juan.*

Damir Uzunovic was born Sarajevo in 1965. He has published two collections of poetry, *Brod sa talismanom* (Ship with a Talisman,1992) and *Madjionicar* (The Magician,1994), as well as a collection of short stories *Kesten* (Chestnut, 1996). He currently works as a manager of the Buybook Bookstore in Sarajevo and edits a cultural magazine *Lica* (Faces) and is a member of the Bosnia and Herzegovina PEN.

Aglaja Veteranyi, born 1962 in Bucarest, Rumania, now lives in Zurich. She grew up in a circus family and traveled with the circus, performing in Europe, Africa, and Latin America, and since

1982 has worked as a freelance actress. In 1996 she founded with Jens Nielsen the performance group "Die Engelmaschine." Veteranyi, whose work has appeared in anthologies and literary magazines, has received several prizes including the literary award of the City of Zurich, the "Kunstpreis Berlin 2000," and the "Chamisso Förderpreis," Munich.

Eileen Walliser-Schwarzbart was born in New York City in 1947. The daughter of refugees from Nazi Germany, she grew up bilingual. After completing her degree in Philosophy at New York University, she went to Switzerland, where she "fell" quite nautrally into translating. Her work has been published by OUP, Rizzoli, and Yale University Press. Walliser-Schwarzbart is also on the editorial board of *Passages: A Swiss Cultural Magazine*. She lives in Riehen, Switzerland, with her husband Stephan.

Elisabeth Wandeler-Deck, born in 1939, lives in Zurich. Apart from being a writer, she has pursued a successful career as an architect, and as a Gestalt-analyst. Interested in combining different media, she frequently collaborates with composers and musicians and has given musical performances herself and ventured into filmmaking. Her latest book, partly set in Haïti, received the Central Switzerland Literary Award.

Wallis Wilde-Menozzi lives in Parma, Italy, and publishes widely. Her recent publications include a memoir, *Mother Tongue, An American Life in Italy* (North Point Press, 1999), essays and poetry in *The Mississippi Review*, *The Southwest Review*, and *Agni*, among others. Her poems appeared in **Frank 6/7**. She is on the Board of the Ledig-Rowohlt Foundation.

Publisher's Notes

Frank wishes to acknowleges the following publishers:

Duff Brenna's *The Altar of the Body* is forthcoming from Picador; Alain Campos' drawings appeared in *Gros Plans*, Musée de Lodëve, 1998; José María Mendiluce's "Leila" was published in Spanish in *Armed Love* (Editorial Planeta, 1996). Bedri Baykam's *Kemik* was published in Turkish by Piramid (Istanbul, 2001); James Baldwin's "Telegram" belongs to the Ledig-Rowohlt Foundation, Lavigny; Paul Nizon's *The Year of Love* was published in French by Actes Sud as *L'année de l'amour*, 1986; Monica Cantieni's *Herr Pillwein and Frau Kulanek* is from the 2001 novel *Die Nebeltrinker*; Aglaja Veteranyi's *Why the Child is Cooking in the Polenta* was published in German by Deutsche Verlags-Anstalt, Stuttgart; Claire Genoux's *Saisons du corps* was published in French by Editions Empreintes, 1999; Laurent Schweizer's *Naso Lituratus* was published in French by Actes Sud in 2001; Anne-Lou Steininger's "Sickness of Being a Fly," translated from the French *La maladie d'être mouche* (Eds. Gallimard, 1996), is published here with the permission of the publisher. Acknowledgement also goes to the highly creative Swiss publisher Ricco Bilger with whom the first discussion of a Swiss Foreign Dossier was explored.

Frank also wishes to acknowledge the following Swiss and Swiss-based authors whose work is not represented in this collection: Adolf Muschg, Alain Rocaht, Franz Hohler, Thomas Hürlimann, Gisela Widmer, Peter Bichsel, Franz Hohler, Martin Suter, Paul Bilton.

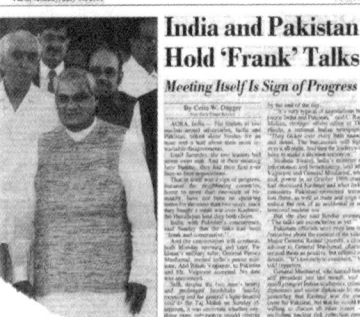

Ticking Along free

Join these thirty-eight authors who are coming and going, climbing cliffs, finding jobs and a plot, exploring the myth of lousy lovers, plunging in and out of trouble and on the wrong trains, making new friends on benches, or in places for women only. Discover a dog that drives a car and a cat that saves Christmas, feel how cultures sometimes clash when you're stuck between two worlds. Grab some tips for doing business, have fun with Swiss German, figure out how Switzerland works with the laundry room key.

The authors come from Australia, Canada, the Caribbean, England, Ethiopia, Ghana, the Philippines, Switzerland and the USA. Some simply can't remember. Some have always been and will always be Swiss. All are at home, yet foreign, and making the best of it.

Ticking Along Free, stories about Switzerland, edited by Dianne Dicks ISBN 3-905252-03-1, 224 pages, paperback, CHF 29.80.

This is only one of our many books that focus on Switzerland to make the best of intercultural living. We also distribute Frank, an international journal of contemporary writing & art.

Bergli Books
 Great gifts!
particularly for anyone interested in Switzerland
Ask for a free catalog or visit our web site:
Bergli Books, Eptingerstr. 5, CH-4052 Basel, Switzerland
Tel. +41 61 373 27 77, Fax +41 61 373 27 78
e-mail: info@bergli.ch   web: www.bergli.ch

Achevé d'imprimer en octobre 2001
sur les presses de la Nouvelle Imprimerie Laballery - 58500 Clamecy
Dépôt légal : octobre 2001   Numéro d'impression : 109096

Imprimé en France

mosaic press

1252 Speers Road, Oakville, Ontario, Canada, L6L 5N9
mosaicpress@on.aibn.com

Books of International Importance from Mosaic Press:

SECOND PRINTING after 7 months!
The book that says more about the
'secrets' of Leonard Cohen
**The Song of Leonard Cohen:
Portrait of a Poet, a Friendship & a Film**
By Harry Rasky
Including the unpublished Bob Dylan Diaries
160 pages with previously unpublished photos
ISBN 0-88962 742-8 PB   **$15.95**

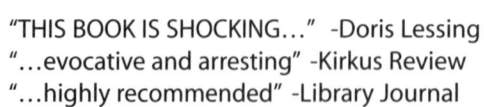

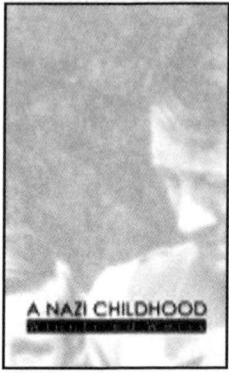

"THIS BOOK IS SHOCKING…" -Doris Lessing
"…evocative and arresting" -Kirkus Review
"…highly recommended" -Library Journal
A Nazi Childhood
By Winfried Weiss
A moving and evocative memoir of World War II
as seen through the eyes of a young German boy.
Originally published in 1983 to rave reviews,
now published in a complete, uncensored version!
240 pages
ISBN 0-88962-727-4 PB   **$15**

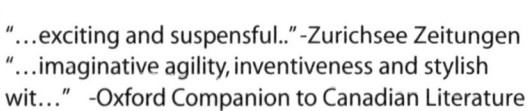

"…exciting and suspensful.." -Zurichsee Zeitungen
"…imaginative agility, inventiveness and stylish
wit…" -Oxford Companion to Canadian Literature
**The Man Who Knew Charlie Chaplin
A novel about the Weimar Republic**
By Eric Koch
October 1929…Berlin…the characters, the
decadence, the intrigue… Which way will
Germany fall – communism or fascism, or what?
150 pages
ISBN 0-88962-718-5 PB   **$15**

Order our books from your local bookseller, www.amazon.com, Roundhouse Group in the U.K. and western Europe, roundhse@compuserve.com; Wakefield Press Distribution in Australia and New Zealand, www.wakefield.com; or SCB Distributors in the U.S. www.scbdistribtors.com.

Cuba's greatest poet now in bilingual edition:
Parables poems/Parabolas poemas
By Pablo Armando Fernandez
Introduction by Margaret Atwood
The first major collection of the esteemed
poetry of the man who has won
every major Spanish language literary award.
220 pages
ISBN 0-88962-754-1 PB   **$15**

"...very fine writing, brilliant juxtapositions and deeply moving meditations on the nature of memory and death"   -Library Journal
On a Flying Fish
A novel by David Applefield
David Applefield's second novel after his highly praised *Once Removed*. Set in Frankfurt, Germany and a Caribbean island, a story of mystery, intrigue driven by an obsessive American book editor.
200 pages
ISBN 0-88962-687-1 HC   **$24**

Just reviewed in *Publishers Weekly!*
Stations
By Winfried Weiss
A story about friendship, loyalty and loss,
AIDS and the author's selfless devotion to
his dying lover Bob.
128 pages
ISBN 0-88962-728-2 PB   **$15**

Visit us at the Frankfurt Book Fair, the London International Book Fair, the Guadalajara Book Fair/Mexico, BookExpo America, BookExpo Canada, or www.mosaic-press.com

"A BRILLIANT NEW VOICE AMONG PARIS EXPATS!"

"Multimedia on the printed page!"
— Paris Voice

Dale Gershwin

A novel for readers with yearning for physical love, compulsive jogging, and above all the unending beauty of Paris.

Set in Paris and Singapore (home of the Seven Deadly Goldfish), animated by a magnetizing set of very off-beat characters, spiked with dizzying twists up to its very last word, OUR LADY is a blend of *The Perils of Pauline* (crime! adventure! suspense!), *Basic Instinct* (sex!), *A Moveable Feast* (romantic Paris! exotic Singapore! glamorous Marbella!) and *Marathon Man* (running for sport! running for life!).
In OUR LADY almost no one and nothing are what they originally seem: friends turn out to be enemies turn out to be friends, men to be women, pawns to be perpetrators, servants to be masters. As we switch countries, continents and cultures in rapid succession, we continuously discover who knew what before the other guy...who is not a guy at all...or is he? Only Notre Dame is what she's supposed to be, but then again someone wants to blow her up!

For a signed copy by the author send 20 Euros or $20 US
Plus 6 Euros or $6 US for First Class Postage anywhere in the world

Please make checks payable to:
Association Kilometer Zero
3, passage de la Vierge · 75007 · Paris France

OUR LADY is published by Mosaic Press (Oakville ·New York)

470 pages · ISBN: 0-88962-692-8

Also available at www.amazon.com and www.bn.com

the **writers** are the **readers**

the performers **are** the audience

the **artists** are the **critics**

the kilometer zero project

www.kilometerzero.org

Don't miss Writers' Forum now available at all good newsagents

FREE SAMPLE

Writers' Forum is a major resource for writers, from beginners to established authors. It covers the who, why, where, what and how on the craft of writing.

Fiction, faction and feature writing. Scripts for television. Comedy and biography.

It costs just £18 a year for six issues and if you would like a a free sample copy send us an sae (80p) 12 x 9 inches and we'll post you a back issue AND a copy of World Wide Writers.

Writers' Forum, PO Box 3229, Bournemouth BH1 1ZS.

See our web site:
www.worldwidewriters.com

Wanted

Frank is actively recruiting concerned, culturally-minded lawyers to join its honorary Publishing Board:

•

Lawyers for Literature.

•

Annual meeting in Burgundy!

For details, write, email, or log in:
www.ReadFrank.com and click on Publishing Partners.

Frank Association
Lawyers for Literature
32 rue Edouard Vaillant
93100 MONTREUIL
France

lawyers@ReadFrank.com

Oui, I want to Subscribe

Name: _____
Address: _____

City: _____
Country: _____
Postal Code: _____
Phone: _____
Fax: _____
Email: _____

Please start my subscription with:
Frank: 18 ___   Frank 19 ___

Enclosed please find a check for: $38 US or 38 Euros payable to: Frank Association. Or: debit my VISA or MC
N _____ Exp: _____
Signature: _____

Send to: Frank Association
32 rue Edouard Vaillant
93100 MONTREUIL / France

Fax: (33) 1 48 59 66 68
Email: order@ReadFrank.com
Website: www.ReadFrank.com

www.ReadFrank.com

If you read Frank, subscribe to Frank, submit work to Frank, or have published in Frank, you are entitled to Frank citizenship! Publicize your literary events, new publications, and reviews online to Frank compatriats everywhere.

A community of writers, poets, translators, artists, and culturally-engaged readers around the world.

●

Subscribe (4 issues/$38 US or 38 Euros)
- Order copies or back issues
- Correspond with Frank writers
- Sign up for the Mini-Frank

(We deliver Frank to your printer)

Frank Association
32 rue Edouard Vaillant
93100 MONTREUIL
France

painting, François Lamore, 2001
www.ReadFrank.com

"If you haven't read Duff Brenna yet, well... you should." – Frank

The ALTAR of the Body

A NOVEL

Duff Brenna

AUTHOR OF TOO COOL

"Available in leading bookstores and at www.ReadFrank.com